Paul Ferguson the Fighter

"The Man with the *Knock-out Punch* In the Ring and in the Pulpit!"

Southern Welter-Weight Boxing Champion
232 professional fights
BY DAN CARR

FOREWORD

Paul Ferguson—one of the most unusual men in the pulpits of America.

Dan Carr has given us a very scholarly picture of this amazing person.

I knew Paul Ferguson. I helped him get his education. I encouraged him in his hours of difficulty. Paul was a man of prayer, determination, and a love for people. He was used in a very unique way to win souls and to strengthen the weak and troubled.

Paul never varied in his preaching of the Word of God, nor did he vary in his compassion for the lost.

Dr. Lee Roberson
Founder and Chancellor
Tennessee Temple University
1815 Union Avenue
Chattanooga, TN 37404

Paul Ferguson the Fighter
Appreciation

Thanks to Pastor Bill Boruff for his gentle but persistent encouragement to finish the manuscript from aging, brittle tapes and for his substantial monetary assistance to make the printing possible.

I appreciate Dr. Lee Roberson reading the manuscript and writing the *Foreword*. He insisted on the title, *Paul Ferguson the Fighter*, suggested with enthusiasm that the cover should feature an upcoming boxing glove, and offered to put me in touch with his publisher. He was much interested in the project because he loved Paul Ferguson and was convinced of God's strong hand upon him. He believed in Paul's integrity and truthfulness.

Thanks to Gerri Smith who proofread every inch—thrice—and dealt with my misplaced commas and quotation marks and capital letters. I think of her as Mrs. Sherlock Holmes of grammar and punctuation.

Thanks to our son, M. Anthony Carr, who made several suggestions concerning page format, organizing the writing and options for publishing.

Thanks to Craig DeSpain for many hours of on-hand emergency room treatment of our sick computers. And thanks to his wife, Claire, who was willing to be a computer widow while Craig performed computer resuscitation many times.

My wife, Barbara, listened at the adjoining desk for many hours and helped me decipher difficult audio passages from the fragile tapes. Her advice on "the best way to say it" was good. She gave me gentle encouragement many times toward the computer, and helped me when the tapes broke and had to be spliced, or the tape cases jammed and had to be opened and repaired. In the beginning, when the Word Perfect 5.2 software program devoured hours and hours of work—without a trace two or three times—she was there to help me start all over again. I am thankful for her prolonged help and ncouragement.

Thanks to Cooper Francis for providing website lodging on a big computer somewhere in Texas, for being our Webmaster, and for his private tutoring of me in email "101."

The Ferguson family has been patient with me in getting this

project done, as it dragged out far too long. Thanks to them for their review of the manuscript.

I enjoyed reviewing *The Life Story of Dr. Paul Ferguson,* as released on Moody Radio's popular *UNSHACKLED* program. The early and updated dramatized versions of this program were very enjoyable, and I recommend them to those who are interested.

I am grateful for the patience of everyone who has been waiting for this report—FOR YEARS— and has refrained from getting pushy or giving up altogether.

By faith, I am grateful to everyone who will take hold of this project in reading, praying, and helping distribute it to wherever it's supposed to go.

Last, but not least, I am thankful to our Lord and Savior Jesus Christ for the privilege of being a part of this serious, enjoyable, and at times...hilarious work.

Dan Carr

Paul Ferguson the Fighter

IN THE RING - IN THE PULPIT
July 10, 1916—November 15, 1996

Preface

They called him "Country Ferguson." Paul Ferguson fought his way through scraps with his sister and in school yard fights to the Southern Welter-Weight Boxing Championship in 1939 at age 23. He defended that title for eleven years, fighting 232 professional fights, losing 10, with 7 or 8 draws, and was _never_ knocked out. Two thirds of his 214 wins were knockouts.

Boxing and the Split-second Advantage.
In the boxing ring, Paul focused intensely on the face of his opponent. He said that many fighters would give themselves away in their facial expression a split-second before they would strike. Paul's lightening reflex enabled him to duck or block the punch and deliver his own powerful blow before his opponent could recoil. "That put the lights out for several of my opponents," he said.

Everybody knew he was a natural-born fighter. His competitive, fighting spirit was obvious on the elementary school playground, in high school sports, in boxing at King College in Bristol, Virginia, and throughout his eleven-year career of professional boxing. He never tired of boxing, nor had he aged beyond fighting ability in his boxing circle when he hung up his gloves after his 35th birthday. He had simply found something that interested him far more than boxing – the call of God upon his life to be a Christian evangelist.

His giving up boxing in 1950 surprised a lot of people who knew Paul. He had defended his Welter Weight Championship title for eleven years, was still in his prime, was still laying out his opponents on the floor, and was still alive in the hearts of his fans. It was not so much a sudden, conscious decision as it was a tide that flowed in and swept him in another direction.

Since boyhood days, Paul was a born-again believer in

6

Christ's death on the cross for his sins. But after eleven years of professional boxing, he discovered from the Bible, especially in John 5:24, that he could not lose his eternal salvation. This single truth completely changed the direction of his life. Suddenly, instead of his daily training routine, he ignored his punching bags and spent the time in Bible reading and prayer. Paul was unusual in boxing, and he would continue to be unusual in the years ahead – in a different arena.

Becoming an evangelist did not stop his keen interest in sports. Until he was almost seventy years old, he was the Handball Champion in the Chattanooga-Cleveland area at the YMCA. He defended that title with as much vigor and discipline as he had demonstrated in the boxing ring. After age 70, he continued at a less vigorous level until he became ill with a blocked artery a few months before his death at age 80. For many years he coached Little League ball teams in Chattanooga as much as his schedule would permit.

This book highlights part of his earlier life, and then explores some of the details of his unusual ministry as a Christian evangelist. As an evangelist, he was still fearless, and continued to study the facial expressions of his opponents as he encountered some of the meanest and toughest of men in trying to win them to Christ. He won many men to Christ, and some died in his meetings in connection with his sermon: *God's Last Train to Heaven*.

Unusual Power with God.

It was obvious that he had unusual power with God, but less obvious as to *why.* My six days of interviews with Paul revealed a substantial root system of study that focused on the Scriptures and the lives of many outstanding preachers of the past. He was familiar with the great preachers at the time of the American Revolution. The lives and written sermons of E. M. Bounds, Charles G. Finney, and D. L. Moody were prominent in his spontaneous conversation. I already knew he had memorized over 8,000 (eight thousand) verses of Scripture.

One day when he came to our carport office for another day of remembering, he brought me a pocket-size paperback book written by Miles J. Stanford, *Principles of Spiritual Growth*,

7

published by Back to the Bible. It was really beat up. Its 101 pages were heavily marked and underlined in red. The cover was encased in packaging tape and scotch tape. The pages are finger-smudged from frequent and long-term use, and the edges of the first 37 pages are rolled up. I consider this little book one of the most valuable books in my library. It was Paul Ferguson's private, secret treasury of "spiritual vitamins."

In the Foreword, Theodore Epp, founder of Back to the Bible Broadcast, explains: "The various parts of the book were originally prepared as short letters and were sent to a number of interested friends. They were then compiled into the book which was known as *The Green Letters*. But in order to make this new printing meaningful to a new audience, the title has been changed to *Principles of Spiritual Growth*." The book's printing record states: "555,000 printed to date, 1987." We don't know when the letters were written and circulated, or when they were compiled into *The Green Letters* collection.

Most of all, Paul Ferguson was familiar with the lives and preaching of the great preachers in the Bible and what Jesus had taught about salvation and the power of the Holy Spirit. Some of his Bibles are in worse shape than *The Green Letters*. His life as an evangelist focused on this Bible passage:

"Draw Nigh To God, and He Will Draw Nigh To You" (James 4:8a).

The text continues: *"Cleanse your hands, ye sinners, and purify your hearts, ye double minded. Humble yourselves in the sight of the Lord, and he shall lift you up"* (James 4:8b, 10),

---

Sir Winston Churchill, the Prime Minister of England during World War II, once said, *"Occasionally a man stumbles over the truth but, usually jumps up quickly, brushes himself off, and hurries on as if nothing has happened. Please don't hurry on. Study this book carefully".*

Paul Ferguson died November 15, 1996. In 1992, I interviewed Paul one day per week for six weeks – six days of intense conversation. I tried to x-ray his life, his fighting and his ministry from his own words. There is more in the Appendix.

Most of the material here was transcribed word-for-word from interview tapes with him. It was necessary to slightly alter some of the quotes to make complete sentences and to explain the meaning within the context of the conversation. He worked hard to remember things that happened many years ago, things he did not dwell on through the years. Every effort has been made to let Paul speak for himself. No sentences were twisted; no liberties were taken. If quotations are not otherwise identified in the text, they are quotes from Paul. Conversations between Paul and the writer will be obvious.

[WARNING: This book is written to encourage you to *Draw Nigh to God*. We do not encourage you to try to be like Paul Ferguson or to portray him as the norm of Christian living and service. If his life and work can encourage you to walk with God and discover His will for your life, the book will have served its purpose. We can all listen to the Word of God. We can all pray at least 15 minutes a day and obey what God shows us. God may want you to pray more than 15 minutes a day.]

Dan Carr

About Dan Carr

Daniel Dewey Carr was born September 16, 1934 in Alpine, Tennessee, in the living room of an unpainted house built by his great-grandfather several years before the Civil War. Bullet holes were in the ceiling of the dining room. His great-grandfather farmed the land in the summer and made shoes in winter. One fall, he made a hollow shock of corn and hid in it when Union guerilla soldiers were in the area. Tinkers' Men, they called them. A hundred years before that, Medlock Hollow had been a rich hunting ground for Indians. Arrowheads could often be found in the spring of year as the fields were turned.

Dan attended Tennessee public schools in Alpine; Mountain City; Elizabethton; Crossville (Homesteads); and Stevenson, Alabama, graduating from high school at the Homesteads High School in Crossville, Tennessee, 1952.

He was enrolled in Tennessee Temple College 1952-58 and pursued a major in piano for three years until he tired of Bach and Beethoven; switching to a major in Bible with a minor in social studies.

During his college years, he was challenged by the great preaching of many visiting preachers and missionaries. He was particularly drawn to the elderly preacher-songwriter, Dr. Charles Weigle, in his 90's, who lived on campus in the Prophet's Chamber. Dan ate breakfast with him many times in the school dining hall.

Dan preached often with teams on the streets, rescue missions, tents, jails, and weekends in churches, and dabbled in radio. In the summers of 1954 and 1955, he traveled with a team to Jamaica where they preached and sang in Scottish Presbyterian churches. They preached in fish and produce markets and streets, and climbed many hills to give out pocket-size Gospels of John to families in thatched huts.

He preached on the streets of Chattanooga with various open air teams, and recruited a team of young men who sang as a male quartet with the aid of an accordion. Trumpets and trombones formed a brass quartet. They held open-air meetings in the towns surrounding Chattanooga. A junk milk truck was purchased for $200. The old truck housed the yard goats. They were forced out and the truck was pulled with a chain until it fired off—in a great cloud

11

of blue smoke! The truck was repaired, painted bright red, trimmed in white, and equipped with sound equipment. The team lived a lot in the truck that summer during meetings, "meals" and all.

Upon becoming the pastor of Centennial Baptist Church in Stevenson, Alabama, he was ordained at age 19 to the Gospel ministry in 1953, by the Highland Park Baptist Church in Chattanooga, Tennessee, along with three other young men. The ordination service was incorporated into the mid-week prayer meeting of the church. Pastor Lee Roberson preached on "Four Foolish Fellows."

With the aid of a ragged school bus, the Centennial Baptist Church grew in attendance from 9 to 110 in six months, with many people making professions of faith and being baptized in Crow Creek.

Dan was married to Shirley Martin in February, 1956, and served as associate pastor or pastor in Pensacola, Florida; Jacksonville, Florida; Bay Minette, Alabama; Tallahassee, Florida; Johnson City, Tennessee; Bristol, Tennessee; Tennessee Ridge, Tennessee; Jacksonville, Florida (Music, Principal, Christian High School); Winston-Salem, North Carolina; Raleigh, North Carolina (lobbyist for Christian schools 5 years in North Carolina and Washington); and currently serves as an Interim Pastor at Southern Pines, North Carolina.

Four children were born to Dan and Shirley: Joy, David, Paul, Anthony. Shirley died at age 49 in her sleep. Dan and Barbara (Goforth) have been married 20 years and make their home in Flat Rock, Alabama.

Dan and Barbara together produce *The Encourager*, a free email newsletter, and operate Web sites: www.dancarr.org and www.firebuilders.org. Since long-time Pastor Kent Kelly suffered a severe stroke April, 2003, Dan and Barbara have shuttled the 475 miles from Flat Rock, Alabama to Southern Pines, North Carolina, where Dan serves as Senior Interim Pastor. They are usually at the church two months and home for one month— now into the third year. Dan will be 72 in September, 2006.

Lessons learned: Life is short, and there is a final exam. The hope of the world is the crucified and risen Christ. Everything done for self-glory will burn as trash. The Jewish Christ and our Savior is coming to reign on the throne of David, and we shall reign with Him. Our best days are yet to come!

12

Paul Ferguson the Fighter
Chapter 1

The Flood.
D.C: *The flood waters rose steadily in North Carolina as it rained, and rained, and rained. The rising water swallowed up farm land and property. Paul Ferguson could not have cared less about the flood or the rain. His mother was carrying him around in her womb with a motherly eagerness to get the birthing behind her - but not in all the rain and flooding. It was a devastating flood that marked the memory and talk of people in that area for the rest of their lives.*

In time, just as it did in Noah's day, the water receded and dry land appeared. Not long after the flood, Paul Ferguson discovered America on July 10, 1916. People around there took notice of the birth and referred to him as "the child that was born right after the flood." Paul considered it a valuable heritage to have been born and raised up on a farm and to have had six sisters and three brothers. He especially considered it a valuable heritage to have had a Christian mother and father. It's a good thing his mother and father were Christians, because Paul would prove their mettle of patience.

The Times.
Another side of the story is that 1916 was in the middle of World War One. Thousands of our young men were dying "over there" and being shipped home in boxes, and sometimes there were huge losses. Many of our dead were gathered up and buried "over there" in hastily-dug graves and then moved to large cemeteries crowned with a striking array of white crosses, where they remain to this day.

On top of that was the massive epidemic of Spanish Flu that would kill 600,000 in this country and millions around the world. During the winter of 1918, the death

13

toll outpaced the grave diggers, and in some places the dead were laid out on the front porches and froze until the undertakers could take them to the cemetery and dig graves through hard, frozen ground.

Paul Ferguson was born into America when the birth of every baby was a breath of fresh air; a strong, healing symbol of hope and relief from death and suffering - so different from today, when the same country has voluntarily slaughtered over forty-three million inconvenient babies and accepts an American industry that buys and sells human baby parts from late-pregnancy abortions, making some merchants wealthy. When Paul and I discussed this dark side of America, he boiled with disgust and indignation.

Paul's parents taught him from his earliest years about God and the Bible. By the time he was twelve years old, it all began to come together. He knew he was quickly growing into a young man and he had to get some things settled. Of that time, he said: "I was saved when I was twelve years old. I went out into the woods and prayed. While I was praying to be saved, I also prayed God, don't ever let me cause my mother any trouble from drinking whiskey, or anything like that. God answered that prayer. I've never put a hand on it. I give Him the glory. I've never smoked a cigarette in my life. I believe God used my training as an athlete to keep my life clean morally."

Before I Was Born.

Before I was born, my mother prayed I would be a preacher. Somebody said that if she had prayed for a prize fighter, I would have been an outlaw. I had a fighting spirit at an early age and was ready to fight my teacher my very first year in school.

I started boxing with boxing gloves on when I was twelve years old. More important to me, I was saved at age twelve, not long *before* I started boxing. Some preachers have announced that I fought for a long time, got saved, and quit fighting to preach. That's not like it was. I got saved at age twelve and after that I took up boxing.

There were boxing clubs for kids in those days, and I continued to box right on up through high school. Actually, my boxing began to really develop in high school. I taught my sister, Margaret, to box and she got really good at it. She had some of my fighting spirit and had a natural inborn ability to learn boxing. I was much interested in other sports as well as boxing. I ran a lot and played football. Sports built discipline into my life that helped me in my ministry.

> D.C.: *Paul believed that participation in sports was an important building block in the development of self discipline, pursuing goals, and taking tough licks without quitting. He wanted to see young people learn how to live without whining and complaining and making excuses for not doing their best. That was it. Doing their best! Regardless of the outcome. He believed that when you've done your best, you can look into the mirror without looking down on yourself. But not doing your best is a shameful thing.*

King College.
At age 18, I went to King College in Bristol, Virginia to sign up in their boxing program. I didn't care anything about college. I just wanted to box. The next year, at age 19, I left King College to begin professional boxing and won the Golden Gloves at High Point, North Carolina.

Altogether, as a professional fighter, I fought 232 pro-fights and lost ten of them. There were 7 or 8 draws. That leaves me winning about 214 out of 232. Of the 214 fights I won, two-thirds of them, 143, were knock-outs. They named me "Country Ferguson." I became the Southern Welter-Weight Champion.

I was a good fighter, as the ones on the floor would probably agree. I was never knocked out. I was in real good physical shape in those days. I could jump rope for a half-hour at a time, and sometimes I would fight twice the same night. You had to be in good shape to fight twice on the same night.

Professional fighting is a world of its own. Not only are there the fighters - there are also the promoters. Promoters get either a part of the box office receipts or part of the contract price agreement for a given fight. They want to make money over the long haul, but they may get in a pinch and risk their man losing a fight by matching him with someone that outweighs him.

I was matched several times with fighters that outweighed me by twenty pounds or more. Some of my losses came from that. I never weighed in at more than 147 pounds.

The Big, Mean Dude.

Once I was matched against a big, hairy boxer who outweighed me by 25 pounds. Three or four of my sisters came from Wilkesboro, North Carolina to Greensboro to see the fight. They were worried to death that this guy was going to really beat me up - hurt me bad.

Not only did my sisters fear I would get beat up, so did everybody else. This guy looked, talked, and acted mean. My sisters wouldn't go inside to see the fight. On the sixth round I put out his lights; knocked him flat on the floor—out cold. Everybody was surprised. In fact, they were shocked! Someone ran outside to tell my sisters. When they saw the messenger open the door, they just knew it was bad news. I reckon everybody got their money's worth that came to see me get beat up.

The Fork in the Road.

D.C.: *The road ahead was completely hidden from Paul Ferguson. He was heavy into boxing and was very good at it. He knew the Lord as his Creator and Redeemer, but the farthest thing from his mind—ever— was that Paul Ferguson would become a preacher. Not Paul Ferguson. It wasn't that he was dead-set against preaching. He loved good preaching. It was just that it never occurred to him that he, Paul Ferguson, might ever become a preacher.*

He certainly would never have taken it upon himself to be a preacher, as preachers were thought of—standing

16

behind a pulpit and going through the expected procedure known as preaching. It just didn't fit him. Lena, his wife, had not married a preacher. She was a Christian, but it was another matter to become a preacher's wife. He had never thought about all the changes that would be required if he should become a preacher. Paul had never thought of all these things. But, he would have to think about them—soon.

Actually, becoming a preacher was not the first thing confronting Paul beyond the fork in the road. Something else, a life-changing thing would happen to him that would completely change his life.

In The Ring with Lena Mae.

At age 23, in 1939, I married Lena Mae Doggett. That's pronounced *DOG-et*. The Yankees pronounce it *DAHG-et*. Besides being saved and learning I couldn't lose my salvation, marrying Lena Mae was the best thing that ever happened to me. I was already married to her when I learned about *eternal salvation*. Lena Mae was saved when she was young, grew up in a Baptist church, and still believed she could lose her salvation.

My Pastor Was a Big Help

Lena Mae had joined the McConnell Road Baptist Church before I learned about eternal security of the believer. J. T. Ellis was the pastor. Pastor Ellis had attended Davison College for about three years, with no formal Bible training. He was one of the best Bible scholars I ever saw. He just studied the Bible, and prayed, and became educated that way. (More later.)

You Can't Lose Your Salvation.

I didn't know you can't lose your salvation after you are truly saved. After I was saved, part of the time I thought I was saved, and part of the time I thought I was lost. I thought you could be saved and lost, saved and lost, saved and lost. The greatest thing that ever came into my life after I was saved happened to me when I was thirty-two years old, twenty years after I was saved. At age thirty two, I learned that you cannot lose your salvation.

I heard a Baptist deacon say, "You can live perfect, without sin," which is impossible - but he said that "You could live forty years without sin, say a little word like *hell, damn*, or *dadburn,* and you'd go to Hell."

Now, I never was a real curser. I don't say I didn't curse some in my life, but I did have a habit of saying *dadburn*. Really, I don't think that's any worse than many preachers who say *cotton-pickin'*. It's a slang word, not pure, clean English, but it's a long way from cursing or foul language. But the Baptist deacon said that if you said *dadburn*, you'd go to Hell.

Go - Go - Go.

I went to the pastor and he tried to explain to me that once you're saved you can't lose your salvation. I couldn't get it. I just couldn't understand it. Then I went to the chairman of the Board of Deacons, Brother Cleatus Yow. He showed me the same thing and I still couldn't get it.

So I went to the Lord. I was hungry to know. I was desperate. I should have gone to the Lord in the first place. I remember right where I was, in the old woodshed, close to where I had my things for working out and training for boxing.

I began to pray. I said, "Now Lord, if this is so, I can't get it, 'cause I was saved in a Methodist church." (Believe me, I'm not intending to throw off on them, but they're just wrong in their belief that Christians can lose their salvation.) You can't lose your salvation if you are truly saved, but I still thought you could. Christians are not likely to feel much saved or have any assurance of their salvation if they are living in known sin and rebellion against God.

Bible Flipping.

I opened my Bible and flipped through it, as if that would do any good. Just flipped through it. Now, I don't believe flipping through the Bible is God's appointed means of finding His will and direction for your life. But on the other hand, God sometimes seems to delight in doing un-standard things.

I heard about one man who flipped open the Bible every morning to *get his verse for the day*. One morning he flipped to Matthew 27:5: *"[Judas] went and hanged himself."* He said, "Boy, I better get another one." He flipped over to Luke 10:37: *"Go and do thou likewise."* He flipped over to another one and it was John 13:27: *"That thou doest, do quickly."*

My experience wasn't quite like that. I flipped over to John 5:24. I read it real fast, and didn't get a thing out of it. I was by myself. I said, "Lord, now I want you to show me," and He brought me to that verse. I read it too fast - just skidded through it.

The Lord spoke to me there in that woodshed, not in an audible voice. (But I believe He could speak to anybody in an audible voice if He chose to do so. God is sovereign, and does as He pleases.) The Lord spoke to me in my spirit, in an inaudible voice: "Now read like somebody that's got some sense."

I started reading slowly: *"Verily, verily I say unto you, he that heareth my word, and believeth on Him that sent me, hath everlasting life"* (John 5:24). I said, "Hold on now. 'Hath' is present tense."

I Saw It! I Saw It!

I just saw it all at once! And I said: "Hath! Well, if it's hath..if you have...everlasting...life now, how are you gonna lose it? It wouldn't be everlasting. Then I came to the word "condemnation." That's the judgment of the soul. "Well, Lord, if you paid for it, then I couldn't pay for it. It's all of you." It just came to me.

And then I read: *"from death unto life."* When we accept Christ, anybody that's truly saved (I'm not talking about a false profession), anybody that's truly saved, and truly trusts Christ's dying on the cross for our sins, right then and there, God in His foreknowledge sees that person walking down the streets of Glory!

Boy! That's enough to make a dead Baptist shout!

Boxing Loses Out.

I was still boxing. I had hurt my hand earlier, but I was able to continue boxing. I usually went out and ran several miles a day and worked out to keep in shape and train for the fights coming up. But when I learned from God's Word that a Christian can't lose his salvation, I lost all interest in boxing. Instead of working out, I'd go off and pray and read the Bible for hours. It wasn't long 'til I started witnessing. This happened a couple of years before I was ever called to preach.

> D.C.: *Paul did not suddenly stop boxing. But his keen interest in boxing stopped suddenly, immediately. He had trained long enough that he coasted along for a while. But his heart was no longer in boxing.*

Transforming Power.

The thing that really transformed and changed my life was learning I couldn't lose my salvation. Some people say, "Well, if I believed that, I'd live like I want to." They've got a head knowledge of eternal security. They don't have heart knowledge.

There are people that know all about Christ, could tell the plan of salvation as good as you or I, or maybe better, and yet they've never been saved. They've never depended on it; never received; never trusted; never truly believed in Him as dying in their place. They have head knowledge of Christ, but no heart knowledge; and if they die like that, they'll go to Hell.

In the same way, there are people who have head knowledge of *eternal salvation—eternal security*—and it hasn't changed their life. But I say, and I won't take it back, anybody that truly has a heart knowledge of *eternal salvation* will be changed and transformed. It changed me, and it will change others.

Mama and Dad were both Christians for years, but after I learned you couldn't lose your salvation, my mother learned it. She was an old-fashioned Methodist. She accepted the truth of eternal salvation. Before that, she had never won souls, but after she accepted that truth, she won souls and witnessed to people the rest of her life, 'til the time she died.

Some of the experiences that I've had, somebody else might not have. God uses all of us in a different way. But I *know* that if people have a true experience of *eternal salvation* and come to know they can't lose it, it'll change their life. They'll appreciate it. They'll love the Lord better. They'll start thinking. And the people that don't experience these changes, they just don't have the heart knowledge of *eternal salvation—eternal security*.

Heart knowledge makes all the difference in the world."

Weak and Useful.

Brother Dan, you were asking me why God called me. I guess one reason was because He knew I was weak and wasn't much.

In the Word of God we read: *"For ye see your calling, brethren, how that not many wise men after the flesh, not many mighty, not many noble, are called: But God hath chosen the foolish things of the world to confound the wise; and God hath chosen the weak things of the world to confound the things which are mighty, And base things of the world, and things which are despised, hath God chosen, yea, and things which are not, to bring to nought things that are: that no flesh should glory in His presence"* (I Corinthians 1:26-29).

The things I tell you that God has done in my ministry, God did it! I didn't do it. God gets the credit. To God be the glory!

God is still looking, in this day, to find people He can use. We read in the Word of God: *"I sought for a man among them, and found none" (Ezekiel 22:30)* . I think He will still use people today that are willing to be used of Him. We can still have revival.

God Called Me To Preach.

I still don't fully understand why God chose me, but He did. I know I had a specific calling of the Lord, and He blessed me and used me. I was called to preach a couple of years after I learned about eternal security and had spent a lot of time in prayer and reading the Word of God. I had quit boxing then, and I worked on the railroad. I witnessed to men and won some of them to the Lord. A lot of them that I witnessed to were not saved then, but were saved later.

You don't have to be a preacher, a pulpit preacher, to witness and win people to Christ. I spent a lot of time in prayer and the Word of God, and witnessed to people, and won people to Christ before I was ever called to preach.

My Pastor Calls an Extended Prayer Meeting.

I hadn't been called to preach yet. Brother Ellis, my pastor in Greensboro, N.C., called a meeting for people to come and

21

pray. He said, "God's willing to do something in this church. Some of the people don't want anything to happen. We're going to have a meeting and pray 'til God blesses, or until we know what to do." Sometimes, you don't have to have a feeling to pray. You just pray. That night, our oldest boy was sick. My wife would have gone to the meeting to pray, but she didn't want to leave him home sick. It was too late for us to get anybody to come and stay with him so she could go. I went by myself.

We started to pray about 7:30 p.m. We prayed one after the other. It was easy to pray, and I prayed pretty long. Brother Bullock prayed the longest. Brother Ed York prayed long. Brother Don Summers' was a pretty long prayer too. We prayed around and around. It was about 2:00 o'clock in the morning and we had been praying since 7:30 p.m. There was no great emotional praying. It was one of those prayer meetings where it is easy to pray.

When we started that last round at 2:00 a.m., I couldn't pray a word - not a word could I say. They prayed, BUT every one of them cut their prayers short – those men who were in the habit of praying for long periods in public - Brother Bullock, Brother York, and Brother Summers. Summers was next to me. He was a long-praying man, and I thought he would pray long enough that I wouldn't have to. I knew I couldn't say a word. But Brother Summers said only three or four words. It was my time and I tried to say, "Lord, I can't pray. You'll have to do it for me." I didn't know it then, but that's what He wanted me to do, to pray by the Holy Spirit.

All at once the power of God came on me from the top of my head to the soles of my feet. I had never had anything like that to happen in all my life, and I knew it was God; and everybody else knew it. They all began to pray. I couldn't hear a word they said. They told me later that the whole building was just stirred by the power of God.

I said, "Lord, I'll do what you want me to do." I hadn't been called to preach yet. God was getting me ready to answer Him. I went home and hugged Lena, and she said the Spirit of God went all over her. She said my face was white. She kept hugging me and said to me, "Honey, God's touched you tonight!"

I had never led many people to the Lord before that. I wanted to, and I witnessed some; but, boy, that changed my whole life! After that, I started winning people to the Lord. It wasn't long 'til I was called to preach. Of course, I had wanted to preach. But He was calling me to be an evangelist, and I wanted to be a pastor. I didn't want to be an evangelist. God dealt with me at the railroad switch yard not long after this night of prayer.

Paul Ferguson jumping his horse "Quicker". 1946

Paul at Bill Rice Ranch in 1956.

Another jump by "Quicker" and Paul - 1946

Paul Ferguson shown punching the bag in early forties.

1936 King College Boxing Team, Bristol, TN. Paul Ferguson 2nd from the left

Paul Ferguson served a term in the Coast Guard in the early forties. During that time he did some boxing. Here in Hilton Head, SC.

Paul Ferguson the Fighter
Chapter 2

My First Full-Length Meeting.

When I preached my first full-length meeting, I had previously preached seven sermons. The church was in North Carolina, and my uncle was the pastor. Some of the deacons had gotten into a fight, the way I understood it, and one of them took a swing at the pastor but didn't hit him. He tried to black the eye of the pastor! I preached my first sermon at that church, and they wanted me to come back for a revival meeting. So there I was.

The revival meeting went along pretty good, and we had some people saved. Oh, they were eulogizing and building me up, and saying how great I was. I had an uncle that was saying I was greater than Billy Sunday, and I was going to be one of the greatest, big preachers in the world. Well, the Lord had to let me down in that meeting. I mean, He had to *bring* me down. The Lord doesn't *let* anyone down. He *brought* me down.

The meeting hadn't really broken the way it should, but we'd had some people saved, and the people were bragging. I didn't then know the different words in the Greek language about love. I didn't know about the *eros* love, which is a fleshly love, nor *phileo* love, the root word used in the word *Philadelphia*, called *The City of Brotherly Love*. I didn't know that.

And I didn't know about *agape* love, the love of God. If you're not saved, you can't have that love. But I didn't know all that. So I just said, "You don't love your family if you're not saved." Boy, there was one man that jumped up and said, "I love my family as good as you do!" I didn't know how to explain to him the difference. I said, "I know you don't." He said, "I do!"

That broke up the service, and the people got mad at me. One of my sisters went home and told me I'd disgraced the Lord, the church, and everybody else. Everybody was mad at me but my daddy; he was there that night. I mean *everybody* that was there was mad at me. They said, "We'll never come back. You can come back tomorrow, but there won't be a person here. Not one person will be here tomorrow."

Lower Than A Snake.

I went to Dad's home where I was staying for the meeting, and I could have walked under a snake's belly wearing Abe Lincoln's high hat, and never touched a scale. I was low. I usually ate a little snack after I preached. As I was eating, Daddy said, "Paul, I don't know exactly how to explain it, but I know you're right." I thought I had made two men mad, in particular, and I did. My brother was there, and he might have been mad at first. But I knew for sure that the man who stood up and opposed me was mad. He was really mad!

I went upstairs and went to bed. I was crying and praying. I prayed, and I prayed, and I prayed.

When God Tells You.

But there's more to it than that. I had been walking that day, and God told me to say that. I knew I had obeyed Him, but I didn't expect it to turn out like that.

As I was praying upstairs in bed, the Lord said to me, "Paul Ferguson, quit that cryin', and shut up, and go to sleep. You haven't slept any for a whole week crying and praying about the souls that are going to Hell." And He said, "I told you to say it. I'll work it out. You quit worrying, and go to sleep." And I did.

D.C.: *More about this kind of thing later.*

In Jail.

My brother had said he would drive me to the jail where I was going to preach the next morning. I thought he wouldn't go, but he went. The Lord told me to apologize to him and to the Scott man that got so mad. So I told my brother, "I apologize." He said, "Why? You didn't say the wrong thing. You was right."

I went to the jail, and there were about twenty-five or thirty saved that morning. They said they'd never had anybody saved there before.

They're Going to Hang Me!

I went back to the church, not knowing if anybody would be there. I looked up on the hill where the church building was and saw so many cars you couldn't even get to the church without

31

walking a long way. There were all these people standing outside.

I said to my brother, "I guess they're staying outside 'til I get there so they can hang me. I don't know anything else. Maybe they'll crucify me, but I'm goin' on up there, and see what happens." When I got up there, the church was full, and these people couldn't get in. I've never seen or heard of anything like that in my life.

God at Work.

I walked in, and the man that said he'd never come again, Mr. Scott, was standing there. I walked up to him, and started apologizing, and he said, "You don't have to apologize to me. I was wrong, and I realized you was right, and God had you to do it to wake me up."

So he was there, and he got saved. My brother got saved. One of my oldest brothers was also saved that morning. When those two brothers of mine and the Scott man walked down the aisle together, my mother went to shoutin'. She was an old-time, shoutin' Methodist. When she started shoutin', about twenty-five people came that morning, and were saved.

We were supposed to close the meeting, but they said the meeting couldn't close. They went on a whole week without me and had people saved that whole week. Many people were saved, but I'll tell you, the Lord humbled me.

That was in my home county, Wilkes County, North Carolina, the bootleggin' capital of the world. Wilkesboro was the County Seat. North Wilkesboro was a separate town. Each town had its own high school, and these two high schools were the main rivals in playing football. The high schools were later combined, a few years after I left.

Dressing Like a Bum.

In this first meeting there was a man who asked me to go and talk to his daddy. He said, "Now, he'll run you off. He runs all the preachers off. Daddy says, 'Preachers come over here with a collar and tie. The big shot preachers think they're better than I am.' So, he'll run you off."

My Uncle Peter, who had been an awful rough man in his

day, was burdened about this same man, Mr. Scott. He said, "Paul, now, he'll probably run you off, but will you go and see Mr. Scott?" I said, "Well, he won't run me off. If I preach many years, I'll be run off a whole lot of times."

So, in spite of what had been said, I was dressing up, and the Lord talked to me, but not in an audible voice. He said, "Don't wear that junk that you've got there. You've got a pair of overalls there, put them on." I put them on. Then He said, "These shoes, don't wear them." So I went and got my dad's work shoes. They were a little too big for me but I put them on, put on a blue shirt, and a huntin' cap and huntin' coat. It was a little too big for me, but I got my Bible and went on.

My oldest sister said, "Paul don't go like that. You're a disgrace to the ministry. Don't go like that. Put on some decent clothes." I said, "No Pansie, God told me to go like this and I'm going like this." She said, "It'll never work. You'll be out of the ministry."

So I went on and met my uncle and his eyes got great big. He said, "Paul, are you going like that?" I said, "Yes sir, I'm going like this." And we went on. Mr. Scott was down below his house, about a hundred yards or more. He'd been down to a spring.

He was coming up from the spring and Uncle Peter walked up to him and said, "Mr. Scott, I've got somebody I want you to meet. Paul Ferguson is my nephew and I want you to meet him. He's preaching a revival up here at the church."

He looked at me and pointed his finger at me: "That thing right there, a preacher? Are you a preacher?" "Yes sir." He said, "You mean that…wearing that hat?" I said, "You see it don't you?" He said, "Well, a shirt like that and that coat, those pants, and those shoes?" I said, "Yeah, you see 'em don't you?"

He said, "Well, I've longed to see a preacher all my life that I thought I could talk to, and I can talk to you. Come on in the house and let's talk a while."

I didn't say anything thing about salvation. I just sat there. He started talking. And he talked, and he talked, and he talked. I guess he talked 35-40 minutes. He said, "I never enjoyed talking to a man so in my life." All I said was "yes" and "no." I didn't talk. He kept on talking and finally, after about an hour, I said inside myself, "Now Lord, you let me know when I should talk to him."

He started telling me a story about one of his real close friends, the closest friend he had ever had. The man was coming down a hill on a mule. The mule turned and threw him off and broke his neck. The Lord said, "Speak to him."

I said, "Mr. Scott, that's right. Hebrews 9:27 says, *It is appointed unto men once to die but after that, the judgment.*" I started talking to him. He sat there and listened. I showed him that we are all sinners. He said, "I know, I'm the worst sinner that ever lived. I've always bluffed preachers to get away from me, but I'm a lost sinner. I know there's a hell and I'd go to hell if I died. I'm getting close to it. I'm 92."

After I went over the plan of salvation, I prayed. Now, sometimes *before* I pray, I say, "Will you accept the Lord?" But I didn't that day. I prayed *first.* Then I said, "Will you accept the Lord?" He said, "I WANT to." And he accepted the Lord. Man, it shook that whole country for miles around there, about him getting saved. He gave his testimony the rest of his life.

Looking For a School.

A certain school had been recommended to me (I'll not give the name of the school), and I decided to go visit. The president of the school invited me into his office and we began to talk. He asked me what I wanted to do when I finished school. I told him that God had called me to be an evangelist. He replied that he would not let an evangelist preach in his church; that 90% of it was emotionalism, and that he didn't believe in the second coming of Christ. After that remark I realized we didn't have anything to talk about, so I excused myself and left immediately. Oh, I didn't act ugly with him or argue with him; I just left.

Wrong School - Right Hitch-Hiker.

On my way to the school that day, I had picked up, and won, a black boy to the Lord. He got out of the car and went on his way. Going back home, one of the greatest experiences I ever had took place. A teenager had gone to the school with me. The night before, I had preached at McClainsville Baptist church. This young man was in the service and wanted to start preaching. He wanted to go with me on the trip to the college just to be with me.

As we drove along, we looked on the side of the road, and there stood a big tall man. I decided to pick him up. We drove along a little while with the man in the back seat. (I learned later not to let anybody in the back seat when I pick them up.)

I said, "Mister, do you know the Lord as your Savior? Have you been born again? If you died today would you go to Heaven?" He said, "No sir, I wouldn't. But I'd like to be saved more than anything in all the world. I'd like to be saved."

Good Scripture Verses to Share.

"Well," I said, "Mister, you're at the right place." I pulled the car over by the side of the road and showed him from the Bible that he was a sinner, (Romans 5:12, Romans 3:22, 23), and then I showed him that Christ died on the cross to save him.

I didn't show him, but I think one of the best Scriptures to show this is I Peter 2:24: *"Who his own self bare our sins in his own body on the tree, that we, being dead to sins, should live unto righteousness: by whose stripes ye were healed."* But, though I didn't show him this particular verse, I did tell him that Christ died for his sins, and was willing to save him.

I showed him Romans 10:9-13. When I am dealing with people, I don't quote Scripture to them. I show it to them or read it to them. I read that to him, and brother, he didn't get it. He couldn't get it.

I usually don't show a person John 5:24 until after he or she is saved. That's the verse that changed my life. But I read him that verse. He took the Bible, and read it and read it. I didn't know it then, but *seven* is the perfect number. When he read it the seventh time, he jumped, and threw his hands up, and said, "Praise God! Jesus died for my sins! I'm Saved! I thought I was going to Hell! I'm so happy!" I showed him some other Scripture.

Going to Hell from a Wreck.

When I got through, he said, "Now, I want to tell you something, preacher. Two weeks ago my buddy and I were going down the highway, and both of us were drunk. My buddy was driving, and the car turned over. He was pinned under the car and was dying. But, as he was dying, he was screaming, 'Get these Hell flames out of my face! Get these Hell flames out of my face! Get these Hell flames out of my face!'"

"I said to him, There are no Hell flames here! This car's on fire! He said, 'There's no car on fire! It's the Hell flames! I'm going down to Hell!' (The car was NOT on fire.) He said, "My buddy died like that, and for two weeks I've not been able to eat or sleep."

A Sinner Prays In The Woods.

And then the big hitchhiker told us, "I went out into the woods today and told God, 'God, I'm a low-down sinner. I know I'm a goin' to Hell. I'm goin' to die if I don't get saved. God, will you tell me what to do? The Lord said to me, 'Go out and stand by the road, and a young man will come by driving a 1939 Dodge, and he'll tell you what to do to be saved.' And when you came by, God said, 'That's the man.'"

I was so thankful that God knew what He was doing, and I knew then why God sent me down to that school. He knew I wouldn't go to school there.

Running from God and Reading Books.

I ran from God about being an evangelist. I didn't want to be an evangelist. It had been two years since I had learned about *eternal salvation*. I had prayed. I had studied the Scriptures. I had witnessed to many. I wanted to be a pastor. I didn't want to be an evangelist.

My wife went by Phillip's Book Store in Greensboro, one day, and bought me some small books written by Dr. John R. Rice. One was on Hell; one was on The Holy Spirit. I read them, and began writing to him and getting more of his books. I read his book on prayer.

The church I attended was Southern Baptist, and the first school I thought about attending was Southwestern Seminary in Texas, where Dr. John R. Rice had attended years before, and spoke of in his books.

Letter from Dr. John R. Rice.

I had written John Rice, and asked him where to go to school. He hadn't answered me. Well, while I was gone, his letter came, and he said, "Southwestern is all right. I went there. But it's not as good a school as it was. I would recommend Bob Jones University because it's nearer to you. But there's a Baptist school over in Chattanooga, Tennessee, and I believe, it being nearer, that you ought to go there." I said to myself, "Thank you, Brother Rice, but I'm going to ask the Lord now." I asked the Lord, and He just plainly told me to go to Tennessee Temple. That's where I went. I had four years of Bible school and four years of college there.

I had been to school previously at King's College in Bristol, Virginia, and got my science and math out of the way. I had gone there for boxing, and I hadn't cared about anything else. Oh, I had taken a Bible course, but I made my best grades in science and math, the subjects I needed most to transfer to Temple.

At Tennessee Temple.

So I ended up going to school at Tennessee Temple Schools in Chattanooga, Tennessee. I believe schooling can help you. I needed it and got a lot of training there, but you don't learn how to be a preacher from formal schooling. I enrolled in the 3-year Bible School course in 1951 and finished as Valedictorian of the Graduating Class of 1953. In 1954 I finished the 4-year Bible School course and graduated as Salutatorian. I graduated from the college in 1955.

D.C.. *I was present when Paul gave the Salutatorian Speech.*

God Sometimes Speaks Into Our Spirits.

We are not accustomed to God speaking to us in our spirit. We are more comfortable with the idea that God only speaks to people from the written Word of God today. That is God's main tool of communication with us; however, it does not violate the Word of God if God decides to communicate with us in our spirit.It will never be contrary to the written Word of God. Furthermore, the written Word of God nowhere says that God will never speak to His children directly. I have found these words from the written Word of God:

37

And thine ears shall hear a word behind thee, saying, This is the way, walk ye in it, when ye turn to the right hand, and when ye turn to the left (Isaiah 30:21).

For as many as are led by the Spirit of God, they are the sons of God (Romams 8:14).

"But the manifestation of the Spirit is given to every man to profit withal. For to one is given by the Spirit the word of wisdom; to another the word of knowledge by the same Spirit (I Corinthians 12:7, 8).

We are not talking about "wild fire" or using this as a license to add to the written Word of God. Not at all. Not only do we find God's Spirit leading His children by a variety of ways in the written Word of God, we also find a variety of ways God leads His children, as evidenced by their spoken and written testimonies.

It is true that some people may mix this up to think that anything they think up is from God. What a catastrophe! We must not play the fool in putting words in God's mouth. We must not add to His Word, and we must not take away from His Word – especially His written Word. But His leading word is sometimes spoken into our spirit. It does not happen often, but sometimes it does – only a few times in my entire life.

Dan's Similar Testimony
I have hesitated to include my testimony in Paul's book. But I think I must add my personal testimony concerning this issue of how God sometimes…SOMETIMES… leads His children today. The above story is a delicate matter, and some think that God always leads only by the way they have it figured out. Neither Paul nor I are Pentecostal or Charismatic. Genuine Christians may serve God all their lives and never experience God speaking to them in their conscious spirit. But I would be lying if I denied the following story.

Once, I burned up a transmission many miles from home. I was semi-paralyzed from French Polio. I was pulling a U-Haul trailer loaded with books and a piano. It was heavy! On a long pull on I-40 heading west toward Asheville, NC, the car lost power and the transmission began to flame. A trucker pulled in ahead of me and jumped out with a fire extinguisher to put out the flames. He had watched the car flame all the way up the long grade until the transmission fluid was burned out and the power was lost. After putting out the fire, the truck pulled away and I was left as a sitting duck, alone in the dark at 2:00 a.m. So I explained to the Lord how things were and earnestly committed my keeping into His hands.

A highway patrolman awakened me and wanted to know if I wanted him to call a tow truck. In my spirit I knew not to do it. I waited until dawn and another patrolman stopped. This time, I let him call a wrecker. As it turned out, there had been a time change in their system of which wrecker was to answer the call. A tall, lanky guy pulled up in a Ford wrecker, a chaw of tobacco in one jaw, and I asked him to hook it up. I got in the wrecker cab with him, and he towed the car and trailer to a garage and dropped them off. The mechanic was off for the day.

I went with the wrecker to the mechanic's house, and the mechanic agreed to work. The driver then took me to a restaurant and bought my breakfast. Then he took me to his home and put me to bed on a couch in the basement overlooking I-40. The sound of his footsteps disappeared up the steps and I was alone, very alone, and exhausted. This stranger, this lost man…I wondered if I could pay the bill.

As I began to get sleepy, the Spirit of God spoke into my spirit as clear as a hi-tech telephone: "Do you see how I can take care of you?" *Ten words. Not an idea.*

Ten words. I drifted off to sleep. I was awakened six hours later as the man came down the stairs and said, "I think we've got you ready to go!" He took me to a restaurant and bought me another meal. There was one transmission in town in all the junk yards that would fit my car. The junk yard mechanics said they couldn't get to it that day, but he bribed them with a six-pack of cold Pepsi, and they took care of it.

The man who showed me all that kindness was not saved, but his mechanic had been witnessing to him. I've thought of it scores of times, rehearsed the words God whispered to me that day, counted the words, and cherished them. When there's a problem too big, I sometimes go back to that day and remember: "Do you see how I can take care of you?" That does not make me a super Christian. That's just the way the God chose to handle it on that day. His words to me did not contradict the Word of God.

God's Private Preacher Schooling. (Paul continues…)

I believe the real schooling for preaching is from God. Moses was a highly educated man, in the best university of his day, in the strongest nation on earth. But God put him on the back side of the desert for forty years. The Apostle Paul was highly intelligent and highly educated, but before he was really used of God, he was removed from his human advantages and was schooled and shaped by God for several years in a remote desert place.

Education and formal schooling are fine. God places no premium on ignorance. When God calls a man to preach, it is God's Word that is to be preached. God expects the man to read and study and memorize His Word. How can a man preach what he doesn't know? But *formal schooling*, as we think of it, is not absolutely necessary to be a good preacher.

Some of the best men, who loved the Lord, depended on the Lord, had the power of God, had better services than some others, and did so without formal schooling. Oh, they may have made a few mistakes in the English language and other things, but they had the power of God. Please understand, I'm not against education, but I don't think you have to have a lot of formal education to be used of God.

Get All The Formal Schooling God Wants You To Have.
But don't depend on your education. Depend on God. Thank God for all the education you can get. Work hard at it. But don't love your education. Don't wallow in your education. Don't make a fool of yourself admiring your education. Let's don't glory in education. Glory in God!

If a lot of formal schooling and training were an absolute requirement to be used of God, a lot of effective preachers through the history of Christianity wouldn't have made it. The training Pastor Ellis had was not for preaching. Finney, Moody, Spurgeon, and many others had no formal schooling for preaching, but they saw the need for schooling and studied hard on their own. Some of these men, who were self-taught, started schools to help preachers shorten the time of their education and to get a better quality of education.

Moody - Spurgeon.
Moody was known for his life-long practice of arising before dawn to read and study the Word of God. Few today could equal Spurgeon's disciplined study and mastery of the Bible. His printed sermons are today found in almost every preacher's library. Who can equal his eloquence? But Spurgeon, and Moody, and Torrey wouldn't be allowed in many Baptist churches today because all of them had a beard.

Formal schooling is a short-cut, a means of buying discipline to study that we might not otherwise have. It will save you a lot of blunders and mistakes, but won't give you the power of God. The Holy Spirit is the only source of God's power.

Greek, and Hebrew, and the Power of God.
A man can speak good English, and know the Greek and the Hebrew, and not have the power of God. The power of God is the one thing that's needed today. That's our biggest problem. We're without the power of God. We cannot get the power of God from any school on earth. God's power does not come

41

through training.

The apostles had the best teacher in the history of the world, but Jesus plainly told His disciples that they would receive power when the Holy Spirit came upon them. They got no power from their training, though their training was extremely useful. If the apostles got no power from the best training in the history of the world, from the best teacher in the world, we should not think we will do any better today.

God's power does not come from schooling and training or books that we read. That includes this book. No one can get God's power from reading this book. You may be encouraged by this book to seek God, and God may give you His power. But you cannot get God's power from this book.

Jesus did everything He did in the power of the Holy Spirit. No powerful work is recorded in His biography until after the Holy Spirit descended upon Him. Then, why do we think we can bypass the need for God's power through the Holy Spirit today by going through some kind of educational process? Again, God's power does not come through schooling, and training.

Some of the things that happened to me (Dan, you were in one of those times) years ago, didn't come to me from education, and formal schooling. They came from God.

You don't win people to Christ unless the Holy Spirit convicts them. They can't be saved without it. I believe in studying, and I believe in education; but I believe the power of the Holy Spirit has got to do the work.

God Has Chosen to Work Through People.

In our dispensation, the day in which we live today, God works through people. He has always worked through people. He works through instruments. I've found people being saved that had not been to church, but they had heard the Word of God somewhere.

One man had been going to church forty years or more, and nobody could move him. This man came forward in a meeting and was saved. A young preacher that hadn't been preaching long was preaching. The young preacher went to the man and said, "Brother, what was it I said, what did I do, what words did I say that made you be saved?"

42

The man said, "Son, I didn't hear a word you said. Forty years ago I heard Billy Sunday preach, and I've not got it off my mind since. But, by what he said, I've accepted the Lord as my Savior."

That's like Ecclesiastes. 11:1, *Cast thy bread upon the waters and thou shalt find it after many days.* Many times we'll talk to people, witness to people, and it'll be a long time before they'll ever be saved. I believe it's important for us to realize that it's the Holy Spirit that does it. If He doesn't do the work, it can't be done.

What Is the Call of God Today?

Dan: *"Brother Paul, what is the call of God? Is it sudden? Is it gradual, something you drift into? Is it clear and self-evident?"*

Paul: "I don't think it's something you drift into. I didn't. I think so many people think they're so bad they can't preach, and that's the kind God uses. People have different callings, and some may drift into their calling; but with me it wasn't that way. With me it was specific. I didn't want to be an evangelist. I didn't think I could.

"I didn't know the Scripture we read in I Corinthians 1:26-29. I thought you had to be a great intellect. I thought you had to be something on a stick with a paddle and shovel, and a spoon thrown in – something great and mighty, and I knew I wasn't that."

God and Self.

But God doesn't want someone great and mighty. God wants somebody He can control - somebody He can guide by the Holy Spirit. The main thing in all the Christian life is *self* – being controlled by the Holy Spirit.

You can have experiences In the call of God, and I believe in experiences. You don't have to have the same as someone else. But in my calling, God started putting it on me. I already wanted to be a preacher like the ones I was around. I had been around Pastor Ellis and other preachers. I wanted to be a preacher like them.

I wanted to preach around, and have a job, and work at secular work like the other preachers I knew. A lot of preachers did it that way. I studied the Scriptures.

But He called me specifically. He put it on my heart just as plain as could be, *"You're going to be an evangelist."* He didn't speak to me audibly, but He came pretty close to it. The message was, *"You can forget about being a pastor. You'll never pastor a church. You're going to be an evangelist."*

Paul Ferguson the Fighter
Chapter 3

Summer School is Over, so what Do I Preach?

After attending Tennessee Temple for the first summer, I went back home to Greensboro and the McConnough Road Baptist Church. I didn't know what to preach.

The Lord put it on my heart to pray. I prayed, and prayed, and prayed, and prayed all night. Then about 6:30 in the morning, God gave me the message: *The Last Train to Heaven.* I had worked for the railroad, and a lot of people rode the trains then. So God gave me that message. We'll talk about that message all through this book, and what God told me about it when He gave me the message. That message, *God's Last Train to Heaven*, preached at McConnough Road Baptist Church, was the first time I had ever seen the power of God move like that, in people being saved.

Back To School and Revival Meetings.

During the next four years, while I was a student in Tennessee Temple Bible School, I preached about thirty-five revival meetings. At Pine Set, Tennessee, I had about forty saved in a meeting. I had talked with three men, in particular, during the meeting. Two of the men told me they would get saved when they got ready. I said, "No you won't." I was pretty rough then. I said, "God will stop your heart from beating and drop you into Hell." They cursed me and walked away. The meeting hadn't been over for more than a week when both of those two men were killed in a car wreck near Chattanooga, drunk.

> *D. C.: I remember the wreck at the intersection of Hwy 11 and 64, west of Chattanooga, 3-4 miles. A tractor-trailer turned over onto the car. I think of the wreck every time Barbara and I go that way to the Cracker Barrel about 200 yards below the intersection. Hwy 11 is the Lee Highway, named after Civil War General Robert E. Lee.*

I talked to another man in the same meeting, on the same

45

day. He was drinking, but not drunk. I told him about being saved. He said, "Preacher, I believe that's all right, but I've drunk a lot of liquor. I love liquor better than anything in all the world, and I'm going to drink whiskey 'til I die. I'll go to Hell, but I'm going to drink it. I'll get saved when I get ready."

Of course, I told him the same thing I told the other two men earlier. I said, "God may cut you off and drop you into Hell." The very next day after the other two men were killed, this man was walking down the street and dropped dead with a heart attack.

Sherwood, Tennessee.

In Sherwood, so many of the young people got saved that they had to close down the movie theater. It may have reopened later. I don't know, but for then, it had to close. Sixty or more people were saved in the meeting. Sherwood was a small community. The effect of the meeting went far beyond the sixty or so who were saved. In the years that followed, I returned to Sherwood six or seven times for meetings, and people were saved in every meeting.

During that first meeting at Sherwood, I witnessed to two men who said they would get saved when they got ready. I told them the same thing: "God may stop your heart from beating and drop you into Hell." Not long after the meeting a train hit their car and killed both of them. They were drunk.

Missing God's Last Train - A Special Message.

Perhaps I should again give the background of this message and God's dealing with me. This happened early in my ministry, and it was NOT merely a matter of my coming up with an interesting theme to entertain a crowd, as you will see.

God plainly told me, when He gave me the Last Train message, that He was going to follow it with judgment. Sometimes I gave it the title of *God's Last Train to Heaven* or *Missing God's Last Train to Heaven*. He told me that it wouldn't be popular, that it would make people mad, but that I would have more people saved through this sermon than all the rest of my sermons put together.

It happened all through the years, especially when God would

46

direct me to preach that message after much prayer. It happened at Stevenson, Alabama, where Dan Carr was pastor. A truck turned over and killed a man we had talked to in that meeting. Near Dayton, Tennessee, in a meeting, one man died during the meeting and one died right after the meeting. Both of the men had been witnessed to. Pine Set, Sherwood, Stevenson, Dayton - these are only a few samples of what God did in many other places in my meetings, where God directed me to preach on *God's Last Train to Heaven*.

Pastors and "God's Last Train."

The majority of pastors believed the message was God's doing as they observed what was happening. One pastor in Mississippi got mad at me during the early days of my meeting in his church. He didn't like me and criticized me all week. He had said he would never publicly go talk to anybody during a church service invitation to come forward. Now, I don't believe in just slipshod badgering and button-holing people for show. But if God tells you to go, you'd better go.

When I preached that message, that pastor was crying and going all over the church begging people to be saved. People were stirred. Not only the pastor, but others in the church were going to lost people in the church, begging them to be saved, and many responded. Lost people responded because they believed the presence and power of God was there and because people were genuinely concerned about them. On that day there must have been forty or more people that made professions of faith.

D. C.: Be Careful about Writing off these Accounts as Mere Emotionalism.

There is an emotionalism that can be documented as mere emotionalism. It has no other observable characteristic than the display of emotion. Emotionalism, as such, is not necessarily a movement of God. On the other hand, God's work is not limited to the intellectualism of an accurate dictionary or a book on math or science. God is the author of accuracy of fact and, also, the author of emotion in the human spirit. Some people are addicted to wallowing in emotion for its own sake. But it has been well established, by people known to be endowed with honest insight, that God often combines His convicting power of the Holy Spirit with strong emotion. Joy and sorrow are contrasting emotions often produced by the Holy Spirit.

Cleveland, Tennessee - Message on the Holy Spirit.

I preached a whole message on the Holy Spirit. I said that if anybody had a concern, would cleanse their life, claim the promise of the fullness of the Holy Spirit, you can be filled with the Spirit. Then, whatever God leads you to do, do it. You'll be filled with the Spirit.

I gave the invitation and a man walked forward. He said, "I heard your message today. You said a man can't be filled with the Spirit if he's unsaved. I'm unsaved, and I want to be filled with the Holy Spirit after I'm saved, to be used of God." He accepted the Lord, and it seemed like he had a pretty good experience. He said, "Go over those words.'" I did, again. He went through it and asked the Lord to fill him with the Spirit.

I'm not exaggerating. It seemed like a light from Heaven came down on that man. I'd never seen anything like it in my life. You could see a difference. I'd heard Holiness people talk about a light from Heaven settling upon the face. It happened to him! I saw it! It was not my imagination.

Hot Worker for God.

He said, "I've got some people where I work, unsaved." He went out of that meeting and began working on those people. I don't remember the exact number, but I believe he brought twenty-some the first day after he was saved. The next day he brought a few less. The next day he brought about half the original number. The last day he brought about eight, and then about four. And all those people he brought were converted in the meeting. They never missed another service during the meeting.

Worker Disappears.

The funny part about this story is that the man who recruited all those people dropped out. He didn't come back. The people he had brought to church were begging him to come back. He got drunk! He continued to drink. The people were trying to get him to come back to church. He never came back. I never knew what happened to him. That's the strangest thing I ever saw in my life. Every one of those people joined the church and was baptized. Every one of them went on and continued with the Lord for years.

Eugene Michael - Low-key Man.

I was preaching in the Chester Baptist Church in Ohio. Brother Cook was the pastor. A woman came forward every night in the meeting, praying at the altar for her husband, Eugene Michael. She asked me to go see him.

He was sitting in a pickup truck. I said, "Mr. Michael, your wife is burdened about you, and I came over here to talk to you about being saved. Will you let me talk to you?" "Oh yeah. Yeah, I'll let you talk to me." He sat there just like a knot on a log. Didn't seem like it touched him a bit.

I said, "Well, I'll pray." And I prayed.

"Mr. Michael, are you ready to accept Christ as your Savior?" "Yes, I am." He accepted the Lord right there in the pickup truck. I had gone through the plan of salvation with him in the Scripture. "Now, Brother Michael, you need to follow the Lord and be baptized."

He said, "Well, I work on the second shift, and I can't come 'till Sunday; but Sunday morning I'll be there, and I'll come forward, and I'll be baptized when they baptize." So the next Sunday he came, but he didn't come forward. I went back to him and said, "Brother Michael, were you saved the other day?" He said, "Yeah." I said, "Well, don't you want to be baptized?" "Sure, I want to be baptized." "Well," I said, "why don't you come forward?" He said, "I will." So, he came forward and presented himself for baptism, but he was very low key and laid back about the whole thing. Unimpressive.

The Steam Engine - Walsh.

In that same meeting, there was a lost man named "Walsh." When he got saved, he ran all over the church, jumped up and down and shouted "Praise the Lord," etc. He brought in fifteen people or more during the meeting, and they were all saved. If I remember right, we had sixty-something saved in that meeting. It was a real meeting.

Sunday night, the last night of the meeting, everybody that had made a profession during the meeting came forward and stood at the front. Michael, who had just presented himself that morning, just stood there like lice was falling off of him. Walsh was there that night, running all over the church and praising God.

My Convert and God's Convert.

So I went back to Chattanooga, and I said, "Lord, have mercy. Michael is my convert. He's not saved. But that Walsh fellow, that's a real converted man. When I go back there on my next scheduled meeting, I'll find that Walsh man still a'goin, and Ol' Michael will be 'Gone With The Wind.'"

When I got back a year later, Michael was faithful, and Walsh was no where to be found. Michael has been faithful through the years. He goes out and witnesses to people everywhere. He goes to the State Fair and puts up a booth and wins people to the Lord, even to this day. All these years he's never backslid a bit, just going on real steady for the Lord.

We've not seen Walsh since the day he was shouting and running all over the church. The last time I was at that church in a meeting, he would hide and not let me see him. He ran from me. That shows you that you can't go by the display of emotion all the time.

Baptists on the Left - Methodists on the Right.

In another church in Tennessee, I held a meeting with Baptists and Methodists meeting in the same building. The crowds were good. I preached two weeks. The Baptists sat on the left side of the building, and the Methodists sat on the right side (looking from the pulpit). The Methodists didn't care if everybody went to Hell. They just wanted to have as many or more than the Baptists. The Baptists didn't care if anybody went to Hell. They just wanted to have the same number or more than the Methodists.

As you know, I tell a lot of jokes to warm the people up and relax them from their cares and worries. They'll listen better if they're relaxed. But in this place, I'd tell a joke and their face would get so long they could eat butter out of the bottom of a churn and have fifteen feet of their long face left over. That was the deadest place I've ever seen.

During all that time I didn't even have anybody to get mad at me. I preached on *God's Last Train to Heaven*, that had been used everywhere. But nothing moved them. Nothing happened.

In No Mood To Eat.

People asked me to eat with them, and I wouldn't eat. I went out into the woods, and prayed, and prayed, and prayed, and prayed. I said, "God is there anything on earth I can do?" And I said, "Oh me." It came to me what to do. I said, "Lord, that's awful unusual." He said, "Well, do it." And I said, "All right. I don't much want to, but I'll do it. I'll try it. If that don't do it, nothing in this world would ever move this church. We've been all this time, and nothing has moved, so I'll do it."

They had a curtain that served as a makeshift divider. We could take people behind the curtain and talk to them about being saved, if anybody ever came forward. I'd go back there and pray every night. A young man, Charlie Marshal, was leading singing for me, and he played a trumpet.

I was going to preach on the Second Coming of Christ, and I said, "Charles, you hide that trumpet back there. And, when I say, 'The trumpet sounds!' You blow that trumpet." I said, "Maybe it'll wake these old hypocrites up a little."

Preachin' and Forgettin'.

I got into my message on the Second Coming with great earnestness of soul and forgot all about ol' Charlie being back there. In my sermon I hollered real loud: "AND THE TRUUUUMPET...SOOUUUNNDED!!" Charlie hit that trumpet! It was like dynamite going off, it was so loud! Those ol' hypocrites began throwing up their hands, and moaning, "Oh God! The Lord has come and we're not ready to go!"

They started getting right with God and running all over

the church, hugging each other, apologizing to each other for thinking more about Methodists and Baptists than they did the Lord. People were getting saved. Everybody we knew about being lost in the church house got saved that night. During the next week they had over fifty-six people saved. The pastor said that spirit went on for two or three months, with people being saved in every service.

God used that trumpet to really wake them up. Now, that's the only time I ever did that. I've never used a trumpet like that since. This was a once-in-a-lifetime thing. You don't go around practicing those things because somebody else did it. I had never heard of it. God told me to do it. When God tells you to do something and you do it, He'll honor it. If God don't tell you to do it, and you do it on your own, it'll flop every time.

Does God Ever Speak To A Man In His Spirit?

Let's return to this subject again. We need to do some thinking about this. There are some good men, sincere men, who believe God does not go beyond giving a man a burden; that God will never speak words to a man as a means of leading him today, because that would be adding to the Scriptures. But God can do anything He wants to do. I believe in dispensations. But I believe God can do anything He wants to, anytime He wants to, any time He chooses to do it. When God speaks to a man in the man's spirit and gives him directions, that's not adding to the Scripture.

One of the best Bible teachers that ever lived was Aubrey Martin, who lived in Chattanooga and taught Bible at Tennessee Temple University. Mr. Martin was blind, but, my...how he could teach the Word of God! Aubrey Martin believed like I do. He believed that God could even speak audibly to people today.

God NEVER audibly spoke to me, but He came pretty close. Sometimes I'm so dumb I have to be told, so I don't go by that theory, and that's what it is - a theory - that God cannot or will not speak definite words to people today. If you talk to many missionaries today, you'll find many of them telling you of times when God spoke to them on the mission field.

We Can Make a Big Mistake Here.

As with many of God's gifts and dealings with His people, we can abuse or misuse what God places in our hands. You can make a cult out of making up a bunch of stuff and saying, "God told me this and that," when God hasn't told you a thing. We'd better not go that route. God might decide to cut us down for that.

A Good Pastor Learns a Great Lesson.

I was in a meeting in the Chattanooga area, and we were having people saved. There was a woman in the church who was in the hospital on her death bed. She sent word to the pastor that if the visiting evangelist would come over and pray for her, she would get well.

The doctors had already given her up to die. They said there wasn't a power in this world that could help that woman. They said that if anybody could heal her it would be God, and they didn't think He would do that. That's what the doctors said.

So the pastor and I went to the hospital, but on the way over there, the pastor told me, "Brother Ferguson, this woman is dying. She's got to die. But we want to please her. You go pray for her. She thinks she'll get healed, but she won't."

When the pastor said that, I started praying, not audibly, just within myself. I said, "Lord, do you want me to go in and pray for this woman?" He said, "Yes." I said, "Well, are you going to heal her?" And He said, "Not by you, because you're not going to pray. The pastor will pray. You tell him to pray."

We went on to the hospital and went into the room. The pastor punched me and whispered, "Now, Brother Ferguson, it won't do any good, but you pray." We bowed our heads and I didn't pray. The Lord had told me not to. We waited and waited. The pastor said, "Aren't you going to pray?" And I said, "No, I'm not going to pray. You go on and pray. The Lord wants you to pray." He said, "I can't! I don't believe God can heal her." I said, "I know God can if He so wills. Brother, I don't believe in all those healing lines they're puttin' on, but God is still on the throne and He can heal." We were right in the room with the woman while this was going on, but it was real low so she wasn't supposed to hear us. But she did hear, because we were right beside the bed.

53

So, he started to pray, but he didn't believe anything would happen. I looked up, and the Lord just shook the daylights out of the guy. He was just shaking all over like he was one of those machines that shakes you. He was really shaking. All at once he cut loose, and I never heard such praying in my life, thanking God for healing the woman. And then it happened! She was healed!

The doctors came running in and she was standing up in bed, jumping all over the bed and shouting and praising God. The doctors that had run into the room said, "Don't be disturbing this woman! She's not going to live, and here you are...you'll kill her!" And she said, "They won't kill me...nobody will kill me because I'm healed! God healed me!"

The Doctors Get in on a Good Thing.

The doctors examined her and couldn't find a thing wrong with her. As far as I know, she's still living today, and that must have been twenty years ago. Now, I'm not a healing preacher, but I believe God CAN HEAL; and if we had more faith, He might heal more than He does. It is not always God's will to heal. I'm not a Pentecostal or a Charismatic. I don't believe healing for everybody is in the Atonement. Everybody can be saved who wants to be saved, but everybody cannot be healed by God's power. But God certainly does a lot of healing here and there, and if we would pray more earnestly, we might take hold of God's willingness to heal some of these people. Not everybody, of course, but some.

Preaching and Putting Down the Town Bully.

There was a preacher at Temple who knew about me, about my being a boxer. He had boxed a little. He went to a place in Virginia and there was a man in the town named Hirsch Wright. He didn't bother any of the church services in the town except when the Baptists had revival meetings. There wasn't but one Baptist church in the town and that's where the meeting was being held.

If the Baptist church had a revival meeting, he would bother them. He'd go down there and tell the preacher that if he didn't leave, he'd whip him. All the preachers would leave. Well, this preacher called me for a meeting, and I said, "Sure, I'll take it."

The meeting started. I preached all the first week and nothing happened. Sunday night, I preached *The Last Train to Heaven*, and nothing much happened - two or three saved, some young people. On Friday night of the second week, I was going to preach on *Why Heaven and Hell Are Alike*. Some people say, "Oh, that can't be." But, for example, both are everlasting. I know twenty-some reasons why they're alike.

I got up to preach and I noticed that right down in front of me there was a pretty-good-size man, real tough looking. He had on a checked shirt that stood out in the crowd. Earlier in the week, the people had been laughing at my jokes and opening remarks that I make to break the ice in the beginning of my message, but on this night I noticed that nobody was laughing. I decided that I had better go ahead and preach.

You Can't Preach That Here.

I began by saying that I had announced that I was going to preach on why Heaven and Hell are alike. A man in the audience spoke up, "You mean, why they're different." I said, "No sir. Why they are alike." He said, "Well, you're not goin' to preach that here." I said, "Well, I am. He said, 'You're not.' I said, Well, you listen to me preach, and then if you don't agree with it, that I'm right in what I say, I'll apologize to you in front of everybody." He said, "No, you're not goin' to preach that." He stood up and said, "I mean it. You're not preachin' that."

I just moved over on the platform, right in front of where he sat in the audience, drew my fist back, and said, "Buddy, I'm gonna count to five and if you don't sit down, I'm gonna come down there and knock the living devil out of you." That's what I said, and I was going to do it. I got mad. I mean, I was mad. I was gonna jump over there and knock that guy's head off. I said, "One, two..". - and he sat down.

"I started on, read the text, preached the sermon. Lord have mercy, I didn't think that anything like that would happen. I told that to a group one time and somebody said, "Oh, I know what happened. It broke up the meeting." I said, *It sure did, but not the way you think.*

I finished the sermon and gave the invitation for people to

come forward to be saved. They started coming forward, and I had a little room where I took them. But there was nobody there to deal with them but me. There were 25-30 that came that night, and I dealt with them personally, one at a time. I went through the plan of salvation with each one individually, not as a group.

I was there a half-hour or more, and after I had dealt with the last one, I came out of the room and there stood the preacher and this man, Hirsch Wright. He said, "You put me in my place didn't you?" And I said, "I sure did, and I don't apologize for it. You were wrong." He said, "I know it, and I apologize to you, and will you forgive me?" I said, "Yes sir." We shook hands and he left.

The Town Bully Dies – Many People Saved.

He died in less than two weeks. I had preached *The Last Train* there, but he didn't hear it. Sunday morning, people came from everywhere for miles around. We couldn't get them in the building. They said, "Any preacher that could come and tell Hirsch Wright that he would come and knock his head off if he didn't sit down, and him sit there and listen to you preach, we'll come and listen to you preach anytime."

The meeting broke loose and people were saved the next morning. That night, people came from everywhere around there to see the preacher that told Hirsch Wright he would punch him and Hirsch sat there and listened to him.

I had to leave and go to another meeting. They continued the meeting and more were saved. After Hirsch Wright died, more were saved. That went on for a month or two after I left, people being saved from miles around.

Never Had to Hit Anybody During a Meeting.

I didn't have anything like that to happen many times. It shook me up that time, because I got mad. If I hadn't gotten mad, I wouldn't have done it. God knew what I would do. In South Carolina a man said, "I believe I can whip you." I thought he was joking. I said, "Well, I don't care." He kept on, and I said, "All right, I'll just beat the devil out of you." He left. He got out of there in a hurry. I was gonna do it.

Judo and Teenagers.

I had to learn JUDO in the Coast Guard when we worked with the Marines. I remember to this day how to tie somebody to a tree without using a rope. One time in the Coast Guard, a bunch of them did me like that and went off and left me (not very far), and I couldn't get loose. In rank, I was over them, and they laughed at me. I just let it go and didn't report them.

I've had a whole lot of teenagers come to my meetings, and low fellows wanting to try me. I was pretty good in JUDO. I'd get them by the arm and make them cry "Uncle," and they'd never bother me any more. I didn't want to hurt them. I could make them think they were dying without hurting them. If you hit them, you might do them more damage. If you get a JUDO hold on the arm just right, they don't know how to break it. I knew how, but they didn't. That happened several times, and I never did that a time in my life that the person didn't get saved sometime during the meeting.

I would tell the boys I could tie them to a tree without a rope, and they wouldn't believe me. So I would take them out, do one leg like this and bend the other one down, and it paralyzes them till they can't move. They can have their hands loose, and they can't move. Somebody has to let them loose.

During a meeting, the church boys began to talk about it to other boys, and one boy came to church and said, "Aw, you can't do it. You tie me to a tree and leave me, and I'll get loose." I said, "All right." He said, "Well, I know I need to be saved, but I'll be saved if you'll tie me to a tree." I said, "Well, you'll get saved then."

I tied him to a tree and he couldn't get loose. He went to hollerin' and I said, "No, I think I'll leave you. You're lyin' to me; you don't want to get saved." He said, "I'm honest. I'm a sinner. I know I'm goin' to Hell, and I know I don't want to spend the rest of the time here."

He was about 14 or 15. He was saved and went on to live for the Lord. I saw him years later. He told the story at different places and went out telling people about the Lord and winning people to the Lord. I showed him how to do the tree "handcuff" after he got saved. God used things like that in my ministry to get people saved.

Billy Graham in Greensboro.

Billy Graham went to Greensboro, North Carolina, while I was in school in Chattanooga, Tennessee. Many of the men I had witnessed to over the years accepted Christ in that Billy Graham meeting, and they're living today for the Lord.

Some people don't like Billy Graham. I've heard preachers say they never knew of one of Billy Graham's converts. Well, as I've gone over the land preaching, I've seen hundreds of people who came forward in my meetings who were saved in Billy Graham's meetings. They came to my meetings and were baptized in a Baptist church after they heard me preach and went through a whole meeting.

Now, in the later years, Billy Graham hasn't much told people which church to go to, or even to be baptized. There's a difference between his earlier years and his later years in several ways. He is God's servant, and I leave that up to the Lord. I've got my own record to face at the Judgment Seat of Christ.

Dan Carr: See a larger treatment of this subject in Appendix II.

Memorizing Scripture Was Hard – God Touched Me.

I first learned about memorizing Scripture from Dr. John R. Rice. Dr. Rice said that memorizing Scripture was very important and that most preachers were lazy and wouldn't memorize Scripture. Dr. Rice said that preachers could memorize if they would ask the Lord to help them do it, so I began memorizing. I had memorized about 150 Scriptures before I ever came to Tennessee Temple.

At Tennessee Temple, I enrolled in the Evangelism class under Dr. Salstrand. He talked about various methods of memorizing, but it took hard work for me to memorize. Now, if you memorized ten million verses, you would still have to review if you keep them. I was having real trouble with it. Memorizing was very hard for me.

So one night I went into a room. I said to myself, "I'm not memorizing the Scriptures as easy as I could. I know it's work, but I just don't think I'm retaining it the way I should." I started praying about memorizing Scripture, without praying around the world for Granddaddy and everybody else like we do sometimes. I prayed for at least 35 to 40 minutes about memorizing Scripture, and I just didn't quit. I don't remember all I said, but I asked the Lord to help me to pray and to memorize. Maybe it was an hour.

All at once, the Lord just came - a different experience than I've had before or since. I don't know exactly how to explain it; it was a special experience of His presence. He made me where I could memorize easier. I had a greater desire and more determination to memorize after that. I started memorizing again and I could retain it better. He made it known to me there in the room that night that He had made a difference - not in an audible voice, but it was just as real. I've never doubted it since.

Sometimes I go back and pray again like that. The Lord will advise me about my memorizing. I can still memorize, and I'm 76 years old. (I was thirty-some then.) Even so, it's not easy work. I still review. You should review. You don't retain it if you don't.

Getting Men Saved.

When men get saved, it's usually after long periods of prayer when people cry out to God and get burdened.

I was in Texas and we were having a pretty good meeting. They gave me the name of a man to pray for, Tom McKean. The preacher and I went out to the store, and the preacher introduced me to the man I had been praying for. He said, "Oh you're that old prize fighter that's been preaching over here." And I said, "No, I'm not a prize fighter. I'm a preacher. I used to be a prize fighter, I don't deny that. But I'm a preacher and tell people about Jesus."

He said, "Well, you talk plain, don't you?" I said, "That's the only way I know to talk." He said, "Preacher, I like you. I want to talk to you." The pastor I was with started pulling my coat and said, "Come on, come on, let's go." I said, "No, I want to talk to this man." The man said, "Well, preacher, I like you. I'll be at church tonight."

The pastor pulled at me and we went out. I said, "What's the matter with you?" He said, "You'll run that man off. We had him ready to come to church and you've run him off now. He'll never come." I said, "Preacher, how many times has McKean ever been at church?" He said, "Never." I said, "How in the world can you run somebody off that's never been there?" I said, "You can't run them off 'till you get them there. I didn't run him off, and he'll be there tonight."

He said, "Oh no," and told me what McKean would do if he came. Well, that night he was there - and every night, including the night I preached *The Last Train to Heaven.* After the message, he came to me and said, "Preacher, you said in the message that if anybody is willing to be saved, they can be saved." I said, "That's right." He said, "Well, I'm willing. Will you take me back in the room and talk with me?"

I went back in the room with him, and the preacher dismissed the service. Some of the people left, but the main people of the church stayed. You know how people will hang around after the service and talk. But they didn't talk. They went to prayin'.

While I was witnessing to Tom McKean, I gave him:

The Lord is not slack concerning his promise, as some men count slackness; but is longsuffering to us-ward, not willing that any should perish, but that all should come to repentance. (2 Peter 3:9)

For whosoever shall call upon the name of the Lord shall be saved. (Romans 10:13)

And the Spirit and the bride say, Come. And let him that heareth say, Come. And let him that is athirst come. And whosoever will, let him take the water of life freely. (Revelation 22:17)

I gave him some other verses and stressed the point that anybody that's willing to be saved can be saved. Now, *Missing God's Last Train* is a good message, but a hard message; and a lot of people get mad at it. But some will usually respond to it.

His wife had prayed three different nights, all night long before we saw Tom McKean in the store. When we went to the prayer room, she went to another room by herself and started praying. I dealt with the man for one hour before he could understand how to be saved. He accepted the Lord.

The Glory Came Down!

When Tom McKean got saved, someone hurried over to get his wife. She had prayed so hard she couldn't walk. SHE COULD NOT WALK. Two deacons assisted her in coming to her husband. She started praying again and thanking God. Now, the Shekinah Glory was for another time. But something greater than that is in II Corinthians 4:3,4: *"But if our gospel be hid, it is hid to them that are lost: In whom the god of this world [Satan] hath blinded the minds of them which believe not, <u>lest the light of the glorious gospel of Christ</u>, who is the image of God, <u>should shine unto them</u>."*

Jesus was there! I'd never been around the power of Jesus exactly like that before in all my life, as when that woman began to pray. I've seen the glory of God come down, but not like that. Some other woman, an old woman, started talking in tongues.

61

I said, "God, stop her!" She got choked and had to leave the room. She was a good woman and believed in praying, but she thought she couldn't get anybody saved unless she talked in tongues. I'm open to anything God does, but I sensed that for this woman to continue would be disruptive. So God stopped her.

That was the last day of the meeting, and Tom McKean was baptized the next Sunday. Over 200 people came for miles around to see him saved and baptized. He told me he had spent a half-million dollars or more on whiskey and rough living. Wasted! He was a wealthy man. He came to Christ by the prayers of his wife.

There was a woman in Annapolis, Maryland that prayed like Mrs. McKean, and I've seen some other women do that. More about the woman in Annapolis a little later.

More About Winning Men To Christ.

We're back to how you win men. Sometimes you have to go - that is, really go - after them. Dave Hartman was 70 years old when he got saved. And you know that after a person crosses 50, it's almost a million to one that that person will ever be saved. It takes long agonizing prayer, prevailing prayer, and people getting concerned - not just little ol' flippy, fleshly concern, but a genuine spiritual concern. There's a difference in a spiritual burden and a fleshly burden. A fleshly burden will wear out. A spiritual burden won't wear out.

It takes the Holy Spirit to do it, working through us. Jesus died on the cross and shed His blood for us. So sometimes these people that are getting up in years were missed by their generation. However, there's another side to the picture. Of the men who look like they're being saved after they're fifty years old, many or most of them were actually saved when they were young, I believe.

They went away from God after they were saved. They think that because they did all the things they have done, they weren't actually saved; but I believe many of them were. God brings them back, changes their lives, turns them around; and nearly every one of them will turn out to be a real man of God the rest of his life.

Sometimes the reason people get saved and go away from God is that they get too proud. They think, "Well, I can do it. I can live for God." God lets them go through a period in their lives to show them they can't do it. It's not what we do in living for God, but what He does through us. He does the saving; He does the keeping. All these things are done by the Lord Jesus Christ. Now, I don't run around hollerin' "Jesus this" and "Jesus that," but I do say that under my breath. I talk to Him.

And I believe that Christ ought to be the center of our lives - the center of all preaching. Now, I'm not against programs, and I'm not against school, but that won't do it. Only the Holy Spirit can do it. People have their programs, and some of them are worthwhile. But what I'm saying is that the main thing is our working with the Holy Spirit.

Old Men.

After these men get that old, to break them down is almost impossible. I think the figures show that, after a man is twenty-five, there's a half-million chance to one that he'll never be saved. As he gets older, the figure rises. If he's saved as a child and goes off, people want to say that he wasn't saved. I don't believe that. I believe that most men that make a profession of faith late in life were saved before at some time when they were young.

I was talking about *The Last Train to Heaven*. I believe that some of those men who have responded to that message were actually saved when they were young. I'm repeating myself here, but I really want to make that point. Many of these old men have told me that they were never saved, and maybe some of them were unsaved. But I believe most of them had been saved at some time.

Among those who hear *The Last Train to Heaven* are those who resist it, and they die soon afterward. They weren't going to turn their lives over to the Lord, and God just cut them off. That principle is stated in a different setting in: I Cor.5:5: *"Deliver such an one unto Satan for the destruction of the flesh that the spirit may be saved in the day of the Lord Jesus."*

Here, God is talking about turning a rebellious Christian over to the devil to be abused by him or even to be killed. And yet, this person would not lose his salvation. However, God would

63

kill him because he would not repent. In the same way, God sometimes kills lost people when He is dealing with them and they absolutely refuse to be saved. This is a hard saying, but I know it to be true. I saw it happen many times after I preached *God's Last Train to Heaven.* God told me from the beginning that that message would be followed by judgment, and it happened that way.

More Men Saved In Longer Meetings.
    In this day, I have to admit that where I saw most men saved over the years was in at least two-week meetings. And for some, we had to go a third week. At one place the pastor wanted to go five weeks. He said, "We'll get 500 saved if you'll stay two more weeks." We had gone three weeks and we had witnessed a bunch of people being saved. The longer you go when the power of God is really working like that everywhere, over the whole town, the more people you will have saved.
    I didn't stay. I had another meeting scheduled and I went to it. The meeting I went to was a super, colossal flop. Later, that pastor told me that he had wanted to cancel the meeting if I had asked him, but was afraid to cancel it on his own.
    A year later, the pastor that wanted to go for five weeks came to a meeting where I was preaching and brought a whole group of people to the meeting and said, "In this past year we've had 500 people saved" - the exact number he said would be saved if I had stayed for two weeks. Now, God saved those people that the Lord had put on that pastor's heart in a year's time. But if I had stayed for those two weeks, I would have had the joy of seeing them saved under my ministry.
    Today, almost all the meetings are much shorter. People think they're too long if you have one for three days, now. Women are now working outside the home and, in increasing numbers, are doing that to help hold the home together.

Another Praying Woman.
    There was a woman in North Carolina who got so burdened that she was spending days and nights in prayer for her husband to be saved. It came to the last night of the meeting and her husband told her, "I'm not going. You can pray all you want to.

I'll never get saved 'til I get ready." She said, "Well, the preacher has said that you don't get saved when you get ready. You get saved when God gets ready, and He may cut you off and drop you into Hell."

She turned, walked out, and went to church. The husband got mad and left the house. But God spoke to him and said, "You heard what your wife said. It's true for you, buddy. If you don't get saved tonight, you are THROUGH! You are gone!"

He couldn't wait to get to church and get saved. He couldn't wait to the end of the service. He came forward in the middle of the service and said he wanted to be saved. I didn't get to finish preaching. He did the preaching. It shook that place. Here's an example of what praying and believing God can do - what one woman can do by agonizing in prayer.

Agonizing Prayer Will NOT Always Result in Salvation.

I'm not saying that there's some kind of rule with God that, if the wife becomes sufficiently burdened, her husband will always get saved. It happens often, but not always. I've seen some men cut off – die – because they will not respond to God's pleading with them. But most of the time they do get saved, especially when a whole group of people become burdened.

When I was up here in Flat Rock, Alabama with Brother Glenn York at Caperton's Chapel Baptist Church, there were a few burdened, and we had a few people saved. But if that whole group had gone on another week and had gotten burdened, it might have been a much greater outcome. I'm not wanting to blame the pastor, but the meeting should not have stopped because two people went off on Friday night. I think we should have gone on and we would have seen some of those men saved. I believe that. I've seen that happen too many times over the years not to believe that.

Christ went to the cross and suffered for us. If we have a loved one that's lost, shouldn't we be willing to spend extra time, extra crying out, and extra praying to God?

Practical Things about Prayer.

The most practical thing about prayer is simply to pray because the Bible tells us to pray. Dr. John Rice used to remind us of that. But, since we are human, sometimes the Lord has to bring things upon us before we will pray like we ought to pray.

As we pray, we will get a burden for prayer, a burden to pray. Sometimes we get a burden to pray as we hear a sermon on prayer. A book may inspire us to pray. John Rice's book on prayer is good. Torrey's book on prayer is one of the best I ever read. E. M. Bounds has an excellent book on prayer. Praying Hyde is one of the greatest life examples of prayer of anybody that ever lived, I believe, except the Apostle Paul.

A drifting mind hinders our praying. I used to go play handball, or go jogging or punch a punching bag, or some other kind of exercise. After that, I would be relaxed and I would go back to praying and sometimes pray three or four hours. This may not work for everybody, but it worked for me.

Praying Is Hindered By Eating.

I could never pray good right after I eat. All these preachers all over the country say, "Let's go eat and then pray." And I would say, "No, I can't do that." I can't pray right after I eat, and I don't think many other people can. I've prayed with preachers all over this country. We'd go to pray and they would eat. Then we would begin to pray. I would pray and they would go to sleep. I don't mean that in a critical manner, but it's just a fact. It's true. Not everybody, but most people will get sleepy after eating a big meal, and it's hard to pray then. I can't eat and then pray.

When to Pray.

The time for prayer varies. The Bible talks about praying in the morning. Jesus prayed in the morning: *"And in the morning, rising up a great while before day, he went out, and departed into a solitary place, and there prayed."* (Mark 1:35)

But all of us are not geared like that. There are morning people and there night owls. Some of the great men of the past, such as John Wesley, prayed early. A group of men wanted to meet with Wesley at night, and he said he had to get in bed by 10:00 p.m. because he had to get up at 4:00 a.m. to meet with the Lord.

I couldn't pray that early in the morning. Sometimes the Lord woke me up and I could pray then. But in the natural way of waking up, I couldn't pray in the morning. I always wait until about 10:00 o'clock to pray. The best meetings and the places where I've had the best results, I've prayed from about 10:00 o'clock to 12:00 noon every day. I could pray that way very easy. There are other reasons why we sometimes get too sleepy to pray well. We may be running so tired from physical labor or from losing sleep that we can't pray.

Sometimes God puts a burden on you to pray and you can't sleep. I've had that to happen many times. I've seen that happen to other people, as well. You go to bed and sleep a little while and then wake up and pray.

Older people are said to wake up in the morning easier than younger people. In my case, I've always thought that that was the Lord waking me up to pray. Usually, if you begin praying when you wake up like that, you'll go back to sleep after a while.

Some people say that it's the Devil that makes you go to sleep when you're trying to pray. I don't think so. I think the Lord puts you to sleep a lot of times when you're praying. I think that after you pray a certain amount, He let's you go back to sleep. I still do that.

> It is vain for you to rise up early, to sit up late, to eat the bread of sorrows: for so he giveth his beloved sleep. (Psalm 127:2)

The Devil doesn't control the children of God; the Holy Spirit does. We attribute a lot of things to the Devil that I don't think he has anything to do with. Of course, Jesus' disciples slept when they should have been praying, when Jesus was sweating drops of blood in prayer before going to the cross.

The Burden to Pray.

We shouldn't expect our prayer life to be the same every day, and it won't be the same with everybody. The Lord requires more from some than He does from others. Now, that's not an excuse for some people that don't pray. But everybody doesn't have the same burden for prayer, even if they want to pray like somebody else or want to have a burden for prayer like somebody else.

Praying, the act of praying, brings on a burden to pray more than anything. Praying, itself, brings on a burden to pray. I've had young preachers to come to me who had heard somewhere about praying. They would come to me and say, "I know you pray. Will you teach me to pray?" And I would say, "No, I can't teach you to pray. The Holy Spirit has to do that. But, I'll pray with you."

Most of them who came to me like that have gone on and turned into people who really prayed and continued to pray. A few quit preaching because they thought if they would pray a few hours they would become great, powerful preachers. I had one good friend that prayed, expecting to find the results in a few hours – no more than a few days. These men didn't understand that what they needed was to dedicate themselves to a life dominated by prayer.

Sometimes It Takes Years of Prayer To Get Results.

Sometimes long, consistent, laborious times of prayer spanning months and even years preceded the greatest revivals - the Welsh Revivals and all the other great revivals in this country and over the world. The great revivals of God's Spirit being poured out came after people started praying and continued praying. Sometimes they prayed for years. Some of the greatest preachers that ever preached found that there was some saint of God that was not known at the time, who prayed days and nights for those preachers.

> *And the LORD said unto him, Go through the midst of the city, through the midst of Jerusalem, and set a mark upon the foreheads of the men that sigh and that cry for all the abominations that be done in the midst thereof. (Ezekiel 9:4)*

One of my prayer warriors was my mother. She prayed before I was born that I would be a preacher. Then she prayed for me and agonized for me. Many of the successes and things that happened in my life over the years happened because of my mother praying so much.

68

After she died, Mrs. Mary Smith in Illinois prayed as much for me as my mother did. It went that way for several years. We preachers are going to find out when we get to Heaven that many of the things that were accomplished through us, the Lord did it through some people who prayed for us. I think we ought to pray for each other.

Why Pray Long?

People may wonder why anybody would pray for three and four hours and longer. What happens, and what do you pray about for that long? Well, if the Holy Spirit is in it that makes a difference.

Also, I have a prayer list of about twenty three hundred Christian people over the country that I pray for - not every day, but at least five times a week. *I read that list of names to the Lord.* After going over those names so many times over a period of time, a period of years, you don't have to be a genius in memorizing to remember many of the names.

The Holy Spirit may bring names to your attention in unusual cases - not usually, but sometimes. I have known people that I haven't had on my prayer list - haven't thought of them in a long time - and the Lord brought them to my mind at certain crisis times in their lives and urged me to pray for them.

Praying in the Spirit.

The Bible tells us to "pray in the Spirit." Many Christians don't know anything about this. It's strange news to most Christians, I'm afraid. Praying in the Spirit is not praying a certain way, loud or soft, etc. We are instructed in the Bible to pray in the Spirit.

> *Praying always with all prayer and supplication in the Spirit, and watching thereunto with all perseverance and supplication for all saints.* (Ephesians 6:18)

This is part of God's prayer plan for us. This is part of our working for God.

> *Likewise the Spirit also helpeth our infirmities: for we know not what we should pray for as we ought: but the Spirit itself maketh intercession for us with groanings*

69

which cannot be uttered. And he that searcheth the hearts knoweth what is the mind of the Spirit, because <u>he maketh intercession for the saints according to the will of</u> God. (Romans 8:26,27)

Hannah prayed (I Samuel), and she didn't utter a word. She just worked her mouth. I don't believe you even have to work your mouth. You can just pray in your heart without an audible word. She was praying for Samuel to be born, and he was born in answer to her prayer. *<u>The first of the great prophets was born from a woman that prayed with her mouth without uttering a word</u>.*

So, you can pray loud, or you can pray low, or no audible words. My personal praying varies. You don't do the same thing every time.

The Greatest Lack in Christian Service.

The greatest lack in Christian service is the lack of prayer. People say, "Oh, we don't need it today. We just believe God." Not so. You pray and pray. *<u>I don't believe we are praying in faith until we are praying in the Spirit.</u>* Much of our praying is merely uttering our desires and wishes into thin air. When we get our earthly, fleshly desires out of the way, *<u>then the Spirit can pray through us.</u>*

I've heard people pray in loud voices, and someone will say, "Oh, that was a great prayer." But some of the greatest prayers that have ever been prayed are not loud prayers. I knew a man in Chattanooga, years ago, who was in a revival meeting, and He would pray all the way to the services, and pray all the way home. During the day he would pray from three to six hours every day.

This man kept praying like that and one night, on his way to the meeting, he had prayed so much he could hardly say another word. He just prayed, "Lord, give us souls, give us souls." He was crying. That's all he could do. That night they had twenty six people to come forward to be saved.

Serving God May Require Hard Work.

People today think that we don't have to put out anything.

70

Jesus went to the cross and suffered for us. Therefore, we don't have to do much. Jesus PAID it all—Jesus will DO it all.

Jesus said: *"For what shall it profit a man, if he shall gain the whole world, and lose his own soul? Or what shall a man give in exchange for his soul?"* (Mark 8:36, 37)

As important as souls are, then, we have to go through some hardship sometimes to get people saved. We take it too lightly today. It takes a terrific burden and agonizing to get men saved. I'll say it again - most of the men that are saved were actually saved when they were young. Children know more about the Lord and about being saved than grown people do.

Praying Through.

There is NO such thing as praying through for salvation. Some think that salvation is like the little boy that cut his dog's tail off an inch at a time so it wouldn't hurt so much. Salvation is instantaneous. Salvation is by repentance toward God and faith toward our Lord Jesus Christ.

However, there is a praying through in other situations. That's for saved people. Jeremiah 29:13 says, *"Ye shall seek me, and find me, when ye shall search for me with all your heart."* So, I believe there is a praying through. You may not want to call it "praying through." You have to pray long enough to get the fleshly things out of the way <u>so that the Spirit can pray through us.</u>

Praying is not to persuade God. Some people think you have to beg and persuade God. God is often willing to answer. He has the answers all ready for us, BUT we're not ready to receive them. And what they call "praying through" is actually just praying ourselves out of the way so the Holy Spirit can pray through us. <u>When we pray in the Spirit, the prayer is going to be answered.</u>

The Old Timers.

Why don't we pray more than we do? Why don't preachers pray more than they do? America is destroying itself. Everybody can see that. The reason preachers don't pray more is that we put too much interest on other things, and we think we can accomplish God's work in a way different than the old-timers did.

Many of the old-time preachers wouldn't preach unless they prayed two hours. Some of them would pray more than that. Then, when the results didn't come, they would pray five or six hours, sometimes all night to see the power of God work. I've done that myself.

I remember a place in Missouri where I preached. We were praying and I preached the message, *The Last Train to Heaven*. The next day three or four unsaved men died. So the people were then stirred up and they began to pray after that. Sometimes it takes tragedy to get people to pray. So these people prayed and some unusual things happened in the meeting.

A Gun to Shoot Me.

In this same town, the preacher and I went into a place to witness to a man. The preacher asked me to speak with the man. The Lord didn't lead me. I was doing it because the preacher asked me to. The man got a gun to shoot me. When he started toward me, the Lord hit him with a heart attack. He almost died and hollered to tell the preacher to get me out of there. I left. Two weeks later he died. The Lord blessed, with many people being saved. We were praying and the pastor and I were spending hours in prayer.

Some of the people there didn't want me to come back for another meeting, but I didn't know it. The preacher asked me to come back. These same people said, "No, all these things happened when he was here, and we're not going to attend the meeting." I didn't know a thing about it. So when I came for another meeting, we just had a few to attend. All the first week we had children saved and some young people. It is amazing how people will react in favor of, or against, what the Lord does. Sometimes the judgment of God will bring repentance, and sometimes people run away from it.

About "Being Saved."

D. C.: *Numerous references are made throughout the book about "being saved." The Philippian jailer brought up the subject in Acts 16:29-31: "Then he called for a light, and sprang in, and came trembling, and fell down before Paul and Silas, And brought them out, and said, Sirs, <u>what must I do to be saved</u>? And they said, <u>Believe on the Lord Jesus Christ, and thou shalt be saved</u>, and thy house."* (Acts 16:29-31)

The Apostle Paul brought up the subject in his classic Book of Romans: "That if thou shalt confess with thy mouth the Lord Jesus, and shalt believe in thine heart that God hath raised him from the dead, <u>thou shalt be saved</u>." (Romans 10:9)

"Being saved" refers to God's judicial act of forgiving individuals of our sins on the basis of Christ's blood, shed on the cross for the sins of the world. We see limited observable things when people are making professions of faith, praying to be saved. We can see our human reactions before, during and after praying that underline a clear change of countenance and conversation. Oftentimes, it involves tears or some change of facial countenance. Of course, that is spontaneous and short-term. The long-term proof of salvation is living the Christian life in such a way that it is observable.

Preaching up North – A New Thing. (Paul continues…)

I had gone to school with Dean Hartman from Bridgeton, Indiana. He asked me to go up there for a revival meeting at his home church. He wasn't the pastor, but he was asking me anyhow. I said, "Why, Dean, I've never preached up north and those Yankees wouldn't like me. Furthermore, I'm just going to preach in the South."

But it turned out that I've had more meetings in the North. The people in the South didn't like me at all when I first started preaching. I would tell jokes and use humor, and the southerners didn't like that.

I told Dean that they wouldn't like me. Dean said, "Whether they like you or not, Dave Hartman, my uncle, will go to Hell. He's 70 years old, and if you don't go to Bridgeton, Indiana, Dave Hartman will spend eternity in Hell." He said, "I've heard you preach that everybody has the key to somebody's heart, and if they don't witness to them they'll go to Hell. If Dave Hartman goes to Hell, it's your fault."

I said, "Well, I don't want to, but if your preacher asks me, I'll go. He hasn't asked me to go." I got home, and there was a letter from his preacher. Dean couldn't have told him what I said, because the letter had already been written and mailed before Dean talked to me. I was to go as soon as school was out.

I took my son, John Paul, with me. He played baseball, and he talked baseball all the way up there. I let him talk. When we got there, Dean's mother had Dean's uncle there, ready to meet me.

I walked in and sat down. Dean's Uncle said, "Oh, this is the prize fighter." We talked about fights. We talked about baseball. I already knew some about baseball, but that was all John talked about all the way up there. I didn't know why I was letting him talk all that time about baseball, but when I was talking with Dave Hartman, I understood. I knew about baseball players and we talked about football and boxing.

This Backslidden Preacher Will Never Win Anybody ...

Dean Hartman's mother got aggravated at me because I was talking to him like that and wouldn't jump on him about being saved. She jumped up and left the room – mad – and said, "A backslidden preacher like that will never win anybody to the Lord. He'll never win anybody. Dave is going to Hell and it's this preacher's fault!"

But Dave Hartman liked me and came to church every night. I hadn't talked to him yet about being saved. I talked to him every day, but I didn't talk to him about the Lord. One night he didn't come to the meeting. He went all over that town – and him unsaved – telling all those sinners, "Listen, you come to church. That preacher is the most 'unlike' preachers I've ever seen. He don't talk all the time about the Lord. You'll love that man. He preaches the Bible, but I love him and you ought to come."

He filled the church with unsaved men that he went out and rounded up. So it came time for me to talk to him. I asked him if he would let me show him how to be saved. He said, "Sure, I'll be glad to." We sat down and went over the plan of salvation in the Scripture. He said, "No, not this time." I talked with that man during the meeting seven times. On the seventh time he accepted the Lord. Now, he had brought all those people to the meeting and they were saved before he was.

Talking with a Rough Woman.

Dave Hartman told me about a woman in that area who had lived a rough life. He said, "You go down there and talk to her about Jesus, and don't let her keep you from talking about Him. You let the Lord lead you. It's a rough place where they sell liquor. I've tried to witness to her and she won't let me. But she'll get saved if you'll go."

I went out to find the woman. Back then, I could change my voice some and I talked like a Yankee. They didn't detect that I was a preacher. I went dressed in a blue shirt and overalls and I was one of the crowd. I was sitting there talking to them and, boy, they liked me, and everything was going fine. The crowd got bigger and bigger. We were talking about baseball and boxing.

Finally, the Lord said, "Now's the time." I said, "Well, we've had a good time talking. I've got to go pretty soon. I'm the preacher down here at the Baptist church and I want you people to come and hear me preach tonight." I mean, it was just like the rapture! They went out of there in a hurry.

This woman was left standing there alone, a great big woman, and she was just trembling. I said, "Woman, do you know the Lord as your Savior?" She said, "No, I can't be saved." I said, "I John 1:7 says: *The blood of Jesus Christ, His son, cleanseth us from all sin.*" You can be saved."

She said, "I'm too mean to be saved." I said, "I John 1:7

says: *'The blood of Jesus Christ, His son, cleanseth us from all sin.'* You can be saved." She told me seven times she couldn't be saved. Seven times I said, "I John 1:7 says: *'The blood of Jesus Christ, His son, cleanseth us from all sin.'* You can be saved."

She said, "Preacher, do you mean that?" I said, "I wasn't beatin' my gums together just to hear 'em pop. I mean, you can be saved." She said, "All right, tell me how to be saved." I went over the plan of salvation and she accepted the Lord. That woman, she won every one of those men to the Lord during that meeting and brought them to church. She quit selling booze. And she ran the place!

Before she got saved she told me that if she didn't sell liquor, she'd go out of business. But she quit selling liquor and she had a better business than she ever had. She put tracts out everywhere.

Mr. Hall Loves His Liquor.

I preached the message, *The Last Train to Heaven,* and there was a man there named Mr. Hall. I talked to him about being saved. He said, "No, I know all these people have been saved, and I know this woman is saved, but I love liquor and I'm going to drink and be saved when I get ready." I told him the same thing I told all the others that said something like that – "No you won't. God will stop your heart and drop you into Hell. Buddy, you better be saved." In less than two weeks, less than two feet from where I talked to the man, he dropped dead.

They scheduled me to go back later for another meeting at this same church. I preached the *Last Train to Heaven* message. There were people there that had been saved before. A backslider lived next door to the church, and we had been to talk with him. He gave a good testimony that he had really been saved. Then up the street a man died. The meeting hadn't done a thing up 'til then, but it took off again, and we had people saved every service after that. I mentioned earlier that God gave me the message on *The Last Train to Heaven,* and that He told me He was going to follow it with judgment. <u>Nine out of ten places that I ever preached it, something unusual happened</u>. People get the message and decide they had better get right with the Lord.

Stevenson, Alabama – Unlikely Place for God to Break Loose.

Stevenson has some Civil War history, since the railroad comes right through the middle of town. The railroad is the main line between Chattanooga and Nashville. The Centennial Baptist Church is located about three miles from town up on Crow Creek. About the turn of the century, there was a railroad repair station near the church and a settlement built up there related to that.

The church building was built in the early 1800's. The church was reportedly the third oldest Baptist church in continual operation in Jackson County, Alabama. When the railroad repair shop moved away, so did most of the people. In 1953 there were only about nine houses within a mile of the church.

A faithful core of church people was made up of those who were born and raised in that neighborhood; others drove a distance "when they could." It was a historic landmark. The first building had been torn down and a smaller building had been built out of the materials. The benches were jammed against the outside walls, leaving only one center aisle. The floor was solid oak and hard with age. Within a few yards of the building there was a cemetery with old and new graves.

Brother Dan Carr had been called to pastor the church at the age of nineteen, and he asked me to come for a meeting. We met and prayed down in the woods. They didn't pray any two or three minutes. The men would get together and pray an hour or more. I preached on prayer, and they prayed in earnest.

We were down in the woods praying, and some boys went down there in the bushes to watch the prayer meeting. We had been praying an hour or more. They began to laugh and make fun. One of the men taught the junior boys. Suddenly, he jumped up and ran up toward the boys. He started beating the bushes where the boys were and began hollering, "These boys are going to Hell! God, everybody's goin' to Hell, they're goin' to Hell! God, save these boys!" They all ran into the church and every one of them was saved that night.

Dan Carr: Burt Reed, a Temple student, led the music for Brother Paul in a lot of meetings. One night Paul had brought one of his sons with him, and the son was acting up a bit. Paul was at the pulpit and called him down and warned him. In a few minutes, Paul laid down his Bible, took his son by the hand and led him out into the cemetery. We could hear "sounds" coming from there. Burt jumped up, flipped open the hymnal, and announced, "All right, everybody open to number so and so, and let's sing: Dwelling in Beulah Land." We sang the first words of the song: "Far away the noise of strife upon my ear is falling...," and that was the end of the singing. From there it was rowdy laughter and chuckles. Burt shook his head and sat down. Paul returned and resumed his sermon as though nothing had happened.

Meeting At the Black School.

The year was 1953, before the Civil Rights Acts had been passed. Segregation of the races was a strong reality. Brother Dan and I went over to Stevenson to a black school. The principal let me come in and preach to the students, and Dan played his accordion. I don't know how many responded to the simple invitation to receive Jesus into their hearts as their personal Savior. Seems like it was close to a hundred. The principal thought there must be some mistake, that many of them were already Christians; but the students said, "No, we've never heard this before." Some of them had attended church now and then, here and there, but had never been saved. They listened attentively to the simple Gospel story.

A Week of Praying – The Pulpit Has To Go.

During the meeting at the Centennial Church, we had been having a few saved along, but not many. I didn't go to my classes at Temple that week, and I spent a lot of time praying. I never slept much that whole week.

On Friday night at the church (the day I preached in the school), I was going to preach on *Why Hell and Heaven Are Alike*. I read my text from Luke 16, the story of the rich man that went to Hell. I started to walk off the low platform at the pulpit.

78

As I walked off, the Spirit of God got a hold of me and took me to the back of the building.

Now, I had heard John Rice and other preachers say that people merely imagine such complete control by the Holy Spirit, that is, that He might take hold of you physically. But I know better. The Spirit of God was all over me and I couldn't do a thing about it. I couldn't stop. I couldn't say a word. He took me to the back of the building. I came back down the aisle to the front of the pulpit. I wasn't doing it. He was doing it. I saw I was going to run into the pulpit, but I went over the pulpit.

My right leg had been bothering me for a long time after a jumping horse fell on me. I was having a lot of trouble with it. I could barely play handball because of that lame leg. I could walk without limping or drawing attention to my walking, but that was the extent of it. Immediately after going over the pulpit, that lame leg stuck out. I thought, "What am I going to do? Go through the pulpit?" The pulpit had been fastened into the old oak floor with 16-penny nails many years earlier, and the oak had an iron grip on the nails. I couldn't think. That leg stuck out and knocked the pulpit down. Song books flew out of the pulpit and went all over the floor, and I said, "There now, I've torn down your god!"

I didn't know that Brother Dan had asked the deacons about moving the pulpit over a few inches so he could walk between the pulpit and the piano while he was preaching without bumping his elbows into the piano. They had said, "No, sir! Grandpa So and So nailed that pulpit down and it will have to stay." And that's the way it was. Brother Dan had said nothing to me about the fuss over moving it. I went around the pulpit, and suddenly it was over. I was back to normal.

> D. C.: *I remember that, as Brother Paul went over the pulpit, he went over it in slow motion. At the time I thought it was strange and said to myself, "How did he do that?" It was so obvious that he was not moving toward the pulpit fast enough to propel himself above it and over, and especially not in slow motion. He quickly turned to face the audience and, with a couple of quick jabs with his foot, the pulpit was lying on its face in the aisle toward*

the congregation with several nails protruding from the base of the pulpit, clean-pulled out of the seasoned oak floor. Pulling 16-penny nails out of seasoned oak is not easy, and especially several nails at one time, spaced as they were in the bottom of the pulpit.

A single young woman was there who had never been married, but she had two young children. She had said that she would never be saved if anyone came to her. She had been riding the church bus to the meetings, and nobody had gone to her during the meeting. She was the niece of Mrs. Maggie Bunch, who was responsible for her being there.

I went straight to her, and with little effort she came charging out of her seat to the front. When she got saved, she went out to the church bus and forcefully brought in her two nieces. She practically threw them into the altar. They, too, were saved. The rest of the meeting we had people saved in every service.

Two Temple students were there that night, Burt Reed and Bobby Oswald. Bobby had lost a kidney in a barroom fight while in the Merchant Marines. He didn't scare easily. But after the meeting he confessed that his hair almost stood up. Several testified that the fear of God fell upon them. Burt Reed's father was a strong pastor in Ohio. The building was packed, and the whole congregation went to its knees at once like they were controlled by an electric switch. Years later, I was with Bobby Oswald for a revival meeting and we talked about it. He told me he was really scared that night.

D. C.: *I remember well the fear of God I experienced that night. I sat toward the front on the right, facing the pulpit. The building was packed with people. I looked around to see what was happening and noticed that everyone, it seems, was on their knees. I fully expected to see someone die that night and realized that it could be me. I searched my heart in a hurry to make sure I was right with God. It was a time for everybody, including the pastor, to take stock.*

An interesting thing happened to me that night. God healed

that lame leg, and it has been healed for about forty years now. Of course, my legs are now giving me some trouble because of age, but the injury that was healed that night has given me no trouble.

After that revival, I went to eight - maybe ten - meetings right in a row, and every one of them had the power of God on them. Every place I went the preachers expected me to kick the pulpit down. Some of them even loosened the pulpit. I'm not exaggerating. They had problems that they thought might be helped that way.

But it never happened again. I've never had an experience like that in my life. A man would be foolish to try to copy that experience. Buddy, I wouldn't copy it! I couldn't. On that night, I couldn't have jumped that pulpit like that to save my life. My leg was not strong enough to kick like that.

> D. C.: *I remember Brother Paul reading his text from Luke 16:19-31. I thought, "Paul will never preach tonight. He's been praying all week; he has lost a lot of sleep; he preached in the black school this afternoon, and that drained him. He'll be emotionally unable to follow through on the text on Hell." But, all at once, he became a different person, closed up the Bible and threw it to the back of the room where it bounced off the back door.*
>
> *He hurried down the aisle to the door and began jumping up and down on his Bible in the floor. He said, "Don't look at me! This is what you people do to the Bible!" He picked up his Bible and threw it again, bouncing it off the pulpit. He ran toward the pulpit and jumped over it in slow motion.*
>
> *After the meeting was over, Burt Reed, Bobby Oswald and I stopped on the side of the road beside the main railroad from Chattanooga to Nashville. We found a large flat rock to sit on and discussed what we had just seen. After rehearsing it, we all decided that we had just witnessed an unusual demonstration of the genuine power of God, upon and through Paul Ferguson, and we*

had been privileged to be there and witness it.

That night, Paul went to my parents' home in Stevenson where he was staying for the week. Burt Reed, Bobby Oswald and I arrived at the house and started inside. It was dark inside. Through the screen door I could hear Paul weeping. He was lying across the bed on his face. When he heard us coming in, he came out onto the porch and began explaining, "Brother Dan, you've got to believe me, I didn't do that. God did that." We quickly assured him that we knew it was the hand of God. There was a good spirit in the church afterward that continued for some time.

One of the reasons I knew it was the power of God and not of Satan, was the number of people saved during the meeting, something like 75. Satan does nothing to help people get saved. I never did anything like that before that meeting or after. I've had other experiences, but never anything like that.

I Wanted To Preach…..My Way.

I would like to go back a minute and review how it was in the earlier days of God's dealing with me. I wanted to work at a job of some kind and preach in a church Sunday morning, Sunday night, and Wednesday night. But the Lord put it on my heart, made it plain to me; He said to me, "You are going to be an evangelist." I said, "I'm not. I just can't. I'm not good enough a preacher to do that. I don't have all the talents that some of these fellows have. I can't do it." He said to me, "You don't have to have that. You'll just have to trust Me and I'll do the work."

I said, "No, I'm not going to do it. I've got two kids growing up and I don't want to be away from them. I need to be at home to be a father to my children. If I'm an evangelist, I'll be gone and I won't be able to take them with me all the time. I just don't plan to do it, now. I'll do anything else you want me to do, but not that."

It went on like that for some time, and the Lord kept dealing with me.

God in the Railroad Yard.

While attending Tennessee Temple, I worked at night on the main railroad switch yard in Chattanooga where they sorted out the freight cars and made up trains going in several directions to distant cities. Chattanooga was a rail center even during the Civil War; and the great battles fought there, with many thousands of soldiers killed on both sides, was because it was a rail center. Anyway, my job was to throw various rail switches to route cars to one train or another. An engine pushed the cars slowly over the hump, and the cars free coasted down a slight grade. They were unhooked and there was no control over them.

One night I was working on the second shift and, suddenly, all the big flood lights went out. I thought I was standing between track seven and track six, but I was not. I was standing right in the middle of track seven. I had a clipboard in my hand with a pad of paperwork on it that I was responsible for. I thought, "I'll catch up on my paperwork until the lights come back on," and I shined my flashlight on the clipboard and looked at the first item. I didn't hear anything, but all of a sudden I was just lifted up and put off the track. It was dark and I couldn't see anything. A loaded coal car went by me and hit into the car down the track below it. Boy, did it make a noise!

The Lord spoke to me in my spirit very clearly and said, "I took you off the track this time. I won't do it the next time. You are going to preach." I said, "Yes, Lord, I'll go. I don't mind what it costs. If it takes my wife, takes my children, or whatever it is, if You say 'Go,' I'll go." And I surrendered right there. I got down on my knees in the cinders and gravel and I surrendered everything. The UNSHACKLED Christian radio broadcast from Chicago featured me in one of their radio broadcasts and used a little of the railroad incident, but they didn't have time to tell the whole story as it's told here.

The next day my friend, Harvey Saunders, called me. Harvey was a good preacher, a Southern Baptist. (Everybody was Southern Baptist back then.) We played handball together pretty regular. (He never did beat me.) I went out to his church the next night and the Lord said "Go forward and tell them." So I went forward and told them I was going to preach as an evangelist. I didn't tell them about God picking me up off the railroad and telling me how it was going to be and threatening

83

me within an inch of my life. I never told people what happened. I didn't even tell my wife for a long time. Later I told my wife and a few others. I didn't tell my boys for a long time. Mark, the youngest one, was the first one I told.

The next Sunday, Pastor Saunders said to my wife, "Mrs. Ferguson, you'll have to be called too, because a preacher can't get along without his wife being called at the same time." She said she was willing to do what God wanted me to do. She would go. I don't know if she would have, had she known some of the things that were going to happen. But she did, and she's been faithful.

Paul's wife, Lena Ferguson - September 1940.

Lena Fgerguson, 2000
Thanks to Lena Ferguson for permission to print these pictures.

Paul Ferguson Family, 1958. Front row: Mark and Tim.
Back row: Lena, Paul, and John.

Family PHOTO - 1972. John, Tim, Mark, Paul, And Lena

Paul Ferguson the Fighter
Chapter 6

Will God Take Care of My Family?

I've finished about forty years of preaching. In the beginning, I worried about Lena some. I worried about how I would take care of her. I admit it. But, to me, worry is a worse sin than taking a drink—and I've never taken a drink—I've never smoked. Worry is doubting God. It's unbelief. I was an evangelist, having a lot of people saved, seeing some great things happen from the hand of the Lord; but I had not committed my wife and my boys to the Lord. I was concerned about how my boys would turn out. One day I said, "Lord, I can't do it. It's going to kill me, and if you can't do it, you didn't call me." I was gone an awful lot, and my wife had to do much of my training job for the boys while I was away in meetings.

Well, today, my oldest boy, John Paul is a preacher. Tim teaches in a Christian school in Virginia. Mark is a Sunday School teacher in a Baptist church. All of them love the Lord. So God can take care of them better than I could, but I had to learn that the hard way. I had to go through it.

Testing Time.

When I began holding meetings after finishing school, it was really a testing time. I had six weeks of meetings and had to pay my traveling expense. I was in South Carolina for two meetings, and one meeting in Georgia. I brought home $152.50, a small amount for six weeks - and from which to pay expenses. My wife told me we had bills. We owed the house rent and $202 or so on other bills. One thing we always did - my wife and I together - we paid our bills. We paid our rent first and then the other bills we had, and if we had any money left over we used that for our current needs.

Well, it came time for me to go to another meeting. I told my wife that I would go pray, so I went in the closet and prayed about two hours. The Lord put it on my heart directly, "You go on with your meeting and I'll take care of everything and you don't have to worry." My wife mentioned to me (not in a mean way, she's never mean - sometimes I am, but she isn't):

"We'll have enough food to do until Wednesday. These bills will have to be paid before you come back from this fourteen-day meeting." I told her I would come back Wednesday, that I had prayed and everything would be taken care of when I came back Wednesday.

So I went to the meeting and things went along fairly good. The night came when I had told my wife I would have the money to pay the bills and food. When I left home, I only had enough gas to get to the meeting. I drove from Saturday 'til Wednesday with the gas gauge on empty. On Wednesday night we had a good-sized crowd. Nobody made a profession of faith. Three or four teenagers were in the back of the church. Right after the service I walked back to them. I had made a public statement that we would have somebody saved that night, and the Lord had told me privately that He would supply the other need. I hadn't had anybody saved, nothing happened, I was broke, and the service closed.

On my way back to talk to the young men, a woman said to me, "Would it make you mad if we gave you some groceries?" She said, "We women were praying today, and God told us to give you some groceries." I said, "No, it would be an answer to prayer." She borrowed my keys. I talked to the three boys and they accepted the Lord as their Savior, and the next night they came forward.

The devil said, "All right, you got those young men saved, but where are all those groceries you were talking about?" I went to the car, and the trunk and back seat were full of groceries. There were more groceries than I thought you could get in a truck the way they had packed them in. Everybody went home. I was rejoicing about that and praying. The old devil came to me again. The devil never gives up.

The devil seemed to get right up on my shoulder. It was so real to me, whatever it was. I said, "Okay, Devil, I've got the groceries, and three young men have been saved, and I'll get the gas if the angel of the Lord has to push me all the way to Chattanooga. I'll get there." I was willing to start out. "You just leave me out. I'm agoin'."

About that time I saw a car light. A man drove up and said, "Brother Ferguson, I own a filling station and it wouldn't make you mad if I put some gas in your car, would it? I was on my way home and God told me to come back and give you some gas so you can get to Chattanooga."

I said, "Praise the Lord! That's an answer to prayer!" I told him to drive behind me so if I ran out of gas he could push me. So we got to the filling station. He filled up the car, and I went on toward Chattanooga praising the Lord. The devil climbed up again. "Uh huh! You got the groceries and you got the gas - but where is the money you have to have for those bills?" I said, "Devil! You might as well leave me alone. I believe God and He's promised to supply the need - and I'm going on to Chattanooga."

I got back, and my wife came to the door and we hugged. I'd been gone a few days, and after we had talked a little while she said, "Well, did you get any groceries?" I said, "Yes." We went to the car and I told her how we got the groceries and how the man had filled up the car with gas. We rejoiced over the groceries and the gas. I never thought of the bills. The mail would come in the morning. We were still rejoicing over the groceries and the gas when the mail came.

I went to the mail box and saw three or four letters in the box. They were all from North Carolina, but they were all from different people. I opened one and it had some money in it. I told my wife and she said, "Well, is there enough to pay that bill?" I said, "No." But, when we opened them all, there was enough to pay the bill and about forty dollars left over. We paid the bill and thanked the Lord. *Sometimes the Lord will let you be tested, but He never fails!*

Preachers Learning to Pray.

Preachers have come to me and wanted me to pray with them. They'd pray and they'd have some results. So they'd say, "Oh, I'm going to dedicate myself to prayer." But, then, the devil would step in. You see, Satan knows what prayer will do. Satan is not omniscient. He does not know all things, but he knows that if he hinders prayer, he hinders the work of God. He'll set in on people who have begun to pray and a lot of them will quit.

I won't tell his name, but I had a friend that started praying. He came to me and asked me to teach him how to pray. I said,

91

"I'll pray with you." He started out praying and had great results. But then he came into some difficulty and he quit the ministry. Anybody that chooses to pray is choosing some hardships. The devil is allowed to test us. I can't tell you why, but I know it's so. He's allowed to test us. If we don't pass the test, then our praying falls apart.

In God's scheme of things, prayer is so very important – even more important than the preaching. God has ordained it that way. All the old-time effective preachers knew that. They said that God had ordained it that way. Christ suffered for us, and we ought to be willing to suffer for Him, enter into His sufferings through our intercessory prayer. We ought to be willing to travail in prayer to get these hard cases saved. God is not calling us to a lot more labor as much as He is calling us to a lot more prayer.

Some Preachers Just Don't Like to Pray.

I know there are a lot of good preachers over the land, men of God. A lot of men had me for a meeting because they heard that I prayed a lot and they wanted to pray with me. But there are a lot of men who would go play handball with me quicker than they would pray with me because they said I prayed too long. Now, they knew I was going to beat them in handball, but they'd play handball rather than pray; I'm talking about preachers. I'm not intending to run down preachers, but it's easy for preachers to get off-center, like the rest of us, and not pray consistently.

Over the years, we've neglected praying. I believe now there's a trend for preachers and churches to get back to praying. My pastor in Greensboro was a praying man. John Rice and Dr. Lee Roberson are great men, and I learned a lot from them; but Brother J. T. Ellis, pastor of McConnell Road Baptist Church in Greensboro, North Carolina, taught me more about praying and about the things of God - the basic understanding of the fundamental beliefs - than they did. One of the differences is that I spent so many hours talking with Brother Ellis, one-on-one, and I could ask him questions about things I didn't understand and get an immediate answer.

McConnell Road Baptist Church was where I joined and where I learned you couldn't lose your salvation (though that didn't come from the church; but from God). I think Brother Ellis was one of the greatest men I ever knew. He never knew much about broader things, but he was a man of prayer, a man of God. The Lord told him things that people today would think he was crazy if he told it. He didn't tell it all the time, but sometimes he would tell things God had told him. He was a great man of God, really - one of the greatest men I ever met; and I've met some of the greatest over the years.

The Best Way to Pray.

When a man faces the need to pray, the best way to pursue a life of prayer is just to pray. Just pray and God will send some followers. I've always prayed - not like I ought to, but I've always prayed. Most preachers thought I was a fanatic, while I didn't think I prayed enough. When I'd pray three or four hours, they thought I was crazy, but there would be results.

Any man that God lays it on his heart for a prayer life may live a lonely life and not be as popular as he would be if he was just a "great preacher." *We don't need great preachers. We need people that pray.* But if a man dedicates himself to prayer, God will give him other warriors that will join in. The big revivals always started with a small group of praying people, and sometimes it didn't always start right away.

When I speak of a man dedicated to prayer experiencing more loneliness, I don't mean that he loses his sense of humor. When you lose your sense of humor, in most cases you're done for in the ministry. When you lose your sense of humor, you start feeling sorry for yourself. The devil will work on you at this point and help you feel sorry for yourself. *That ruins more preachers in their ministry than other main things.* It ruins more preachers than women, whiskey, money, or anything you can mention.

Dr. John Rice listed money and women equally, and being sorry for yourself about third place. But, personally, I think that feeling sorry for yourself wrecks more preachers than money or women. You look around and see other people making more money and getting more publicity; you think you're not appreciated for what you've done. This runs into jealousy, a very destructive thing.

I think the answer to this is to depend on the Holy Spirit and

93

ask Him. You know, they'll think you're crazy if you talk about the Holy Spirit, but He's God. There's the Father, the Son and the Holy Spirit, and to ignore the Holy Spirit is to reject God. We try to do things ourselves instead of working in the Holy Spirit, under His direction and in His power.

Billy Graham's Praying and Preaching.

I don't know what people think of Billy Graham, but I'll tell you this. In years past, in his earlier years, he and his team and the core people they led... prayed. I don't know what he does now. But I do know that in the past he organized prayer meetings and sent men ahead to pray like the old timers did. I know that took place when he started out. I haven't kept up with his ministry and I don't know what he has done in recent years, but in his earlier years he really prayed.

When he was in Greensboro, North Carolina, they had one of the best meetings Greensboro had ever had. People prayed all over town. Groups of people got together and prayed all night long, worked the next day at their jobs, and attended the meeting that night. I know the results of that meeting were the result of prayer. Billy Graham has preached the Gospel every time I've ever heard him - that is, he preached the death, burial, and resurrection of Christ and the necessity that lost people repent of their sins and receive Christ as Savior and Lord. But it was not his preaching that brought the results. It was the praying, and I think that any preacher that has had good success will tell you the same thing. Most of the truly successful preachers will tell you that it was their praying and other people praying. *Praying is hard work. It's a lot harder than preaching.* It's hard physically and emotionally, and the devil fights it more.

America Needs Prayer More than Anything.

That's the answer right now in this country. We've got a lot of problems in the country with homosexuals, the dope, the violence, abortions, teen-age pregnancies, the breaking up of homes and families. Most preachers are against all of these things, but the way to fight it more than anything is to pray. Then, when we go out to fight and work against it, we'll get more done.

Sometimes it takes a while of continued prayer. We've let all these big problems build up, but we don't want to pray long to take them out. When we pray for the lost man, the dope addict, the prostitute, God doesn't override the will of these people. But the Holy Spirit will work on these people in answer to prayer. Nobody can be saved apart from the working of the Holy Spirit.

Praising the Lord and worship should mainly be done in private. We don't know much about it. We think that worship is supposed to take place in church, but the greatest need among preachers and Christians is to have a time set aside to worship and pray and read Scripture before the Lord and to praise Him. I think that praising the Lord, worship, and prayer should be done mostly in private. There are exceptions and people won't like that idea, but I still believe it.

There's a book on worship that helped me: *How to Worship Jesus Christ*, by Carol of Greenville, South Carolina. That's the best book on worship that I know.

Suggestions for Praying.

Today, my prayer life has changed some in emphasis since I don't travel as much. I've always prayed for people, but I pray more now for more people than I used to. I have a big list of names that I pray for. I try to go over the list every day. I've had preachers tell me that I try to pray for too many people. I don't think you can pray for too many people; but as I go over my list, the Holy Spirit may show me to dwell on a certain individual, and I pray for that one until He lets me go on to the next one.

I pray for some people in groups, such as city officials. I call them by name if I know them. When I'm talking with someone, I can't remember names like I can when I'm praying. The Holy Spirit helps me remember names when I'm praying. I've gone over the names so many times, I know them. I have to go over things, even in Scripture, to remember. When I preach and use so many Scripture verses, I make very few mistakes, but I study them. I have to. And you have to study more as you get older.

We should be as specific as we can in prayer. Laying your hand on the phone book and praying, "God bless all the people in this phone book," is not as specific as calling the individual names of people. To say, "I pray for my whole family," is not

95

nearly as good as praying for each individual name. I believe that, in praying for revival, you have better results if you pray for individual names of lost people.

I was in a meeting where the preacher thought that when I came the church could just watch me, and they would then witness everywhere and jump on everybody, saved or unsaved, and just talk to everybody. When I came in, I didn't do that. I don't do that. I pray. I had a list of names I started praying for. When they came to pray, they knew that I was in the habit of praying; so they prayed generally. I said, "No, let's pray specifically. Let each one take out so many names and pray for them out loud."

We don't have to pray out loud, but I told them to pray out loud because they didn't pray much unless they prayed out loud. So we passed out the names, and the prayer list must have contained a hundred names or more. They said that they had never had anybody saved off of a prayer list that they had prayed for. I said, "Well, the people you are praying for are in general and not specifically." During the meeting we saw over twenty-five people saved off their prayer list that they prayed for name by name. I believe it was closer to forty people saved off the prayer list. And what happened there, happened all over the country. One of the major secrets of prayer is to pray for people by name. When we pray specifically, God answers specifically.

There are some people that have been prayed over for such a long time that people have given up on them ever being saved. They have said that their hearts were just too hard. But when we prayed for them specifically and witnessed to them, they were saved. Prayer and witnessing go together.

Today, we have the general opinion in churches and schools that the thing to do is to have a little bit of praying and a whole lot of visitation. If you'll notice in the New Testament, the Holy Spirit was working. The people spent hours in prayer. In Acts 6, when the disciples elected the deacons, in verse 4 they said, *"...that we may give ourselves to prayer and the ministry of the Word."* They prayed for hours and unusual things happened. I still believe that unusual things can happen today if we will spend much time in prayer.

Now, Dr. John Herrmann, who taught philosophy, psychology,

96

and theology at Tennessee Temple Schools in Chattanooga, Tennessee, was a great man of prayer. He rated way up there in being one of the smartest men in the world, was rated by his professional peers as being one of the highest in the fields of philosophy and psychology. He rated high in his overall knowledge. And, yet, that man prayed for hours. He agonized.

I was holding a meeting one time and the meeting wouldn't break like it should. I said, "God what on earth am I going to do?" Sometimes there are special keys that unlock a meeting. So I said, "God, what is it?" God told me to go ask Dr. Herrmann to pray for the meeting. I said, "Now Lord, Dr. Brownlee... he's a man of prayer, a good man." God said, "No, go to Dr. Herrmann."

I named Carl Green and other preachers there that I figured were better. Well, three days went by and nothing happened in the meeting. I said, "Lord, aren't you going to do anything?" He said, "Yes, when you do what I tell you to do. Go to Dr. Herrmann and ask him to pray for it." I said, "Well, I guess I'll have to. I still don't want to."

Dr. John Herrmann and Prayer.

Dr. Herrmann was chairman of the Psychology Department at Temple, and you wouldn't look at him and think that he ever prayed. He was always talking about psychology and philosophy - always kidding, sports-minded - and you would think that he didn't pray. But one day I knocked on his office door. He always called me, "prize fighter" (the only teacher that did that). I liked him, but I didn't think he was a man of prayer.

So I knocked on his door and he said, "Hello prize fighter! How're you doing?" I said, "Well, Dr. Herrmann, I'm in a meeting that won't break and the Lord laid it on my heart to come to you and ask you to pray." He said, "Okay." We got down on our knees and he started to pray. I figured he'd pray three or four minutes. In an hour and forty five minutes, he hadn't stopped. He was cryin' and prayin' and agonizin' and goin' on. And I thought, "My Lord, will this man never get through?"

But, I knew the Lord was in it. He touched me. So Dr. Herrmann prayed about two hours. When he got through he said, "Well, Prize Fighter, the Lord is going to bless. Come back tomorrow and we'll pray again." I said, "Well, Dr. Herrmann, I've got to confess that I knew you were a man of psychology and philosophy and I didn't think you were a man of prayer. I didn't come when God first told me." He grabbed me. (I thought I was pretty strong.) He grabbed me by the neck and dragged me down to the floor and he started praying again and crying and telling the Lord how ignorant he was. *He prayed for another hour and a half!*

I couldn't pray after that. I left and went back to the meeting that night. We had about twenty people saved. I went back to Dr. Herrmann the next day to pray, and that night we had about that many more saved. The remainder of the meeting after that, we had fifteen or twenty people saved. People came that we had never invited; people we didn't even know came in to be saved, some of the hardest you ever saw. And right there is where Dr. Herrmann and I got to be real close friends. When I needed something, I'd always go to him. He was a real man of prayer.

Hard Hearts and God's Tornado.

D.C.: *The place of this meeting is missing from the tape. If you know, please let us know.*

People wouldn't come. Some children were being saved and a few others came. There was a stronger attendance on the second Wednesday night of the meeting. A few people had been praying for hours. Other people over the country were praying, but these people weren't praying much because they wouldn't come to the meetings. They were mad at me over what happened when I was there in a meeting before.

So that night I was preaching on backsliding. I got down to the part that God will chasten His children. I didn't mean to say it. It wasn't in my message. It wasn't planned. I said, "God may send a cyclone and kill all of you old hypocrites!" When I said that - I'm not exaggerating - a big storm, cyclone or something hit right then while I was preaching. It knocked all the lights out. It seemed like the storm picked the church up, turned it around and put it right back on the pillars just like it was. I don't think it

98

happened, but it seemed like that's what happened. But it did pick up a big, old tree on one side of the church, and it went right over the building to the other side and drove up in the ground, way down so that the roots and a good part of the trunk of the tree was down in the ground.

Man, you talk about scaring a group of people - they started to jump up and run out! I said, "The Lord will kill all of you hypocrites if you don't get right with God." They sat down and I went ahead and finished the message in the dark. You know how you can see a dog's eyes at night? Well, you could have counted those people by their eyes, the way they were lookin'.

When I got through, I quit. I try to do that when I'm finished and not to just continue on. I started praying and, when I finished, the lights came on. I didn't have to give an invitation. Everyone in the house ran to the front and got on their knees and started praying. There were six unsaved people there, and they were saved. After that, we had people saved every service. I don't know how many people were saved the rest of the meeting - 30 or 40 people. The meeting closed and I had to leave to go to another meeting. I would usually leave after the morning service.

Has the Pastor Gone Completely Crazy?

During that last morning service, the pastor jumped up and ran out of the room while I was preaching. He came back in and ran out again. He did that three times. I said to myself, "He's gone crazy. He's prayed so much he's gone crazy." That's what I thought to myself when I left. I thought, "I'll hear of him being in a place for the mentally disturbed people, because he has gone crazy, he's flipped his lid."

On the way to the airport he said, "God's going to send a cyclone through here and kill two hundred people or more. I believe the church has repented today in this meeting and God won't destroy the church. God has shown me that He was going to destroy the church, but He won't now." I said to myself, "Now I know he's crazy." He went back to the church and told it to the people after he took me to the airport.

In about two weeks, as he said it would happen, a cyclone came through that city and killed over two hundred people. The church got to praying, and they said when the cyclone came the second time, it destroyed houses in the millions of dollars. When it came to the church, it went up over it and dropped down again, and went on destroying property. Now, wouldn't you figure that was God's judgment? That was God's judgment. *"The LORD is slow to anger, and great in power, and will not at all acquit the wicked: the LORD hath his way in the whirlwind and in the storm, and the clouds are the dust of his feet" (Nahum 1:3).*

They had revival in all parts of that city after that. Hundreds of people were saved. I've told that to a few preachers privately. I've never told it publicly. I told my sons. Some of those preachers said, "Well, God wouldn't do that." My response to that is that God is a God of love, but He's a God of judgment also. When people don't get right and God is about to send revival, many times it takes judgment before real revival can come. You don't hear much about it. I think the judgment of God might help our country now.

Tightwad Pastor and God's End Run around Him.

I went to a meeting in Florida and preached fourteen days; and we had good services and several people saved, a large number. On the last night of the meeting the preacher said, "Well, we've had the best meeting we've ever had. We've had more people saved, good crowds. And there's one thing for certain, Brother Ferguson's not preaching for money because he hasn't mentioned money all week, so therefore we don't have to give him much." They gave me $26.46 for fourteen days, and I had to pay all my expenses and everything, including traveling. They did furnish me a place to stay and my food.

As I walked back to the door that night, I was talking to myself and the Lord: "Lord, you called me to preach and I told You I wasn't going to beg for money and talk about it. But I do have a family and I don't know if I can get home on this much money. You're going to have to supply some way and it's going to have to be pretty quick."

I went to the back door as people were leaving. Men from different churches were coming out who said, "Here's a little gift for you." I put it in my pocket. Then, another one and another

100

one. Several came by and gave me money. I didn't know how much it was. I thought they were giving me a dollar - not over five. I figured, "Well, it'll help out some." I got in my car and went on down the road toward home, which I always did as quick as I could after a meeting. I was tired, and I decided I would look at the money. These men had given me $656. They were all from other churches. Not one of them was from the church that sponsored the meeting. In that day, that was a lot of money.

Paul Ferguson the Fighter
Chapter 7

Dreamy Eyes in Georgia.

In a meeting in Georgia, there was a girl there with real black hair that came down around her shoulders. She was a nice looking girl with real fair skin. I never did just single out people to look at them in meetings, but she was a bit different. Her eye lashes were unusually long and she was beating them up and down. The Lord put it on my heart to go talk with her. She hadn't seemed a bit concerned. She was looking around everywhere. I didn't think I ought to go talk to her, but the Lord laid on my heart to do it.

I went over to her and spoke to her, and she didn't look at me. I didn't know her name. I said, "Dreamy Eyes," and she said, "Who're you talking to?" I said, "Dreamy Eyes, I'm talking to you. You, right here. Are you born again? Are you saved? Do you know the Lord?" She said, "No! Who do you think I am? Do you think I get drunk? Do you think I do all these other things that people talk about?" She said, "No, I don't need to be saved." I said, "Little Lady, you're the biggest sinner I've ever met in all my life." She drew her fist back and I thought she was going to hit me. I was hoping she would go ahead and get it over with. I didn't know what to do.

Finally, I said, "All right, do you believe the Bible?" "Oh yes. I believe all the Bible." I said, "All right, if you believe the Bible, let's turn to I John 3:23 and 24, and we read: *"This is his commandment that we should believe on the name of his Son Jesus Christ and love one another as He gave us commandment."* Then I said, "Do you see that?" "Yes." I said, All right, turn over here to Matthew 22:37,38 *: "Thou shalt love the Lord thy God with all thy heart,.... all thy soul, ...all thy might. This is the first and great commandment."* I said, "What commandment is that?" She said, "The first." I said, "Well, if you've broken the first commandment by rejecting Christ, you must be a great sinner." She said, "Let me see that."

She jerked it over in front of her and read it again and again, seven times. Seven is the perfect number. And on the seventh time, she dropped the Bible, ran back to the prayer room screaming, "I'm the greatest sinner that ever lived because I've shut Jesus out of my life!" She gave her heart to the Lord. She got it right. She was a great sinner because she had broken the First Commandment. I think the greatest sin of a Christian is unbelief. We have enough belief for salvation, but we don't trust Him for daily needs and other things.

The Last Train Runs Again.

Dennis Hannah came to me while I was in a meeting in Lafayette, Georgia. He said, "I want you to come to my church for five weeks." I said, "I can't. I don't have but three weeks. I have another meeting." He said, "Well, if you will cancel the other meeting, I'll pay the pastor whatever he wants and we'll set five weeks." I said, "I don't think we ought to do that." So, we began a three-week meeting.

In the first week, we didn't see much happen. I preached on the church. There was one unsaved lady who was coming every night, and I preached one night on Hell. That's unusual for me, because usually in the first week I don't preach on Hell. The Lord laid it on my heart to preach on Hell, so I preached on Hell. I asked her after the service about being saved. She said, "Well, I wanted to come tonight, but my husband is saved and he's in the army. I'll go get him Sunday. You're going to preach that *Last Train to Heaven* sermon, and I'll get him to come with me and I'll be saved that night and get him to rededicate his life to the Lord, because he's not living for the Lord." Now, that's an unsaved woman talking.

We had meetings on Saturday night. (People don't have meetings on Saturday night now.) Her husband came back from his army base, and she wanted to go to church. He said, "No, I won't go." They didn't come that Sunday morning. That night I preached *The Last Train To Heaven*. We had a fair response. That was the third Sunday night of the meeting. She didn't come. She was taking her husband back to the army base and somehow she fell out of the car and a car ran over her and killed her right on the spot. Pastor Hannah ran out crying and said, "Paul! Lord, it's happened! It's happened! This woman has been killed."

I need to pause and tell what we had been doing the first

week and the second week and the third week. We had been praying a whole lot. But that second week, on Monday, the day after the woman was killed, a man had a car to fall on him. He was unsaved. Altogether there were five deaths during the meeting. One would have died anyway, but even that death added to the others.

Those people got stirred up. Pastor Dennis Hannah and I didn't visit. We prayed. He'd meet me after he ate breakfast. I didn't eat breakfast. We'd go pray. He'd eat big steaks every day. I ate one hamburger a day. He'd go eat and we would pray. He'd go eat and we would pray. Part of the time I would drink a Dr. Pepper instead of eating a meal so I could pray without getting sleepy. Eating makes you sleepy and hinders prolonged prayer. We went on through that third week. I don't know how many people were saved. It got bigger and bigger as we went along.

A Mad Woman.

A woman there was mad at Pastor Hannah. I preached and she came forward. The preacher walked over to her and she said, "I don't want to talk to you. I want to talk to the evangelist." He said, "OK." He called me over and said, "Will you talk to this woman?" I was about to take her back to the prayer room, but I said to her, "Why wouldn't you talk to the preacher?" She said, "I hate him, and I don't want to talk to him, but I want to get saved." I said, "I'm sorry, but I don't want to talk to you. If you won't be willing to give up that hatred and get right with God and with the preacher, I'm not talking to you."

I walked away from her and went back to my place. She said, "Oh, no, no, no. Come on! Come on!" I said, "No, I'm not going. If you'll let the preacher talk to you, then he'll talk to you or you won't be saved." I said, "We've got this idea that we can come to God and force Him to do something. No! You haven't repented. You don't want to be saved." She said, "Yes, I do."

Finally, she said: "Come on preacher (Hannah)." He took her back to the prayer room and led her to the Lord. She became one of his best friends and one of the greatest workers in the church, even after the pastor had died. The pastor that followed Pastor Hannah had me back for a meeting, and she was still strong for the Lord several years later. As it turned out, there was no great thing she was mad at him about. It was a little thing, but she was mad at him about it and she tried to go around it. People will get mad at the preacher over anything. If a billy goat breaks a horn off, they'll get mad at the preacher about it and say it was the preacher's fault.

Another Mad Woman Repents.

Right after that, there was a lady in the hospital in Fort Oglethorpe, Georgia. The doctors pronounced that she was dying. She sent word by someone that she wanted me to come and see her in the hospital. I went over there and walked in the room. She began crying. She asked me to pray for her, and I did. She said, "Brother Ferguson, that was my daughter that was killed (that fell out of the car) a year ago. I've hated you, and I've prayed for you to die all this time. I wanted you to die. I hated you. But God put me in the hospital. I said to God, 'Lord, why are you killing me?' He said to me, 'You hated Brother Ferguson and that wasn't his work. He just preached my message and I was the one that did it. You're mad at me. If you apologize to him, I'll let you live.'"

So she apologized to me, we had prayer again, and the woman lived. As far as I know she lived at least ten to fifteen years. I don't know if she's living now or not. She said the Lord spoke to her in her spirit so strong that it was almost audible. Sometimes God makes things so plain that you may think it's audible whether it is or not, but He'll let you know. I believe that.

About three years after the above meeting at Lafayette, Georgia with Pastor Hannah, I was in a meeting up on Lookout Mountain. This mountain goes for miles across the Tennessee line down into Georgia. There was a woman on the mountain named Mrs. Patterson. She told me that when she was living in Lafayette, Georgia (in the valley) during my earlier meeting, such conviction of sin and the wrath of God had come upon her that she moved away from Lafayette back up on the mountain where she had previously lived. She didn't know what the conviction by the Holy Spirit was at the time, but she was later saved, and then her children were saved.

Another Man Who Said "Don't Come To Me."

When I came to Lookout Mountain for a meeting, her husband was not saved. I went over to the man's house that Sunday night, the pastor going with me. I said, "Why don't you come to the meeting, Mr. Patterson? The rest of your family is saved. Why don't you come?" He said, "Well, I'll never be saved when anybody comes to me in the service. I'm afraid somebody will come to me."

I said, "Mr. Patterson, you are going to die and go to Hell. That's all there is to it." He said, "Wait a minute. Wait a minute. What do you mean?" I said, "You're going to die and go to Hell. You're putting stipulations on God. You're telling God you're gonna be saved your way. And that's why we've got so many false professions in the church today. People are trying to be saved their way and not God's way. And you'll never be saved."

He said, "Well, I'll come tonight if you'll promise not to come to me." I said, "No, I never go to anybody unless God lays it on my heart and I know I'm in line with what God is doing. But, now, let me ask you a question. I'll not come unless God tells me He's going to kill you tonight. Now, if He says He's going to kill you tonight if you don't get saved, would you want me to come?" He said, "Oh yes. I'll give you permission if God tells you that. I believe that you would listen to God."

I said, "All right, come on. I'll not come to you unless I know that God's going to cut you off if you don't come tonight." He said, "All right," and he came. The whole family came. I preached, not on judgment at all. I believe I preached on Heaven that night. Just a little simple sermon. I gave the invitation, and his wife and all the children came forward. They were down at the altar praying.

She said, "Brother Ferguson, God's gonna kill him. He's gonna die if he doesn't get saved tonight." And, I kind of believed the same. A whole lot of other people came up. Some were already at the altar to be saved. Some more came to be saved. Christian workers were dealing (counseling) with all those who had come to the altar. Somebody came to me for me to talk with them a little.

Then, I looked around and there was Patterson down on his

106

knees between the pews where he had been sitting. You could see his head above the pew in front of him. He couldn't talk but he motioned with his hand for me to come to him. I went to him, and he came to the altar and was saved.

Now, you talk about a service! We had people saved, people rejoicing all over the place. A great number of people came, men, children. Then he told me. He said, "Brother Ferguson, I could not move one step (could not move physically). I tried to come but I couldn't until you came to me." Think about that. God showed His power and wouldn't let him come 'til somebody came to him.

Mr. Patterson became Brother Patterson. He went to Tennessee Temple School in Chattanooga, went all the way through school and graduated. God called him to preach and he's still over in Missouri preaching and doing a good work, the Lord working through him. Sometimes we say, "They're doing a good work." But we don't do it. God works through us. There's a lot of working for the Lord that's not going to stand, and I've done it myself - and probably every preacher has. But God has to work through us, or it's sounding brass and a tinkling cymbal.

The Stevenson Woman Who Said, "Don't Come To Me."

That's like it was over there at Stevenson, Alabama. You remember what the girl said, Brother Dan. She said she would never be saved if somebody came to her and the Lord sent me right straight to her. She could not be saved until somebody came to her. I didn't know she had said that, and when the Lord sent me over to her and she surrendered her will, it became possible for her to be saved. God is not going to let us be saved in our self-will. Otherwise, we would say that we did something in our own salvation. It's God's salvation, not our salvation. It's not what we do, but what He's already done on the Cross, and we'll have to accept that.

People can't tell God how they'll get saved. I believe in "whosoever will," but there comes a time when they have to bend. People can't be saved, I don't believe, unless their will is broken. The Holy Spirit has to do the work of putting pressure on them, but they must yield in order to be saved. God knows the future and, if He sees that a man will not repent and bend his will to God's will to be saved, God may cut him off in judgment and send him to Hell. Everyone has a last day, a last time when God strives with their will. Beyond that time, there will never be another opportunity to be saved.

A Woman Drank Out of a Mudhole.

People cannot set stipulations and dictate to God how, when, or where they will be saved. In one of Charles Finney's meetings, a woman told him she wanted to be saved. But she said to him, "I'm not going to be saved down in these woods. I'll be saved anywhere else, but not here." A goodly number of other people had been saved in that spot in the woods. Finney said to her, "You're going to Hell. You'll never get saved 'til you go to those woods." So the woman got down and drank muddy water, rolled in a mud hole, washed her head with mud, and she still couldn't get saved. Finally, she said, "All right, Lord, I'll go down in those woods and get saved." And the minute she got down in the woods she was saved.

Breaking Into Jail Services.

A couple of years ago, I went back to my home town of North Wilkesboro, North Carolina. We lived near there and it brought back some memories. I used to go to the jail there to preach. I asked the lady at the jail if I could preach. "I'm a Baptist preacher and, I want to go upstairs and preach to the men in jail." She said, "Well, I don't think you can preach to 'em. I don't think they'll listen to you. I think it would be a good idea if you would go into the jail and bring them some presents and stuff. They might accept that. I don't think they will, anyway." I said, "All right." That was back in the days when you could get something for five dollars. So, I had five dollars, and I bought them five dollars worth of presents, came back, and she went upstairs with me and said, "Now, here men, here's a preacher that was willing and good-hearted to buy you some stuff and here it is. We'll appreciate it if you'll listen to him."

As she shut the door and went out she said, "You'll call me in about five minutes." I said to the men, "Fellows, I've come to preach to you." They said, "Ha, ha, ha, ha, HA! Preach all you want to but we won't listen." I said, "Look here, you dirty, low-down, hypocritin' cowards you!" I said, "Every one of you is a low-down, dirty coward. I'll fight every one of you, one at a time if you'll fight." I was inside with them where the whole group was. The lady jailer had brought them out into a group together. I said, "But I'd better tell you who I am before you fight. I'm Paul 'Country' Ferguson, the Ex-Welter-Weight Champion of the South, and I just retired not long ago - and I'm still in pretty good shape, and I'll fight all of you."

Boy, their mouths flew open and one of them said, "Country Ferguson, is that you?" And I said, "Yes sir!" He said, "I saw you knock somebody out one time at Winston-Salem. I came to your fight, and turned my head, and when I looked around the fight was over. You probably knocked him out with one punch. What'd you hit him with?" I said, "A left hook." Another one said, "Yeah, I saw you fight somewhere else. Yeah, I remember you knocked a guy out in the third round." I said, "Yeah, that's right." And they said, "Brother, preach all you want to. We'll listen."

They listened and I started in to preachin.' I preached, and when I thought the Lord was through with me, I said, "OK men, now, let's bow our heads in prayer and I'll pray." I said, "Right over here at the next cell the door is open. I saw that when I came in. If any of you are willing to be saved, come over there."

Cussin' Woman Wants Cigarette Money.
Well, I walked by the men to go to the cell with the open door. Over on the other side of the big room was a woman in a cell. She started cursing me, calling me S.O.B and everything else, and said, "I'm dying for a cigarette but a lowdown dirty preacher wouldn't give you any money." I had some money, some change, beside what I had spent on presents for them. I threw it to her and went on. I walked into the cell and waited just a second and one of the men came. I dealt with him very carefully and he accepted the Lord.

Tough Inmates Want to Be Saved.
He went out, and another one came in. And another one came in. And they all came in. One big ol' tall, red-headed fellow

came in. I'll just call him "Shu." He said, "Preacher, I heard what you said. I don't believe that God could save me. I'm too mean." I said, "I John 1:7 says, *'The blood of Jesus Christ His Son cleanseth us from all sin.'*" "Aw," he said, "Preacher, you don't understand. I've made enough whiskey to float a battleship and you think He would save me?" I said, *"The blood of Jesus Christ His Son cleanseth us from all sin."*

He said, "Yeow, but I've stoled and done all this stuff." I said, *"The blood of Jesus Christ His Son cleanseth us from all sin."* Every time, I quoted I John 1:7. He said, "Well, I'm the meanest man that ever lived." I said, *"The blood of Jesus Christ His Son cleanseth us from all sin."* He said, "You don't understand. That's why I'm in jail. My brother and I got in a fight and I shot him. I shot him twice. And then I put the gun to his heart and something turned the bullet away and didn't kill him. I hate him worse than anything. I hope he dies."

I said, "I John 1:7 still says, *'The blood of Jesus Christ His Son cleanseth from all sin.'*" He said, "Preacher, I believe you mean that." "Well," I said, "I wasn't beatin my gums together just to hear 'em pop." I said, *"The blood of Jesus Christ, God's Son, cleanseth from all sin."* He said, "All right, tell me how to be saved."

I told him how to be saved, and he accepted the Lord in a casual manner, not too much excitement or anything. He said, "Now Preacher, now that I'm saved will you do me a favor?" I said to myself, "Oh Lord. I know what this is. He wants me to help him get out of jail." That's what went through my mind. I said to myself, "That rascal's not a bit more saved than a billy goat."

He said, "Preacher, I shot my brother. And he's in the hospital and they say he's goin' to die right away. I want you to go see him, and go see my pore ol' daddy. He's the biggest bootlegger in the whole Huntin' Creek section of North Carolina. He'll die and go to Hell." And tears were coming out of his eyes. He said, "Will you go today?" I said, "Yes, it's getting late but I'll go. I'll have to go back to my mother's first, and then I'll go."

I went on back home and told my mother, and I thought she'd be happy. I told her I was going by to see that man that night. It scared her to death! She called all the neighbors and everybody she knew that was saved to pray for me. There were several people praying at the time, and she was praying. Of course, they thought I'd get killed. I went on and came to a filling station. I knew in a general section of where it was, but I'd never been in that section before.

They'll Kill You!

When I stopped at the filling station, I said, "Mister, can you tell me where Mr. Shu lives?" He said, "Shu?" "Yeah." He said, "You mean that Shu (and he called his name, I can't remember the exact name), you mean him?" I said, "That's the man I mean." He said, "Fellow, you don't look like you want to buy whiskey. You don't look like that kind of man. Why are you going over there?"

I said, "I'm a Baptist preacher and I'm going over there to tell him how to be saved. That's why I'm going." He said, "Fellow, you'd better not go. They'll kill you. You'd better take my advice and go on to where you live." I said, "No sir. If the Lord wants me to die, I'll die. But I'm going over there and talk to Mr. Shu. I'll find the place." He told me the best he could, and I understood it the best I could.

The only person in that whole section that I knew of being saved was a Baptist deacon. I came right to his house and knocked on the door. His wife came to the door. She said, "Brother, what can we do for you?" I said, "Ma'am, I'm a Baptist preacher and I'm on the way over to Mr. Shu's house to talk to him about the Lord and tell him how to be saved. His son was saved in jail and I want to go over there to see his daddy." She said, "Fellow, I - I tell you. You better not go over there. They'll kill you." I said, "Lady, I don't care. If this is God's time for me to die, I'm willing. He told me to go and I'm going."

The old deacon came out; I'll never forget it. He had on the left sleeve of his coat, and he put his hand down and picked up his lantern while he was putting on his right sleeve. He said, "Well, preacher, if you want to die, I'll go and watch you die." We walked down the trail that wound back into the mountain past one place and then another.

Now, I didn't go down that trail as an ex-fighter, thinking that my fighting days would get me through. I was depending on the

111

Lord, and I was talking to Him as I went. I said, "Lord, now if I get killed and you want me to, if this is the time, all right. And if it's not, I'm gonna have to claim Psalm 34:7: *"The angel of the Lord encampeth round about them that fear Him."* And I said, "You'll have to look after me."

So I went on, and I wasn't a bit afraid. The house was one of those old fashioned houses with great big rooms. I knocked on the door and told the man about his boy, Ed, being saved in jail, and that his son had asked me to come by and talk with him. He said, "Come in." It was pretty gruff. There was a big living room and two side rooms. It was a rough place. Everything was bad. Everybody in the house was drunk—the wife, even the children—everybody but the man. As we used to say in North Carolina, "He was sober as a jug."

He sat down. I pulled up a chair, the only chair I saw. He said, "Talk all you want to." I went over the plan of salvation and showed him he was a sinner. He said, "You don't have to show me that; I know that. I'm the meanest man that ever lived. There's nobody in the world as mean as me." I said, "Well, you're at a good place to get saved then. 'Cause most people don't think they're mean." Then I showed him that Christ died to pay for all of his sins. I showed him several Scripture verses, but especially Galatians 1:4: *"Who gave himself for our sins, that he might deliver us from this present evil world, according to the will of God and our Father."* And then, John 1:12 and some others, and Romans 10:13: *"For whosoever shall call upon the name of the Lord shall be saved."*

And then, I prayed. Then I said, "Are you willing to be saved?" "Yes sir." So he accepted the Lord, and he was rejoicing! I had carried a Bible with me. I'm one of the old-timey preachers that carries a Bible as big as the *Encyclopedia Brittanica*. I don't take a little 'ol Bible with me. Now, I have in some cases, but I didn't in that case.

The Door Burst Open and There Stood Ed.

As I was getting ready to leave, the door burst open and in came Ed, his son. He was out of jail! Back in the jail, right after I had prayed with Ed and he accepted the Lord, I said to him, "Let's pray that God will get you out of jail." I said, "You're already free. If God wants you to serve your penalty, you serve it. But, if He don't want you to serve your penalty, you pray and I'll pray, and the Lord will somehow get you out."

Here he was in front of me, and I didn't know what to think. "Ed! Have you broken out of jail?" He said, 'No, the jailer let me out. He said the sheriff told him that if he ever did get anything against me, he would see that I went to the penitentiary for life, or maybe even to the electric chair. He told me I would never be free again!"

Big Gun Battle Coming Up?

I failed in faith when I saw Ed Shu come through the door. I said to myself, "Lord have mercy. He's broke out of jail. I told him to pray and maybe the Lord would let him out, but he's broke out of jail, and the sheriff will be here any minute with men and guns, and there'll be a big gun battle right here at this house." I was doubting what I had told him. Surely God wouldn't get him out of jail that quick.

Ed grabbed me and started hugging me. He said, "Preacher, you remember me telling you today that the sheriff would see to it that I would go to the penitentiary, or if my brother dies, he would send me to the electric chair? Because I meant to kill him?" I said, "Yeah. I remember that." He said, "Well, I prayed, and I know you prayed, and that man - that very man- came today and went on my bond and said I wouldn't spend a day in jail over it."

Ed asked me if I had been by to see his brother. I told him, "No, I haven't, because they wouldn't let me in at the hospital to see him. The way God's working, He'll keep him alive. He won't die. And when I get back in two weeks I'll talk to him. I had to leave, and I couldn't get back until two weeks later.

So I went on and passed the deacon's house. The deacon's wife promised me that she would be praying and getting all the people she knew away from there to pray concerning my return in two weeks. She wanted me to come back and visit some others in that bootleg section of town.

Mothers Are Nice To Have.

I called my mother, or maybe wrote her. I can't remember

which. I told her what had happened and that I was going back to see Ed's brother and was going back to the deacon's house and visit some more in that section.

My mother was excited about it and she called her Methodist preacher and said, "Paul is going over there and they'll kill him." The preacher said, "No, they won't kill him." She said, "Why don't you go with him?" The preacher said, "They'd kill me, but they won't kill him because God sent him over there. God didn't send me. We'll pray that God will bless."

During the next two weeks, over five hundred people were praying for God to bless when I returned. I came back in two weeks, came near the place and saw about five people standing around talking. The Lord laid it on my heart to go over there and witness to them. All five of them got saved.

Max Shu Comes Out of the Woods.

I went on from there, going toward Max Shu's, the man that Ed Shu shot. He was coming up out of the woods. I told him who I was and he said, "Well, I've been looking for you." I said, "Well, did your daddy and brother say anything to you?" He said, "No, I've not seen them during this two weeks. I heard about you being over there. But I wouldn't let 'em come around. But I've been expecting you." I thought, "How in the world was he expecting me?" He said, "I'm willing for you to talk to me now." So I took the Bible and showed him he was a sinner. He said he knew he was a sinner. He just wanted to know how to be saved. He accepted the Lord, and I was glad.

He said, "Now, I want to tell you something. My brother shot me. God turned the bullet away, and God spoke to me. He said, "Max Shu, I've had you in four car wrecks. I've had you shot a couple of times to try to wake you up. There's a preacher coming to you, and when he comes you'll know him. You've never seen him, you don't know who he is, but you'll know him when he walks up." The minute you walked up, I knew it was you.

And, boy! That stirred me up. After he was saved, he went over and saw his brother and they were all right with each other after they had gotten saved.

114

To the Bootlegger's House.

That afternoon I went out and walked up to one man who was one of the biggest bootleggers in North Carolina. He was working on something on his car, and I waited till he finished. He thought I was a salesman or something at first, but then he saw my Bible. I told him I was a preacher. He said that he had heard about the Shus. He figured I was the same one that talked with them. I told him I was. He said, "Talk all you want to."

I went over the plan of salvation with him; then, I turned to Luke 16:19-31, about Hell. That's the same thing I did to Ed Shu's daddy. I said, "That's where you're going." I started praying. I prayed a little longer than I usually do. He patted on my back and said, "Will you please quit praying and tell me how to get saved. I can't wait no longer." I can't remember that happening before. He accepted the Lord, started rejoicing, ran in the house and brought his whole family out and they all got saved.

I went on visiting that afternoon and won sixteen more, some of the hardest bootleggers in that whole section. That's really the first time the Gospel had ever been in that section. The Gospel had come around that section, and near it, but not in that section.

Jerking the Cover Off the Sick.

That night, I got back to the deacon's house and was going to stay all night. I walked in and told the woman what had happened. She rejoiced and then said, "There's something you need to do yet. My son found out you're here and he's unsaved, a teenager." She said, "You can talk to him in the morning, he's in bed sick." I said, "No, I'll talk to him now." I went upstairs and jerked the cover off and said, "Get yourself out of here and let me talk to you about the Lord!" Now, that's not the way they tell you in school to do it, but that's the way that was needed for those kind of people. You had to talk up to 'em. He accepted the Lord, and his mother shouted all over the house and ran up and down. I thought I'd never get any sleep. She went on and on and on, and I went to sleep while she was shoutin'.

The next morning I thought I'd go over and see how the Shus were doing. The deacon didn't go with me. I went by myself that time. I went down the path. It all looked different than the first time. I didn't recognize the house, it was so clean and everything was in place. The man was coming up the path leading his cow and I believe he was singing *Oh, How I Love Jesus.* Boy, he couldn't carry a tune in a tin bucket, no better than I can. I came on up toward him and the cow, and he grabbed me and started huggin' me and said, "I love you better than anybody in the world."

Ed ran out and started telling me how much he loved me. Mac had been over there to see them. The man lined his family all up, about eighteen of them. I'm not exaggerating. That's the kind of family there used to be in that part of the country, a big one. I came out of a big family, myself, with nine children.

He lined them up and said, "Children, the preacher's here to tell you how to be saved. Listen to him and do what he says." He had a leather strap about so wide and so long hanging up in the house. I guess the children knew they had to. No, not really. The strap wasn't what made them listen. They had seen a difference in their daddy for two weeks. That was the thing that happened to those children. Keep in mind also that there were five hundred people who had been praying day and night for two weeks.

I had told the preacher, Brother Ellis, in Greensboro where I was going, and he was also afraid I'd get killed. But when I told him what had happened, they were really happy. The Lord has still got people He can send today if people will pray. All of this came out of prayer and one visit. Now, they were praying kinda like they were in the twelfth chapter of Acts when Peter was in jail. They were praying sincerely for Peter to get out of jail, but they didn't believe it when he knocked on the door. That's the way we do a lot of times, but if we'll pray He'll answer. *God doesn't answer because we pray. He answers because He has promised to answer if we'll pray.* It's God that gets the glory. Not us. God answers prayer.

Paul Ferguson the Fighter
Chapter 8

Nothing Too Hard for God in Salisbury, NC.

I was in Salisbury, North Carolina with Steve Byrd. Now, in all of these stories, I'm not emphasizing as much as I ought to about praying. But we WERE praying, and the Lord blessed. The meeting began to open up and people were saved. Somebody told me about a family that lived right beside the church. "They don't go to church. They're the meanest, hardest people in the world. They may run you off. I believe they will," someone said. "We just believe they're too hard for God." [D.C.: *Speaking for the other church people.*]

I said, "There's not anybody too hard for God. In Jeremiah 32:27, God says: *'Behold, I am the Lord, the God of all flesh; is there any thing too hard for me?'* In Jeremiah 33:3, He continues: *'Call unto me, and I will answer thee, and shew thee great and mighty things, which thou knowest not.'*" I had earlier claimed these verses before I went to the jail and dealt with Ed Shu.

I went to the house next to the church. The man came to the door. I said, "Sir, I'm Paul Ferguson, and I'm preaching a revival over here at this Baptist church. I'd like to come in and talk to you." He said, "Mister, did you say you came from a church? A Baptist church?" I said, "Yeah." He said, "Why, they don't want me. They don't care anything about me." I said, "What do you mean?" He said, "I live right here beside a Baptist church, and I thought it was for social people, rich people. Not anybody from this church or any church has ever been by here to tell me anything about the church. That's all I know. I thought it was for elite people." I said, "No sir. God loves everybody, and He's willing to save anybody that's willing to be saved." He said, "Come on in and tell me about it."

I walked in and sat down, and he went about rounding up his whole family. It was one of those big families. He said, "Now listen to what this man says." I started out the best I could about Genesis. Those people had never heard anything much about God. They had heard it as a curse word but, in America, they had never heard about Christ! They didn't know about it, so

117

it took me a while to go through all of it. I explained it the best I could and prayed. I went very carefully through the plan of salvation. The man and his wife accepted the Lord, and every one of his children - about ten. They came to church that night and followed the Lord in baptism.

> D.C.: *A growing number of people born in this country know hardly anything about God. Many people in America have never seen a Bible, have never sat through a TV program featuring the Bible.*

Smart and Ignorant in Ohio.

In the central part of Ohio, there are a lot of farm sections, and I had several revival meetings up there. In one place, somebody mentioned a boy that was really mean. They thought maybe my going and talking to him as a prize fighter might help him, so I went over to his house and talked to him. He listened to me, and I talked to him about the church. He said, "What do you do over there?" I said, "Well, the first thing we do is to tell people about Jesus and try to magnify Him."

Now, this boy was intellectual about schooling, but about this matter he was dumb. He made good grades in school. He was a good student, but he said, "Jesus Christ? What baseball team is he on?" I said, "Son, he doesn't play baseball. This thing is about people's souls going to Hell." He didn't know what I was talking about. I said, "Come over to the church. Come a while and see how you like it." He said, "I'll come tonight." We sent a man by to get him. He came every service after that.

One night he came to me and said, "I understand now, and I want to be saved." He went back home and told his parents about it. They said, "You can't go over there any more." He said, "I know what the preacher said, to obey your parents. But I believe if you're doing something good and your parents want you to do something bad, you shouldn't do it; and I know it's good to go over to that church and hear all these things." This showed the wisdom the Lord had put in him. "I'm going. I'll obey you on other things, but I won't on that." His parents came too, and were saved.

Now, I believe in children obeying their parents, but I know

118

preachers who say that if a husband told his wife to go out with another man that they ought to do it. I don't believe that. I don't believe God will honor that. We ought to do right even if our parents or our mates want us to do wrong.

A Dead Church Has a Fire.

I was with Pastor Glen Sanders in seven or eight different churches. I was with him in Lima, Ohio. We had a lot of teenagers saved, but a lot of the people wouldn't move. One night I said, "Well people, you know, this thing is so dead, God might just burn this thing down tonight." I quit the sermon right there and went to my room. Nobody thought much about it except to say, "He's crazy." I hadn't intended to say what I said, hadn't intended to stop right there at the end of the sentence; but I did.

That night the church furnace caught on fire and it could have burned the whole church building down. You talk about critical people being shaken up; it liked to have scared them to death! They brought in people from all around there. I don't like to give numbers because I might not get the number right. Anyway, the meeting was a good success with many saved. So the preacher scheduled me for the following year.

There was a man there named Mr. Dollar. He went to the preacher and said, "You've got this man scheduled, and you've got to cancel it because we're not going to back the meeting." The preacher said, "No, I scheduled Paul Ferguson. I'm not going to let him know that you don't want him, but I'm going to have him if there's nobody there but me." Mr. Dollar said, "Well, we won't back it financially." The pastor said, "God will back it. God told me to have him, so we're going to have him."

We started the meeting without many there. The pastor didn't tell me a thing. About Monday night, there was a Church of God group there. Their church had burned down and they were looking for a place to go, so they just came in to our meeting that night. Of all things, I was preaching on eternal salvation that night - that you can't lose your salvation. I guess I quoted extra scripture that night, 65-70 or more verses, with examples of eternal security. I had never done this before, and not many times since.

I said, "Anybody here that has not believed in eternal security, and you'll commit yourself to God if He shows it to you, will you accept it? Every one of those Church of God people came forward! One woman brought twenty-four teenagers, and they were saved. The next night everybody brought somebody else, and they wanted me to preach on eternal security again. I didn't know who was there or from where they had come. They all started giving. We only had one person saved in the meeting that was not a teenager, and they had no money. But in the first meeting I preached there, we had some men saved who started tithing right away. Mr. Dollar had said that the teenagers that were coming to the meeting wouldn't and couldn't support the meeting with money, but the earlier converts gave enough money to support the meeting. Every night the pastor would announce, "This offering will go to the evangelist."

The meeting was over and a lot of people were saved, but all the converts but one went and joined the Church of God Church because the Church of God people brought them. When they started to count the money, this Mr. Dollar said, "That's too much. We're not goin' to give it to him." The pastor said, "Yes, we're going to give it to him." Dollar said, "No." So, the pastor came to me about it. He said, "Paul, I've always treated you fair." I said, "I know that, Glen." He said, "This man says he's not going to give it to you." Then he said, "I'll tell you what we'll do. We'll have a meeting on it and have the deacons to come (they go by the deacons a lot up there); but I'll guarantee you, I'll send you the money."

I said, "Now listen, Glen. If you let them keep part of that money and you send it yourself, I'm going to pray that you'll die." He said, "Oh! For God's sake don't do it! I've seen some of the things you pray for. Don't do that." I said, "Well, I'll still do it unless you promise me you'll not send the money yourself. I'll trust you." He said, "All right."

I rode a bus back home, and Glen called a meeting. When he got up, all the other men were there. Sanders was trying to work it out. Dollar jumped up and said, "People, God's worked on my heart since that meeting. We took that money up for the preacher, and if we didn't give it to him we'd be stealing." That ended the meeting. They sent me the money. That was an unusual thing the way it worked out. The Lord doesn't always work according to our plans. He works His plan.

Giving No Invitations to Be Saved.

In South Carolina, Jesse Pryor has been a friend of mine. He had me for a meeting at the Summerville Baptist Church, and God blessed. In the first part of the meeting, I didn't give an invitation. In the earlier part of my ministry, as a matter of practice, I didn't give any invitations for people to be saved for the first few nights of the meeting. In those days most of the meetings were two weeks or more, and we had time to preach to Christians about prayer and work toward warming up cold hearts.

But one time some lost people came to a meeting where I didn't give an invitation, and they went away unsaved and died. After that, I gave an invitation to unsaved people during the first week of a meeting, but I didn't give an invitation to saved people. So Christians came and they thought, "We don't have to do anything. We're getting off free." This was one of the earlier meetings. I had not given an invitation for lost people to be saved. Several people came around and said, "Look, you're not giving any invitation and we want to be saved." So we'd lead them to the Lord, privately. We'd tell them to come forward Sunday morning and make their profession of faith publicly known.

Through the week several had been saved. The Lord was convicting people with strong conviction. Sunday morning came, and the ones who had already been saved came forward to make it public. In addition to those, there were 22 saved on Sunday morning. During the following weeks we had people saved every night. People were coming from everywhere to the meeting. There were some boys from Columbia Bible College attending the meeting. They said, "We know that the Spirit of God is working here. When things begin to happen, it looks like it's almost a psychological thing, but we know different. We can't understand it." They came every night.

This was one of the best meetings, all around, that did more good, and lasted, that I've ever been in. You're always going to know about the real results. I have been in meetings where large numbers of people would make professions of faith and only three or four would be baptized; but in this meeting, they baptized more than the number making professions of faith. There were some there in the church that had been saved but had not been baptized. Of course, some came from other churches and were saved, but not baptized there in that church. It sort of equalized but, still, there were more baptisms than professions of faith. From that standpoint, it was a very strong meeting.

Farbin, Georgia Didn't Like My Jokes—Didn't Like To Pray.
In Farbin, Georgia, where Ed Cook was the pastor, we had a large number of people saved. There were a lot of women there who didn't like me because I told jokes, but that didn't stop me. Some of them didn't want me to ever come back. As I remember, there were forty-six that were saved and joined the church. Beyond that, there were some who made professions of faith who did not join the church, and some who went to other churches.

There was a strong working of the Lord there. I preached on *God's Last Train To Heaven*. That's when a lot of it broke loose. I had more men saved over the years by preaching that message than all the other sermons put together. Several men came on the night of that message. That was an all-around judgment meeting. The preacher had me to come back for another meeting; but, as I said, some of them didn't want me to come back because I told jokes from the pulpit during the meeting. God didn't stop because I told jokes. These people didn't pray, didn't do anything. But they did get stirred. During the *Last Train To Heaven* message, some of my critics thought they were going to die. By nature, we humans had rather complain as to pray.

Those critics illustrated how we often find some little simple something, not a thing wrong with it, and complain instead of getting concerned over people going to an eternal, everlasting Hell. Our human nature had rather complain than to pray. There were people in the area who said they were just walking along the way and God told them to come to the service and get saved. That was their testimony. That was unusual, of course, but God is my witness that those people told us it happened to them.

122

Signal Mountain —The Man Who Couldn't Read.

The Signal Mountain Baptist Church in Signal Mountain, Tennessee, came out of a meeting I held in a school house there, an all-around unusual meeting. I preached and preached in the school house. There was a man there that belonged to the Masons, and he hated the Baptists because the Baptists didn't agree with the Masons. I preached on "Fellowship," and somewhere in the message it got 'hold of his heart, and he began coming back to the meetings and got saved. He was all stirred up.

Another man was there, Mr. Smith, who couldn't read. He got under conviction and was saved in his home. He started witnessing in that meeting, and he continued witnessing until he died about three years ago. He couldn't read one word. His wife would read Scripture to him, and he would go out and quote verses to people and tell where they were found.

I knew a man in North Carolina who could read the Bible but couldn't read the newspaper or anything else. But this man, Mr. Smith, couldn't read the Bible but could remember it when his wife read it to him. He won many people to the Lord. God used him to win people in the school house meeting.

One night in a meeting, when I was getting ready to preach, just before they were to call me up to the pulpit, the Lord said to me, "This man right over here (house next to the church) that you're praying for, if you want him to be saved you'd better go over there and talk to him right now because this is going to be his last chance. If he doesn't get saved tonight, he'll never get saved. I'm going to cut him off."

So, I went over to his house. I knocked on the door, and he said, "Preacher, aren't you supposed to be preaching?" I said, "Yes sir, but the Lord spoke to me and told me this is your last night. He's going to cut you off if you don't get saved." He said, "You don't mean that do you?" I said, "I wouldn't have come over here and left the service and make them have to sing while I'm gone 'til I get back, if God hadn't told me real plain that this is your last chance. I've come over here to show you how to be saved." He said, "I'll let you talk to me." He accepted the Lord.

He came back to the church with me and sat through the

message. I didn't tell the people anything. They were glad to see him come in. They had been praying and praying for him for weeks. His wife had prayed for him for years, and the whole church had now been praying for him. So I preached the message and gave the invitation.

At the close, the man said, "Preacher, wait a minute. I want to say a word." I said, "O.K." He got up and said, "The preacher told me, and God told me too, that this was my last chance to be saved. And there's some of you in here, too, that'd better be saved." They started coming from all over the church to get saved.

It was a great meeting. After it was all over, a church was formed. From that church several men were called to preach and went out and did other works from that meeting there, and especially from that night. It was the Lord. It wasn't me. I'm not a good preacher, but the Lord is good. That's what we have to keep in remembrance at all times. God doesn't use us *because* of us, but *in spite* of us. He chooses to use some. I don't always know why, but He does.

Paul Ferguson the Fighter
Chapter 9

Enon Baptist Church.

I was scheduled to be at Enon Baptist Church for fourteen days. [D.C.: *Anyone know where this is?*] A few miles away, another church had scheduled a meeting to begin at the same time. Well, they had good results right off, twenty-five or more people being saved that first week. We hadn't had anybody saved. Some of the folks at Enon Baptist began to say, "Well, we know we're obligated to our church here, but we sure would like to go over there where something is happening. There's nothing happening here."

But God was working some of the people hard. I was praying. Pastor Price and I would pray, and some of the men of the church came to pray at 10:00 p.m. and prayed 'til 12:00 midnight, at least. Some other people began to join in with us. I went to play handball some of the mornings for exercise and then come back to pray and study the rest of the day.

But some of the people were like the man who came to a preacher and said, "Preacher pray for me." Preacher said, "Are you saved?" "Yes sir." "How long have you been saved?" "Thirty five years." Preacher said, "Anybody that's been saved for thirty-five years ought to pray for himself." The man said, "I can't pray." Preacher said, "Well, try. I won't pray for you unless you pray." He said, "All right." So, he crossed his arms and said, "Matthew, Mark, Luke, and John, hold my horse while I get on." And that's like a lot of our praying today. We don't get down to business and really pray. That's the way it was going the first two weeks. Some would say a little short prayer like that.

That's the way it went 'til Sunday night. I preached *God's Last Train to Heaven,* and that stirred the people. Some of them had heard me preach that message at several places around where some unsaved person or a backslider had died during the meeting or right after. They said, "We'd better quit playing and get down to business." In the beginning of the meeting, I didn't want them to work at getting people saved. I wanted them to get burdened. If they got burdened, they would do more than they would in six months without a burden. God can do more in one service than people can do in twenty years without Him.

I called for a prayer meeting. The men came to pray and told their wives to go home. While we were praying, the wives became burdened, and they all came back to the church and began praying. The men didn't know their wives had returned to the church. God got hold of my heart that night, and I cried and prayed. We prayed 'til about 2:00 or 3:00 o'clock in the morning. Some of the men had to get up at 5:00 a.m. to go to work, but after losing all that sleep, they said they still had a good day. When we came out of the prayer room, the women came out.

The next day we had about fifteen people saved. That really stirred them up. We repeated our prayer meeting like the night before, and J. R. Cook was the first man to get a burden. The women prayed too. The next night one man brought fifteen teenagers from another church, and they were all saved - and there were others saved. The meeting went on like that every night, with people being saved and the Christians praying up into the morning hours. When people quit looking at the preacher, expecting him to bring the meeting with his preaching, and began praying, the power of God came down. Now, we know that the Bible says God has chosen the foolishness of preaching to save the lost, but what we may forget is that it takes much prayer for the preaching to have power. They go together. That same pattern happened over and over in other places. I would go to a place for a meeting and we never had results until the people started praying, and then things would happen.

In Florida with Pastor Jack Lindsey.

In this meeting a lot of things happened to throw the meeting off. People were not concerned. There was a problem in the church that concerned the pastor. I was going to just leave the meeting and go home. It didn't seem like they were going to do anything. I told them that if they didn't start praying and quit thinking about the problem in the church that I was going to quit after that night. I told them that if they didn't show any burden that it was a waste of my time and theirs, too.

The announcement shook them up a little and they started

praying. They came every night and spent time praying. They didn't do as much visiting as they did praying. The pastor and I had been visiting. God put it on my heart and his heart at the same time: Quit visiting. That's all you do. Get down to praying. We started praying, and things began to happen. People began to be saved. Teenagers and older people were saved.

One night a fellow that no one knew came and sat on the back seat and had his family with him. When the service was over they jumped up and left. The next night the man and his family were there. When we said, "Amen," he started out the door. One of the deacons shook hands with him as he left. He came the next night and was saved. Afterward he went to the back, and one of the deacons began talking with him. He asked him, "What kind of a car do you have?" "I don't have a car." The deacon said, "What? Well, I'll take you home."

The deacon asked him who invited him to the meeting. No one had invited him to come. Then he told his story. He said, "I was getting ready to kill myself. I was lying on the floor getting the gun ready to shoot myself, when something had me to look at a paper advertising the meeting. There was a picture. It interested me because a boxer was preaching. I decided that I didn't know what there was to this thing, but if this fellow gave up fighting and all that, there must be something to it and I'd better not kill myself. I'd better go up there and hear him."

Then he said that he came to church and heard the boxer preach and something just told him he needed to be saved. So he came back the next night. On the third night he came back and was saved and said, "Now I understand it. It was the Lord working in my heart. The Holy Spirit was telling me that I didn't need to kill myself." He said, "I didn't have a job, didn't have any money. The very next morning after the day I got saved, a man called me to come back to my job. Somebody came by and gave me a car. Somebody owed me some money and they came by and paid me. All my needs were met."

It might be that everybody wouldn't get it done that quick, but God knew what that man needed, and He supplied all that need. The man said, "Now I know why it happened. God knew that I'd never be saved if I had plenty. My car was gone, my wife had left me, everything was gone." She came back and she and the children were all saved. All of his pressing problems were solved. Several years later I heard that he was still going on for the Lord.

The pastor said, "I would have expected something like this to happen in the mountains of Tennessee. I would have expected it to happen somewhere in the mountains of North Carolina, but in Florida things just don't happen like that. But it did!"

People may think that things like this only happen in mountain sections, and a few of them did, like the one I'm going to tell you - the thing that happened to Wild Bill.

A Rough Tennessee Mountain Crowd.

I went to a little church in one of the mountains of Tennessee. It was a rough place. The pastor was attending Tennessee Temple. He had asked eighteen different preachers to preach a meeting for him, and none of them would go preach for him. Every night he would get up and say, "Boy, this is the Lord's preacher. The Lord has directed him here. I know He directed him here." He kept saying that, and I got a little tired of it. Finally, I said, "Well, what the preacher said is true. I was God's choice, because he went to eighteen different people and they wouldn't come to this place because of him. I decided to come on anyway, because there were people here that needed to be saved." That's a little rough, but that's what I said. He deserved it.

He had been so mean to those mountain people that some of them wouldn't come inside the building. They would come outside and listen to me. They got so mad at him that they were going to kill him. They brought their guns to church one night during the meeting to shoot him. But they liked me. They'd never been inside the church, hadn't met me, but they had heard me preach. They said, "That man loves us and we'll listen to what he says, but we won't listen to that other preacher. He's a devil. He's a low down scoundrel." He was kind of cocky. He said he was going to build a church up there in that mountain bigger than Highland Park in Chattanooga.

They decided not to shoot him as they had planned, because I was on the platform with him. So they decided to wait until I stepped down and shoot him then. But God was determined to save him. Before I was through preaching, the pastor became burdened and went back to the prayer room. At that point, they decided to shoot him as he left, but the preacher was riding with me, and they were afraid they would shoot me, so they didn't shoot him.

I knew there was talk among the men, but I didn't tell the preacher anything about it. He certainly didn't know anything about it. That night on the way home he started bragging. He started blessing me out for some little something. I said to him, "You crazy idiot, you! I guess I'm goin' to have to tell you. These people are laying beside this road right now to kill you. They're goin' to shoot you in that back seat if you don't get your tail down between the seats and hide. You'll be dead! They would have killed you tonight if they hadn't been afraid they would hit me. They came and told me. You don't have any sense."

Boy, he got down in that seat! All along I could see guns. Some followed us in their cars all the way off the mountain, but they didn't shoot. That preacher didn't go back to the church any more. The church was a mission of Highland Park Baptist Church in Chattanooga. Another man came to take his place. He and the all the people there asked for me to come back.

"Wild Bill" Gets Saved at 92.

I went back to that place and we had a good meeting. Some people were saved and the Lord blessed, but everything I'd heard was about "Wild Bill." Wild Bill ran the preachers off. Wild Bill threatened to kill the preachers. I preached the message about everybody having the key to somebody's heart and that no one else has the key. That explains why you can go to somebody twenty times and not get anywhere with them, and someone else may come along and win them to Christ the first time they talk with them. Sometimes it's children that hold the key.

A woman came up to me and said, "God told me that you have the key to Wild Bill's heart." I said, "Lady, it's a funny thing to me that God told you and didn't tell me. I'm always having somebody to tell me that. Why didn't God tell me?" She said, "I don't know, but, you have." I said, "Well, He hasn't told me." In a couple of days she said, "Have you been to see Wild Bill?" I said, "No."

So, I got my Bible and went up there. He was about 92 years old and was getting feeble, but he still could have shot somebody. I knocked on the door and he said, "Cuum Innn." A great big gruff voice. He said, "Who are you and what do you want?" I said, "Mister, I'm the Baptist preacher that's preaching a revival right down here at this little church, and I came up here to tell you how to be saved."

He said, "Aw preacher, I'll shoot you," etc., etc. He began to tell me what all he would do. I said, "Why you old devil you, I'll knock your head off. I was a prize fighter and I'm not afraid of you, and I'll knock your old head off if you don't let me talk to you." He drew back his fist like he was going to hit me and went to cryin'. "Preacher," he sobbed, "I've wanted to be saved for seventy years or more, and I'd bluff people and they'd all leave me and wouldn't come back. You're the only preacher that ever would stand up to me. I'll listen to anything you say." He accepted the Lord.

I went back to church and told those people. It shocked the whole community. People came from everywhere. The meeting was about over, but people came and were saved. Two hundred people or more came for miles around to see "Old Wild Bill" baptized. I didn't get to go; I was out of the area. That was one of the greatest experiences of my life. That's not the usual way, but God doesn't always use the usual way. He uses different things with different people, and it takes that for some people. Some will respond to the love of God, but others you can tell them about love 'til the end of time and it won't get to them. But some, you can only get to them by standing up to them. Wild Bill bluffed people—tried to bluff me, but the Lord wouldn't let me be bluffed.

Heavy Snow in Detroit.

In Detroit, Michigan, I was with Tom Turley. He had rented an auditorium. He was criticized for having the meeting because it was sleeting and snowing, but we went ahead and had the meeting anyway. Many people came and were saved—and told that the sleet was so heavy they thought God was giving them a message and they had better go to church. Tom Turley was a big tall fellow and was a very good ping pong player. God used

130

Tom. That meeting was my introduction to Detroit, and I went back to Detroit eight to ten times because of that one meeting with him. The heavy sleet and threatening weather showed that God doesn't have to have good weather to reach people.

In Ohio one time, there came a snow several feet deep, and the church was filled every night. I couldn't understand it. Many people were saved. "Well, preacher, we think God sent the snow because people had other things planned and, with the snow, we couldn't go anywhere else, so we came to church and were saved."

Can We Measure God's Work?

Pastor Carter, in Interlachen, Florida, called me to come to his church for a meeting. It was not a big church and somewhat isolated from the town and community. Interlachen is between Jacksonville and Daytona Beach, about fifty miles inland. Brother Carter was one of the nicest men I was ever with. I've had some good meetings with men who were not so nice, but Brother Carter was outstanding in being nice. In this meeting we had about sixty people saved in two weeks. Afterward, I went back to Brother Carter's church three different times and had people saved in all those meetings.

The two weeks following that first meeting, I was in Jacksonville, Florida in a big church. After being in the small church and having such a good meeting, the results in the big church were disappointing. The pastor and I went out visiting and worked hard, but there were only six people saved. Let me change that. Six people made professions of faith. Only God knows how many were saved.

One of those six in the big church was a little boy six years old. I believe his name was Andy Black. I'll have more to say about this church and another meeting later. Andy grew up and went to Tennessee Temple Schools and is now a preacher. But at the time, I thought that the meeting in Jacksonville wasn't anything. Six people made a profession of faith in a big church right after sixty people were saved in a small church, removed away from everything.

A year later the pastor of the big church in Jacksonville called me. He said, "Brother Ferguson, you know the meeting we had last year?" I said, "Yes, I remember it. I'll never forget that." He said, "That's the best meeting....the results of that meeting were the best of any meeting I've ever seen in my life." I said, "What did you say?" He repeated it again. I thought a mule had kicked him in the head. I thought he had gone completely crazy, talking about six people being saved and calling it a great meeting. He laughed and said, "You think a mule kicked me on the head, don't you?" I said, "No, I don't think it. I know it." He wanted me to come for another meeting. I said, "I'm not coming. You're crazy."

He said, "Let me explain. When we were out visiting, you used the verses on *whosoever will* - that if a person is willing to be saved they can be saved." We used:

> Acts 2:21: *And it shall come to pass, that whosoever shall call on the name of the Lord shall be saved.*

> I John 5:1: *Whosoever believeth that Jesus is the Christ is born of God: and every one that loveth him that begat loveth him also that is begotten of him.*

> Revelation 22:17: *And the Spirit and the bride say, Come. And let him that heareth say, Come. And let him that is athirst come. And whosoever will, let him take the water of life freely.*

> Romans 10:13: *For whosoever shall call upon the name of the Lord shall be saved.*

> John 3:16: *For God so loved the world, that he gave his only begotten Son, that whosoever believeth in him should not perish, but have everlasting life.*

The pastor said those verses really stuck to him, and he began teaching that to the church. The church went out *from* the church and, in a year's time, won over a hundred people just using those Scriptures. He said, "I knew you would think I was crazy, but the results took place after you were gone."

I had seen that in other places, where nothing outstanding

132

would happen during the meeting. You wouldn't want to write about some of the results. We like to write about big results and not about little results.

A Tough Man Brags Too Much Before God.

Brother Carter left Interlachen, Florida and went to another church in Florida. I can't remember the name of the place. I was the first one he had for a meeting. During that meeting, a man was there who had boasted that he would go fourteen days to the meeting but wouldn't get saved. He boasted to the pastor that there wasn't enough power to get him saved.

So the people prayed for him. I prayed for him. During the second week, the Lord was blessing and people were being saved. On the second Tuesday night, the Lord told me to go back and talk to him. I don't usually go to people unless I know that it's from the Lord. He didn't act like it, but underneath the surface he got real mad. He didn't come the next night (Wednesday). He had said he would come every night but he wouldn't get saved. Thursday night he was back, and the Lord put it on my heart to go talk to him again. He still didn't get saved. He missed the next night (Friday).

He came back on Saturday night. A lot of people were there, and the Lord was really working. They were just standing around the walls, there were so many people there. The Lord laid it on my heart not to go to that man, but to go to another man. A young fellow was standing in the back trembling. I went to him and asked him if he would accept the Lord, and he said, "I want to, worse than anything in the world. If you hadn't come to me, I just couldn't walk out by myself."

I started back up the aisle toward the front. I did not intend to go to the other man who had boasted he would come fourteen days and not be saved. But as I walked up the aisle, he just turned around and drew his fist back and started to curse. When he did, he fell right on his knees and started screaming, "Oh God! I'll get saved if you won't kill me! Please don't kill me!" You talk about something shaking the place! He asked me to help him up, and he went back to the prayer room. It really shook up the whole place. We had more people saved than we did in the first meeting at the other church with Pastor Carter (sixty in the first meeting).

While he was resisting God where he was standing, the Spirit of God just physically knocked him down to his knees. This man said he would have died on the spot if he hadn't gotten saved.

Let me repeat. You see, he had bragged that he could go fourteen nights - and the day meetings too - to all the services, and not miss any of them, and he could hold out without being saved. Bragging before God like that is a dangerous thing. He didn't count on getting so mad twice that he would miss two nights. He didn't count on God knocking him to his knees and convincing him that He would kill him on the spot. This is not the usual way God deals with people, but people don't usually defy God like this man did. Sometimes God makes an example out of a rebel.

A Desperate Woman and a Strange Preacher.

I was scheduled to be home for a week, and a pastor called me and insisted that I come and hold a meeting for him for just a week. I had to travel by plane to give him a full week. It's hard to have much of a meeting in less than two weeks. The pastor said to me, "Preacher, I want you to emphasize eternal security. It's needed here. You believe it, so I want you to emphasize it." I did.

The meeting was going along pretty good. People were coming. I was staying with a man who believed that, in the Ten Commandments where it says, "Thou shalt not kill," it meant everything. It included bugs, fleas, etc. He said he wouldn't kill a snake. I never stayed with anybody like that before. He was a nice man and tenderhearted. I'll tell you I'd kill a snake if it was going to bite me.

In that meeting seventy-something people made a profession of faith. You'll notice that I don't say there were that many people saved. People make a profession and they might not be saved.

One lady in the meeting was named Mrs. Hardesty. As I often did, I preached that everyone has the key to somebody's heart. Nobody can unlock that heart but the one who has the key. Roman 14:7 says, *"...none of us liveth to himself and no man dieth to himself."* Even with our influence we may win

134

somebody to the Lord and not even know it. I've seen that happen over and over.

But Mrs. Hardesty told me, about Tuesday night after I'd preached that, "You have the key to my husband's heart." I'd been told about how mean the man was and how he was indifferent and nobody could reach him. He was too hard for God. I remember saying: In Jeremiah 32:27, God says: *"Behold, I am the LORD, the God of all flesh: is there any thing too hard for me?"* And *Jeremiah 33:3 says: 'Call unto me and I will answer thee and shew thee great and mighty things which thou knowest not."* He's not too hard for God. But I'll go if the Lord leads me." Really, I just didn't want to go.

She came back on Wednesday night and Thursday night and said, "You've got the key to Hardesty's heart, and he'll go to hell if you don't go." Well, on Friday I decided I would go see Mr. Hardesty. She was a smart woman. Sometimes—many times—when you go to see a lost man in the home, his Christian wife will stay right in the room. I won't witness to a man with his wife in the room if she is saved. If they're both unsaved, I will. The reason is that his home is his castle and his throne, and one should not embarrass a man before his wife. I won't do it. Before I went to the home, I told Mrs. Hardesty that she was to leave the room when I got there. I went over the plan of salvation. I don't just go over two or three verses. I showed the man by the Scripture that he was lost and that if he was willing he could be saved. I went over the whole plan of salvation, that Christ had died on the cross and paid for all his sins and that if he was willing he could be saved. I prayed like I usually do and asked him if he was willing to be saved. He said, "No."

About that time, his wife ran into the room and kneeled down at the bed and went to praying. I'm not exaggerating one bit. The floor was literally wet with her tears. She was crying out, "This is his last chance! He's going to Hell! God, he's got to be saved today." Hardesty went over and put his arms around her and said, "Honey, I can't stand those tears. I'll accept the Lord." And he accepted the Lord right there. Now, these people considered themselves to be Yankees, but they shouted all over that room!

That was one of the best meetings I ever saw. The preacher

was plenty strange. Right before the meeting he had been blasting me out because I preached on eternal security. His wife didn't believe it. Maybe he was trying to score points with her. I gave so much Scripture that most of the people came to accept it, but his wife wouldn't accept it. This was the very man who asked me to emphasize eternal security. Well, he didn't have to ask me to emphasize that, because that's what changed my life. I'd been saved twenty years before that. I was saved all the years I was a prizefighter, and I lived a better moral life than a lot of the deacons. I didn't smoke, drink, and all these things. I thought part of the time I was saved, and part of the time I thought I was lost.

During the meeting he said that I was ruining his church by preaching so hard on eternal salvation, but before the meeting was over, even his wife came to accept it. The key to the meeting was when Mr. Hardesty was saved.

Paul Ferguson the Fighter
Chapter 10

Jumping the Rope Helps Win Two Basketball Teams.

I was in a meeting with Persil Cullens in Ohio. He asked me if I would jump the rope for the church young people. I don't mean it in a bragging way, but the truth is that I was pretty good at jumping rope and punching a bag. I was in my early forties, and I was almost as good at it then as I was when I was fighting in the ring.

I announced a night when I would jump the rope. I went over to the high school to find a good place to practice. It was basketball season, and the coach said I could get over to one side of the gym and practice. It so happened that I was jumping rope while the basketball team was practicing. The coach came over to me and said, "Boy, you can jump the rope pretty good." I said, "Yeah. I'm going to jump the rope over at the church where I'm holding a meeting. Why don't you bring the team over?" He said, "We will." So he brought the whole varsity basketball team to the meeting. The whole team was saved that night. The next night they brought the junior varsity team, and all of them were saved. You understand that I mean they made professions of faith.

Praying brings the power of God. I never emphasized the putting on of shows, but I did jump the rope some; and the Lord used it in the winning of young people to the Lord. We had about seventy-five of all ages to make professions of faith in that meeting. I went back three or four times after that, and every time, at King's Mill, we had good meetings with professions of faith.

Pitching Baseball with Either Hand.

In North Carolina, there was a man who came regularly to the meeting who was a manager of a teenage baseball team. He asked me if I knew anything about baseball. I said, "I don't know so much." (When I was young I had to choose between baseball and boxing, and I chose boxing. I was always glad I chose boxing, but I never lost interest in baseball. Years later I coached baseball in Chattanooga elementary schools. At one time I had a whole system in which I coached baseball, and we had some good teams.)

This man said, "Come out and watch us practice tomorrow." Well, to this day, I carry two baseball gloves in my car, one for the right hand and one for the left hand. I can throw with either hand. I was at the practice and was off to one side throwing with a boy. I would throw one with my right and hand and one with my left hand. The manager came over to me and said, "We're having a practice game today. We don't know what happened, but not one of our pitchers is here today. We need somebody to pitch who can get it over the plate. How about pitching one game with your left hand and one game with your right hand?"

I said, "OK, I'll try it. I haven't pitched in a long time." So I pitched to one team with my left hand and to the other team with my right hand. We went seven innings. The team I pitched for with my left hand won 2-1.

The coach told the boys, "Now, Friday night every one of you boys are going to church, including the pitchers that are not here today. Anybody in the ball club that doesn't come to church on Friday night can't play Saturday. I don't care if it's a pitcher or who it is." There were twenty-something of them and they all came, and every one of them made professions of faith.

Let me say again that I think the main thing in having the power of God is to spend some time in prayer. Some schools teach today that you don't need to agonize in prayer, but I don't believe that. I believe you do have to spend much time in prayer. But a few times I used sports to get people to the meetings. God used it.

I've always heard that you can't reach teenagers. You can't if you can't get them there, but teenagers are the easiest group of people to reach if you can get them to coming to the services. The teen boys are between being a man and a boy. The teen girls are between being a woman and a girl. I've seen more teenagers go into the ministry over the forty some years I've been preaching than any class of people.

Of people coming to my meetings and being saved, I've seen a lot of men, children, teenagers, and less women. As I got older, I've seen a few more women in my meetings than I used to in earlier years. I guess the women didn't like me because I was so ugly.

Why Does God Want Us to Labor In Prayer for HIS Harvest?

The question is sometimes raised as to why God said: *"Pray ye therefore the Lord of the harvest, that he will send forth labourers into his harvest"* (Mat 9:38). If God is interested in getting people saved, why is our laboring in prayer part of God's plan to get the job done? Without our knowing all the reasons, we do know this that God has told us to pray. If we search the Bible, we'll find much about praying. God has chosen it to be so. In our own American history, some of the old time preachers have said that, when they got so busy, they sometimes couldn't pray but three hours a day.

God has told us to pray. I just believe the 'unction' of God, as it was called in the older days, came through much prayer. The filling of the Holy Spirit in power, as we call it today, comes through much prayer. *Much praying is effective in emptying us of self so that the Holy Spirit can fill us*. The genuine filling of the Holy Spirit makes a difference in preaching. You don't have to be an orator. A man that has the schooling and other gifts tends to depend less on the working of the Holy Spirit and the need for much prayer than those who don't have schooling and other gifts. That's just the way it is.

Some of the greatest preachers In power and effectiveness were not the greatest orators. A few of them were, but not many. It's simply a fact that God has chosen it to be this way.

Christ agonized on the cross for us. He prayed much. He is our example. If we don't pray, I don't think we have as deep and lasting results as we will have if we spend much time in prayer. I'm not worthy of God's power and blessing, but in spite of me God has done some unusual things.

Some Preachers Won't Believe This.

I was in an unusual meeting in Florida. I spent much time in prayer, and the pastor and I prayed together. The spiritual results were good with people being saved. A lot of times, when

I would be away from home for two weeks or so, I would drive all night, if I had to, to get back home and see the boys before they went to school. If I could arrange it, I didn't stay away from my family over twelve days at a time.

Sometimes I would be tired as I drove all night. Sometimes I would do a lot of praying during the trip. On this particular trip home at night it started raining, and I believe it was one of the hardest rains I had ever seen. I was driving alongside a river. The car began to drift off the road without my realizing it. I could see water all around me and then I realized the car was plunging into the river.

All of a sudden there came down a light and went under the car. The light lifted the car back onto the road. On the top of the front of the car, a light positioned itself and penetrated the black night that the car lights could not penetrate. That light guided me all the way to the next town. I stopped and got a motel room and stayed the rest of the night. I wondered about what had happened. I couldn't go to sleep for a while for thinking about it. The next day I was still wondering about it.

Still Wondering.

I began to wonder also if maybe the Lord wanted me to witness to somebody. I drove out to the edge of town as I started home. There was a man along the road hitchhiking, so I picked him up and led him to the Lord. He didn't go very far with me. I stopped and picked up another man along the road and led him to the Lord. A lot of people say that picking up hitchhikers is dangerous, and I've had some experiences that were a little dangerous.

One time, as I was going to North Carolina to a meeting, I picked two boys up at Lenoir. When I pick somebody up, I usually try to find out a little about them and then try to witness to them, but I just jumped right on these boys right away. I said, "Where you boys going?" They said, "We're going to Taylorsville, North Carolina." I said, "Well, I'm going down that way quite a bit." And I just turned right on them and said, "Do you boys know the Lord - are you born again - are you saved - are you going to Heaven? I started quoting some scripture. They punched each other and one of them said, "I---I think I've got a relative that lives right down here. I don't think we're going to Taylorsville now. We'll stop." They both got out of the car and I drove on to Greensboro. Tuesday, I was in a meeting in that area.

I picked up the paper and there was the picture of these two boys. I recognized them right away. They had killed a business man that had come along and picked them up right after me. They stole his car and his money. The Lord protected me from those boys. I was not afraid to pick up people. It wasn't because I was a prize fighter. I was not afraid because I figured the Lord would look after me. And that's like some of the other stories I've told. It's not because I'm so good but, because He is. That's what it's all about.

Mississippi Pastor Changes His Mind.

In Mississippi, the pastor I was with had just gotten out of school, and he was a little bit of a smart aleck. It usually takes a preacher ten years to get over school. I'm not against schooling, because I finished four years of Bible School and four years of college at Tennessee Temple in Chattanooga, Tennessee; but preachers are not made by education or training. Preacher schooling comes from God. Moses was educated, but it took him forty years before God could use him, really.

Well, there I was in this meeting in Mississippi, and I realized that I still had some of my habits I had formed in boxing. I just didn't feel comfortable coming right out into auditorium where I was going to preach. I'd stay back in a room and pray and go over my notes and pray. This pastor said that I couldn't do that. He said, "You've got to come out to the front and sit up on the platform." I said, "I won't do it." He said, "Well, you didn't learn anything at school." I said, "Schooling doesn't make a preacher. God makes them, and I don't think you'll ever be one."

I talked back to him. I had my wife with me, or I might have said more. Years later I changed to come into the auditorium where I preach, but I still don't go up on the platform until I'm ready to preach. Most of the preachers don't care that I don't come up on the platform ahead of time. He said that I bragged too much, and back in those days I didn't tell many stories about myself. I never told anybody the river story that I just told you; I think I told my youngest boy and my wife.

Anyway, he said I was living in the past. We went on through the meeting and didn't have much happen. He said that, if anybody ever went to anybody in a service to ask them to come forward where he was the pastor, he would stop the meeting. I said, "Well, you'd better not stop me, because I don't go to anyone in the meeting unless I know I have a message from the Lord. And if the Lord tells me to go, I'll go; and if you try to stop me, I'll knock the devil out of you." That's just what I told him and I meant it. Maybe I shouldn't have, but I did.

Things went on through the week and I told him, "All right, on Sunday morning, I'll sit on the platform. But I will not sit on the platform Sunday night, 'cause, I'm going to preach the message, *The Last Train to Heaven*, and I'm not going to be up there and be still. I'm going to be where I can walk around and exercise and pray, and I won't sit on the platform. He said, "OK." And he said, "I'll be glad when this meeting's over." I preached that message, *The Last Train to Heaven*, and it shook him up so that he was running all over the church talking to people and bringing them forward to get saved.

Now, I don't believe in just running to everybody that's lost. I know of one evangelist - I won't call his name - he'll get up and tell people, "Your family's saved and you're going to hell," and calls the man by name in public. I don't believe in that and I don't believe in going to anybody unless you know the Lord's directing you, but if the Lord's directing you, I believe you ought to go. He'll let you know whether it's you or whether it's Him. He doesn't speak audibly. (I think He could if He wanted to.) In the day we're living today, people say He couldn't speak audibly. God can do anything.

I guess we had forty or more to make a profession of faith that night and the preacher was happy, but I never did go back with him for another meeting. He never asked me, but I wouldn't have gone back there if he had.

Ohio Meetings - A preacher Learns about Soul Winning.

Over a period of time, I was with several pastors in an area of Ohio, with many people being saved. I was at Mt. Gilead, Ohio, and Brother Cook came over to hear me preach. He said to himself, "Well, this is not going to be much of a preacher." He didn't care much about hearing me, but we had some people saved that night. I had preached on soul winning. Later, he said that was the first time in his ministry that he had ever tried to win souls, or even wanted to win souls. He became a good soul winner and a real man of God. I've been with him since in several other churches he pastored.

Byrdstown, Ohio.

Howard Stevens went to Tennessee Temple School and made his way as a barber. He always cut my hair and didn't charge me anything. I liked that. I was with him in three different churches in the Byrdstown area, and we always had at least twenty professions of faith. I didn't preach for money, but when I bought groceries and paid my bills, it was always money they wanted. At Howard's third church there, they gave me the third largest offering I ever received - a thousand dollars. That was a LOT of money then.

Three Baptist Churches - Pastor Threatened With Murder.

Brother Cook, a man about 70 years old, was pastor of three Baptist churches, all at one time. We had about twenty-two professions of faith in one of them. The week before I came, he preached on tithing. A man in the church got mad at him for preaching on tithing and told him he would never come back. Furthermore, he might kill him if he ever saw him again. He told the preacher that. Brother Cook went to Chester to preach at one of his churches.

The preacher's wife told him that the wife of the man who had threatened him had called, and the man wanted Brother Cook to come over to his house. He wanted to talk to him. Now Brother Cook, at that time, was about seventy years old. I never expected to live that long and here I am now, 76 years old.

I was upstairs in Brother Cook's house, and I could hear him praying downstairs. He was walking the floor and talking to the Lord. You could have heard him praying twenty blocks away. He said, "Lord, I'm going over there to face that lion. I'm not only going to face the lion, I'm going over there to face the lion in his own den, Lord!!" I was hearing him and I got so tickled I thought

143

I was going to die. I didn't think I'd ever face him again. He went on and on talking to the Lord like that for about twenty minutes. After I got over my tickled spell, I got to praying for him.

He went to that man, and when he went to him, the man said: "Brother Cook, I treated you mean. I threatened you. But God smote my heart and I don't want to hurt you....I want to be saved." The man accepted the Lord as his Savior. That helped stir up the meeting. I've already told about two other men God dealt with in that meeting and how God used them to stir up the place. There were sixty people saved in that church during the meeting.

I went to all these churches at least two times. Brother Cook left there and went to Barnesville. Brother Jim Gant took over two of the churches, Chester and Harmony. Jim pulled these two churches out of the Northern Baptist Convention. I was with Jim Gant eight or ten times, and we had a lot of people saved there.

Charleston, West Virginia. - My Vacation Was Messed Up.

This was my first year as a full-time evangelist. I had been away from home a lot that year and had scheduled two weeks off in the first part of October. Ron Smith called me and said, "I want you to come for a two-week meeting this year." I said, "Well, I'm booked up for the year." He said, "How about the first two weeks in October? You've got that time off." I said, "I'll kill Gerald Mitton." Gerald and Ron were both from Canada and were friends from their school days at Tennessee Temple. I knew nobody else could have told him but that nut, because I hadn't told anybody else.

I said, "I won't come." He said, "The Lord told me to call you. The Lord wants you to come, and you've got to come." I said, "Ron, I'd have to come on a plane and come back on a plane, and you probably wouldn't want to pay the plane fare." He said, "Yeah, we'll pay the plane fare. We'll guarantee you an offering if you want me to." I said, "I don't do that. I won't do that." And then I said, "I guess I'll come. I don't want to, I'll tell you that." I'll admit that this is one meeting I didn't pray for. I did pray after I got there, but not before I went. God was about to show me something.

All the time I was on that plane, I was studying how I could get out of that meeting and go back home. I'd been away from my family a lot. The boys needed me - my wife too. The meeting started off on Monday, going along pretty good. Now, you know, I always use some humor, so I told some jokes. They had a nursery, and it was a pretty good-size church. The preacher's wife didn't like me because I told jokes.

Pastor's Wife Pinched Her Baby So She Could Leave.

The preacher's wife would bring the baby into the auditorium, pinch the baby and have to take the baby out so she wouldn't have to hear me preach. She later came to me before the meeting was over and told me what she had been doing. She apologized. I knew what she was doing.

The meeting was going along pretty good and the pastor said to me, "Brother Ferguson, we have a children's meeting on Thursday. We were wondering if you had anything you can do that might help draw the children into the meeting." I said, "Well, naw I don't think I could....I might make 'em mad." Now, I'm telling you,—I'm not bragging on myself—I was really trying to make them mad so I could quit the meeting and go home.

I said, "OK, I know something I can do. I can jump the rope." He said, "You can't jump the rope, now." He meant he thought my rope jumping had been too many years ago. I said, "I'll show you." So I put on my shoes and jumped for him. He said, "Man! That's just what we need." This was still early in the week. He said, "We'll have you to jump the rope."

He printed up posters with a picture of a man jumping a rope and a caption that said, "Come See the Preacher Jump the Rope." That was in the early fifties, and in those days people could preach in the schools. The pastor and I went over to visit the principal and we talked a while. He said, "We'll put them all over the school." So they did.

The Thursday meeting had the biggest attendance they had ever had. I jumped the rope, gave a little simple message. Children began to come forward, so many of them, I thought it was psychological. I stopped one little boy and said, "Son, you're just going 'cause the rest of them are." He said, "Preacher, I don't believe you believe what you preach. You told me in that message that I was a sinner and that if I'm growed up enough to know right from wrong that I'm old enough to be saved. You don't believe what you preach, do you?" I said, "Go on."

They kept coming. I don't know how many, maybe about sixty-five. That didn't end it. Those children went home and told their parents and every one of them came, bringing their parents, and the children were baptized during the meeting. One little plump girl came to be saved and went home to talk with her mother about it. She said, "Now mother, I know that children are to obey their parents, but you're going to obey me now. You're going to church with me tonight." The mother said, "I can't go.... I've got something else." The child said, "Mama I'm going to be baptized and I mean you're going." And the mother came.

The preaching was over. The pastor was baptizing. That mother started crying and said, "Lord, have mercy. Here my child is getting saved and I'm not saved." So the mother got saved. The children had brought parents and relatives to the meeting and many of them were saved by being brought there by the children. That's one of the best meetings in numbers of people being saved that I had had up 'til that time. There's a special man in this meeting that we'll discuss in the next chapter.

My Vacation Was Messed Up. (continued)

I didn't want to be in this meeting. My vacation was messed up, and I didn't know how to get out of it. I was stuck there and decided to make the most of it, and God worked in spite of me. Jonah didn't want to go to Nineveh, but God saw it through and it turned out good in spite of Jonah. I keep telling you that God used me in spite of myself.

Miles Upland had never been saved and had said he was too hard for God—God couldn't save him. I told him that he wasn't too hard for God. He came to the meetings and got under deep conviction. Many people who have never been under conviction by the Holy Spirit don't know what it is, what it means. The Bible says of the Holy Spirit: *"And when he is come, he will reprove the world of sin, and of righteousness, and of judgment..."* (John 16:8). I went over to his house four or five times and dealt with him, counseled with him, one-on-one. I had dinner with him several times. The last night came and about everybody was sure that Miles was going to be saved.

But there was one man in the church that had a special burden for Miles. He said, "I know the meeting is over, but you go over and talk to Miles Upland one more time. This is his last opportunity." I had preached the message, *The Last Train to Heaven*. The man with the special burden for Miles said, "He'll die in a short time if he doesn't get saved." I said, "Well, I was planning to go anyway, but, I'll go. And, you can go with me."

This concerned man took me over to the house of Miles Upland and knocked on the door. The wife came to the door. "Where's Miles?" His wife said, "He's in the bed and he can't come out. He's sick." The man said, "We've got to talk to him." She said, "You can't!" The man just pushed the door open and walked in, and I followed him.

We went in to his bedroom and Miles was covered up in bed. I pulled the cover off of him and said, "Man, don't you know the Lord's going to kill you if you don't get saved?" He muttered "mmuh mmumph mmuhh." I thought he was drunk. I said to myself, "This man'll never get saved. He's drunk. He's crazy. But, this man's brought me over here. I'll deal with him."

So I went ahead and showed him he was a sinner and showed him that if he'd accept the Lord, that if he was willing to be saved, God would save him. And then I prayed. I always pray with a man at the end, when I'm showing him how to be saved. I asked the Lord to touch him and save him. He said, "Yes, I'll be saved!" So he accepted the Lord. He immediately jumped up and started jumping on the bed and shouting and running around in the room, hollerin'.

His wife came running in. She grabbed him and said, "What's the matter with you?" And he said, "I'm saved!! I'm going to Heaven!! Glory to God!! Hallelujah!! Amen!! I was dying, but now I'm on my way to Heaven!!" He said, "Preacher, do you know why I didn't come to church tonight?" He said, "I didn't know what it was then, but I was under such conviction that I couldn't walk. I would have died tonight. The Lord had let me know that this was my last night. I knew I couldn't pray much of anything. And the Lord wouldn't let me pray unless you came. And praise God! I'm saved! I'm saved! I'm gloriously saved!" For years after that he was of the most faithful workers, one of the best men in the church. After he was saved, he said that the preaching touched him, but not like my personal dealing with him.

Now, I prayed some during that meeting, especially after I got there. But I'd have to say that it was somebody else's prayers that helped that meeting. God showed me He could have a meeting without me. He used me as the instrument, but that was one of the outstanding meetings I've ever been in. Unusual. In looking back on it, children are often the key to a fruitful meeting, but the situation with the children I talked about in the last chapter was just altogether different than most meetings.

Praying for a Sleeping Bag and Tent.
John Paul Ferguson, our oldest son, was pastor of the First Baptist Church at Johns Town, New York. I was there for two or three meetings with John Paul. There were some good people there, and we had a good meeting with about twenty-

five professions of faith. I don't think in any of them did we have less than twenty professions of faith.

It was an independent church and John Paul was having a hard time financially. They had prayer meetings in the morning and prayer meetings at night in their home devotions. They would pour out the needs they had to pray for, and then they laid them out on the table when they ate, while the family was all together. There was the oldest, Pam, and John Paul, Jr., whom they called "Ji." Ji put out that he was praying for a sleeping bag and a tent.

After John was called to preach, they sold their house in Chattanooga and paid off bills, and they moved to New York. Up there, they just weren't making enough to get by. The people were good people, but they didn't see the need of taking care of a pastor so good, so they just had to pray in their needs. They knew that we had lived that way for many years.

Well, I was coming for a meeting with them. They told Ji that if he asked Granddaddy for a sleeping bag and tent, they would whip him real good. "Oh," he said, "I won't ask Granddaddy for a sleeping bag and tent. Y'all ought to know better than that. I won't do it." The meeting went on two or three days, and it was picking up pretty good. People were getting burdened to pray. Ji said, "Granddaddy, I think we better pray today." I said, "Sure, Ji, I'll be glad to pray." I thought he was stirred up about the meeting, had some concerns about it.

I said, "Let's go in the room. Now, I lie down when I pray, so I got on the bed and was lying there ready to pray. Ji started out. I'm telling you that I never heard so many descriptive words in all my life that he was saying – how imperative, how essential it was that he right now get a sleeping bag and a tent. I'm not joking. He prayed for over an hour and never ran out of words to tell the Lord. He was talking to me, but was pretending to go through the Lord.

I got tickled. I pulled out a handkerchief and like to have got choked on that. I got the corner of the bed sheet and held it in my mouth. I couldn't pray – I laughed the whole time. And when he finally stopped – I didn't think he'd ever stop – he said "Amen." I prayed - about a half-dozen words was all I could pray. I said, "Well, Ji, go get your coat." His daddy had borrowed a car for me to drive while I was there. He said, "Where we goin' Granddaddy?" I said, "To get a sleeping bag and a tent." So off we went, and he got his sleeping bag and tent.

Why I Tell These Stories.

Now, all these things I tell about meetings and people being saved is to say that they happened because of prayer – not just because of my praying, but others prayed. I've been in meetings where I would pray and pray, a lot of praying, and see a few people saved. But in the outstanding meetings I had in Virginia, New York, Florida, Alabama, and other states, the people got under the burden of prayer. If I went into a place where nobody was praying much, it would usually take two weeks to get the people to really praying, to get really concerned about their lost loved ones.

John Paul Ferguson, my son, said that he got different things from different preachers, and that the main thing he got from his Daddy was that he prayed a whole lot and that God answers prayer. He read good books on prayer, too.

Non-denominational Churches.

The second time I was with John in a meeting at Vestal Center, I had a meeting already scheduled over at Jamestown, New York with Harley Akers. It was a non-denominational church. There are some good non-denominational churches. Usually, they call them Bible churches. I had checked out the pastor and knew that he didn't believe you could lose your salvation.

I've told this on another tape, but I repeat it here because this brought a big change in my life—to know I couldn't lose my salvation. I was saved early, but for twenty years I thought you could lose your salvation. By reading John 5:24, the Lord showed me you can't lose your salvation. I've always emphasized that. Jesus wouldn't have paid it all if we could lose our salvation.

I touched on that along all week. There was one lady in the meeting, 86 years old, a fine, dignified lady with quite a bit of money. She asked the pastor if he would invite the evangelist to come over and eat dinner with her on Friday. I agreed to go. I've always been careful in meetings not to go into a home where women were unless someone was with me, but in the

150

home of an 86-year-old lady, I decided it would be all right. She had said she didn't want anyone else there, that she wanted to talk with me privately.

So, I went to eat with her. She was a good cook—a Yankee and a good cook. I ate and enjoyed it. Then she said, "Will you quote me all the Scriptures you know about eternal salvation. You've preached that you can't lose your salvation. I've been brought up the other way, and most of the people in the church. The pastor believes like you, but we don't. I just want you to quote me all the Scripture that you can quote on that."

Well, I didn't quote all I could quote, but I started on John 3:36, John 5:24, John 6:37, John 6:47, Phil. 1:6, II Tim. 1:12, I Peter 1:5, then in Jude 24: *"Now unto Him that is able to keep you from falling, and to present you faultless before the presence of His glory with exceeding joy..."*

She said, "Preacher, stop there a minute." I said, "What is it?" She said, "Quote that again." I went over it again. And that lady said, "Praise God, Hallelujah!" Now, remember, she's 86 years old. I'm not exaggerating. She jumped at least a foot off the floor, slapping her hands, running all over the house, shouting, and rejoicing. She said: "God! Thank you! Thank you! You showed it to me! I can now rest in peace and know that if I make a little mistake I won't go to Hell!"

She just kept on and on, running around. I thought she never was going to wind down. After it was over, I was glad she didn't. She got on the telephone and called everybody and either quoted or read that verse to all the people. That night in the church, I guess we had 15 or 20 saved—people who had heard about this lady learning she couldn't lose her salvation. People came forward, and the place was filled every night the rest of the meeting, on Friday and Saturday and Sunday morning.

I was leaving to go over to Vestal, New York by plane that Sunday afternoon, although they wanted me to stay on. But, after I left, for weeks and weeks people were being saved. That woman was the leader in keeping it stirred up. It just shook that place up. When she learned she couldn't lose her salvation, it made the difference.

Not Boasting.

I realize that when I say this, it may sound like boasting to some people, but in spite of me, God does some unusual things. I'm not a great preacher – I know that. But I do pray. It doesn't take a great theologian; it doesn't take great preaching. It takes great praying to bring the power of God. Especially if a church gets to praying and gets burdened, you can see unusual things happen. So many people don't see it today. They don't believe it can happen, but I believe it can still happen right now.

People say, "But, how can it happen today?" Remember that when the Bride of Christ is complete, Christ is coming. I believe it's possible to have revival today.

Lollypops and Suckers.

I usually buy lollipops and suckers and give them to the children. We had one woman in New York who was a busy-body type. Now, when you've got a busy-body southern woman, she's bad enough, but a Yankee busy-body woman is a whole lot worse. This woman was always telling everybody what to do.

She told me I ought not to be giving the children lollipops. Now the reason I've always done it is real simple. Especially in the past years, if the children got a little treat of some kind, it gave them a good feeling about the church. I suppose it's not so much that way now as it was years ago, but I still give out lollipops to the children.

I've had men to say to me, "Do you give lollipops? Somebody gave me a lollipop at church when I was a boy, and it made me want to go to church and I was saved."

Well, this busy-body woman said to me, "You ought not to be giving out lollipops. You ought to be giving out apples." I said, "Well, apples would be better for 'em, but the children would probably rather have the lollipop. Now, if you will buy the apples, I'll give 'em one." That was the last of that. She never mentioned it any more while I was there. The next time I came back to the church for a meeting she was there, but she never said anything about lollipops. She didn't want to pay for them. I thought if she wanted me to give out apples, she ought to be willing to pay for them, don't you?

Crew, Virginia - Belfast Baptist Church.

Brother Gordon Morris was the pastor at the Belfast Baptist Church. He had me in Belfast maybe six times, and I went back a couple of times after Brother Morris went to Blackstone at the Grace Baptist Church. One of those meetings was snowed out with 2-3 feet of snow.

Brother Morris was a real good friend of mine. He attended Tennessee Temple Schools, and his wife was there with him. But when he left school and began to pastor, his wife left him. She said she couldn't be the wife of a pastor. He went ahead and preached 30-40 years at two different churches. He never had any bad stories told about him, although it could easily have happened. He stayed faithful to the Lord. At Blackstone, he started a Christian school. He had me scheduled in meetings until he died. I never went back to the church after he died. As of today, his wife is still living. I'm repeating myself, but it's strange that nothing ever happened against him - against his name - in those circumstances, but the Lord just held it down.

> D.C.: *Consider this: "And there shall be a great cry throughout all the land of Egypt, such as there was none like it, nor shall be like it any more. But against any of the children of Israel shall not a dog move his tongue, against man or beast: that ye may know how that the LORD doth put a difference between the Egyptians and Israel" (Ex.11:6,7).*

Grant Carter had a similar experience. He came to Chattanooga to go to school and had to work a job to pay his expenses. His wife left him. He's still preaching and is now at Harriman, Tennessee. I've been in five or six meetings with him over the years. He's just going right on, and I've never heard any bad stories against him. Sometimes bad stories will get out on preachers, especially if they don't have a wife. Jim Gant was another preacher like that. His wife left him when he began to preach. All three of those men went on and did a good job preaching. They are good fellows.

Seat Belts – Good, But Not Always.

Clyde Singer came to some of my meetings and, later, became a pastor between Farmville and Crew, Virginia. I was with him several times. We always spent time in prayer, coming and going in the car, and the people prayed. We always had people saved in meetings in that church. His daughter, Peggy, forgot to fasten her seatbelt and had a wreck. The car was on ice and skidded into a telephone pole. It split the car in two and threw her out and hurt her but did not kill her. Investigators commented that if she had had a seat belt on it would have killed her. Now, I wear seat belts most of the time, but that is one case that no seat belt saved a life. It would have split her in two. God's power and leading is our greatest protection.

Paul Ferguson the Fighter
Chapter 12

Farmville, Virginia—The Jimmy Dunn Case.

I was at Farmville, Virginia with David Pruitt - small building, small place. The people from Belfast Church brought several unsaved people over to Farmville for a service. The Belfast people had visited my meetings all around that area and had heard me preach *The Last Train to Heaven* several times. They brought Jimmy Dunn with them, who had promised his wife he would come after she had begged him. Well, I preached on *The Last Train to Heaven* that night, and Jimmy accepted the Lord along with about twenty others.

I've seen some good results in meetings - good numbers, etc. - but I've never seen a man turn so quickly and thoroughly as Jimmy Dunn did, with such fruit bearing in his Christian life. After all these years, he's still a good friend and teaches Sunday school at the Grace Baptist Church in Belfast, pastored by Gordon Morris. Jimmy visits every Saturday for the church. He's retired now. Before he retired, when there was a revival meeting somewhere, he sometimes got off from work with the railroad to witness and win people to the Lord. The railroad paid him good money, so it cost him something to do that.

Jimmy Dunn is not a preacher as we think of them, but he's a true preacher who preaches with his life and personal witnessing. He's won more people to the Lord and has been responsible in other ways for more people being saved than any one person I've ever seen who was saved in one of my meetings. There have been several outstanding people like him coming out of my meetings, but he's the top one.

Later, our second son, Timothy Andrew, taught school in Pruitt's church, but as far as I know now, Pruitt has given up the ministry and isn't preaching.

David Foot's Big Church and Little Church.

David Foot pastored a large church in Richmond, Virginia, and a smaller church on the side. I first held a meeting in the smaller church and then in the large church in Richmond. I don't see how we ever got anybody saved there, but many were saved in that meeting in spite of the way we went about it. The preacher wanted me to sit in the car while he traveled around and talked to people. I did have a little time to study some and prayed some. We put on a little play where somebody dressed up like the devil and we put on a fight for three rounds. It drew a lot of young people, but not many of them made a profession of faith. The whole meeting just wasn't my style. What I really needed was time for study and prayer.

Carbondale, Illinois.

I was in a meeting in Carbondale, Illinois where a good number of people made professions of faith. There was a woman there named Mrs. Melancey that comes to mind. I had announced I was going to preach *The Last Train to Heaven*. Now, when I would preach that message, oftentimes it would be followed by the judgment of God. People we had been praying for, people we wanted to see saved, some of them would sometimes die because God had been patient with them long enough. (God's patience ran out with the world of sinners in Noah's day, and ran out at Sodom and Gomorrah; and God's patience runs out with individuals when they have had their last day of God's mercy and grace.)

Mrs. Melancey wanted her husband to come and hear the *God's Last Train* message. He worked on the third shift. This is the longest message I ever preached in meetings. I got it down to where I could preach it in fifty minutes; I preached it that night in about fifty minutes. He was under great conviction. It was the only time he came to the meetings because he worked on the third shift, but he promised his wife he would come and he came.

He had a few words to say as he went out the door that night about it being a hard message. It shook him up. He wasn't mean, but he was just talking about it. The next morning when he got home from work he told his wife, "I couldn't be at rest. I couldn't work. I was all messed up. I couldn't get that message off my mind, and I believe it's my last opportunity to be saved. I want you to call the preacher to come over here and show me how to be saved." So, she called me.

I went over there and led him to the Lord. He came back to the meeting that night and made a profession of faith. He didn't get too sleep much during the day, but he meant business and he went on faithful to the Lord for years. He became a preacher, and he had me later in a meeting in Arkansas in his home community.

In this same meeting in Carbondale, Illinois was another man who came to the meeting and got under conviction. He wouldn't get saved. He drove a beer truck and told his wife, "I drive a beer truck and I can't be saved." He let me talk to him, but he wouldn't be saved. I was preaching in another place in Illinois, and this same man came over to the meeting and heard me preach on *Seven Reasons Heaven and Hell Are Alike*. I told in the message about a man getting saved, giving up beer and whiskey, changing jobs and making more money than he did before.

When he went out the door that night he said, "Preacher, you were preaching to me." I said, "Not intentionally. I didn't know you were coming." He said, "I'll tell you what I'll do. If you'll come back over to Carbondale and preach that over there, I'll come and listen to it." I was scheduled to preach again in Carbondale, so I preached that same message and he was saved. He said, "Brother Ferguson, I've signed a contract that has three more months on it to drive that beer truck ...for three more months. What do you think?" I said, "Well, it would be better if you didn't, but since you've signed the contract, just give it to them. Keep your contract agreement. Tell them you love the Lord." So he'd go in to the beer place singing every morning, *Oh, How I Love Jesus*, witnessing and praising God. Now, I don't do that myself; I can't sing much at all. But this man was gloriously saved and he just sang all the time.

So when the company saw what was happening, they paid him for the rest of his contract and laid him off, saying he was ruining all their business the way he was carrying on. He went around to all the beer places singing *Oh, How I Love Jesus* and witnessing to everybody. The company officials said, "We can't stand it," and laid him off. People began calling him that very day, and they even called me and said, "Oh, he won't have a job." I said, "The Lord will supply his needs, more abundantly than you can ask or think, so don't worry about it." The very next day, a man called him from another town and said, "I've got work right there close to where you live and I need a man bad. Will you work?" It was a good job and paid more money, plus he had already collected the money the beer company had paid him to just quit and get out of their way. God takes care of people if they will honor Him. This is another man that has gone on, faithful to the Lord all these years—faithful, witnessing, and being instrumental in winning many people to the Lord. It all goes back to the glory of Jesus and His power, and not me. It goes to the Lord.

Julius Talmon, the Business Man.

Julius Talmon was a business man, not a preacher. He had been saved after a rough life. He said the thing that kept him from being saved for a long time was that he thought he had to tithe. So many Christians he knew tithed, and he thought he would have to tithe to be saved. But finally, when he was saved, that man was really sold out to the Lord. He said that in his area they weren't preaching true salvation, and he wanted to have a meeting for the area around where he lived.

He had a big store building in that area, and he converted the building into a place to have a revival. He had me to come up there for two weeks. He said, "I'll pay your expenses and pay you for the meeting. We won't receive an offering." So I went and stayed at his home. There was a little building out from the house where I stayed, and I ate in his house.

People came from as far as Columbus, Ohio. They thought it was so unusual that a businessman would sponsor a revival meeting, wanting to get people saved. People came from Cleveland, Ohio and Mt. Gilead, Ohio and Chester, Ohio —and even from Columbia—to see a meeting put on by a businessman. The meeting had no connection with any church. I never had many meetings like that before, and I usually didn't want any meetings that were not connected with a church.

But this man sponsored his own meeting, saying he would not even include the church he went to. It was an outstanding meeting, with 30 to 40, maybe more, professions of faith. This man was saved, loved the Lord, but not a preacher. He felt that

158

if no churches were named, he could get some people to come that would not come otherwise. The results from that meeting lasted for several years.

The Kind of Churches I Preached In.

When I was preaching in meetings, I liked to go to Baptist churches best, but I have preached in a Methodist church in North Carolina where I grew up as a boy. Over a hundred people made a profession of faith in that meeting. The pastor, himself, did not believe in eternal security, but I didn't know it. I just took the meeting because it was the church where I was saved.

The pastor called me in one day during the meeting and said, "You must lean toward being eternally saved, can't lose your salvation." I said, "Yes sir. That's what changed my life." He got on to me about it—said I was preaching wrong, preaching heresy, preaching false doctrine. I said, "Brother, I can't help it. I know this is right. You think you're right. You're more educated – you're a school teacher and all that, and I respect you. You taught me in school, Brother Bumgartner, and you think you're right. But I know I'm right, and I'm not going to change."

And I said, "We'll close the meeting right now if I can't preach it, 'cause I'm going to preach on this in the afternoon meeting and the night meeting, both. So we'll just close the meeting." And he said, "No. We won't do that. I want to hear it. I want to see what you've got to say." So I went on and preached. There were a whole lot of people that didn't believe that, including some of my own family. So I went ahead and preached on eternal security.

The first part of the meeting, hardly anybody had come. Just my own family was all that was going. The weather was bad, and the preacher couldn't come one night or two. We had started early in the week and had gone through Sunday with just a small group of people. My oldest sister said, "Well, Paul, it's just our family that's been going and we're not going tonight." I said, "You may not go, Sandy, but I'm going. I said I'd be at that church and I plan to be there."

I had told a story in that meeting about a man that had been real wicked. I never did the things he did. Now, I was a sinner saved by the grace of God but had lived a good moral life. But this man had been just as wicked as he could be. He got saved and went back to this town. God had told him to preach, and he preached. When he got there the first night, few were there; the Lord was there, and the devil was there. It seemed like the devil had about won out, but he got up and preached just like they had a house full. He did that for three or four nights.

A man came by that owned a store and heard him preach. The next day he went to that store, and he told everybody that came in, "You ought to be ashamed of yourself. Here's one of our own boys that lived a wicked life, and after he's gotten saved he's come here to preach and we won't back him up. And it's a disgrace." That night the preacher said, "The devil has worried me all day to quit, but I said I'm going to preach if I have to preach to myself again tonight."

He said, "The house was full, and I preached and had fifteen or twenty saved the third night. Through the meeting, about a hundred people or more made a profession of faith." I had told that story one of the earlier nights of my meeting with just a few of our relatives there. When my sister told me she wasn't coming, I told my sister, "I'm going tonight." Well, that night it was dark and rainy and a big crowd came in; and when I preached we had people saved. I preached in the school and had about a hundred saved.

So, back to the conversation with the Methodist pastor and my telling him we would just close the meeting if I couldn't preach on eternal security. I told him, "I know the Lord has led me to preach it." And he said, "Go ahead." When I preached the message, nearly every point was about eternal security and the falseness of people that don't believe it. They believe in works, they don't believe in the eternal power of God. I gave the whole message on eternal security of the believer, and I stopped at the end and prayed.

I said, "Now, I've preached the truth, and how many of you will come forward and accept it?" Remember that the preacher, Brother Bumgartner, had just bawled me out about it that same day. The preacher was the first one to come forward. He came forward and said, "Good people, I've been wrong all these years. This boy has just preached the Bible. It's true. If eternal life is not eternal, then God would be lying to us." He told the people he had been mean to me and wanted me to accept his apology. Well, this broke it loose and between 150 and 200 people made a profession of faith during the meeting.

My Daddy was there that night. He told me that the last sermon he heard Brother Bumgartner preach, he preached totally in favor of what I had preached that night in the meeting. He said, "I know it's true. I don't know how to explain it. I know it's against the Methodist doctrine, but you can't lose your salvation." That was a great meeting, and it was in a Methodist church in Wilkesboro, North Carolina. I was saved in this church when it was in another location. I have preached in Presbyterian churches, but I've always preferred to preach in Baptist churches."

Bill Boruff—My Longtime Friend.

Brother Bill Boruff is one of my great friends. All preachers I've been with, just about, are my friends, but Brother Bill Boruff is kinda like Dan Carr and some others—special friends. I first met Brother Boruff when he was with Dan Phillips in Knoxville, Tennessee, and I was at that church four or five times in meetings. Brother Phillips moved his church two or three times, and I think I was with him every time, except maybe the last time he moved. He had a real school and a big church and everything going, and we had good meetings with many professions of faith.

Brother Boruff was a deacon in the church and led the singing. He had a good job nearby as an engineer in the aluminum plant. He played handball with me some, but never did beat me. We were close friends. He moved to Waverly, Tennessee and started a church and built a building. I was there in a meeting with him, and we had people saved. Then he moved the church to another location, and I was back for another meeting and stayed in his home.

He moved to Greenbrier, Alabama, just outside of Huntsville, and I was with him in a meeting there. In Greenbrier, the people treated me good. I was an Alabama fan, and there weren't any Auburn fans in the church. Brother Boruff was the only Tennessee fan. We had good attendance and a few professions of faith, but never a great revival.

The last time I was with Brother Boruff was on a special

Sunday in Greenbrier Baptist Church. I just fell out on the floor and they took me to the hospital. They couldn't find anything wrong. Dan Carr was there that day to take care of the music, and he came down with a severe stomach virus. Between songs he rushed to the men's room, and at last he curled up in the back seat of their little red Plymouth, and Barbara had to drive them home. He was down a few days.

I Didn't Always Have Good Meetings.

This is a good place for me to say that I didn't always have good meetings. In making these tapes, somebody might get the impression that I always had good meetings or that I'm making out like I did. I never preached in many meetings that we didn't have a few people saved, at least two or three. But I also had some extraordinary, good meetings. I also had some super-colossal good meetings. In some places unusual things happened, and you know of one of them at Stevenson, Alabama.

> D.C.: *Brother Paul wanted to set the record straight that some of his meetings were just common ordinary meetings. He always knew that his first job was prayer. His messages were mostly Scripture verses he had memorized through the years. He had memorized over eight thousand verses, and he spent a lot of time reviewing, keeping those verses in good shape so he could quote them.*

Dr. Paul Ferguson, 1962.

McConnell Road Baptist Church, Greensboro, NC
Paul beginning a sermon, 1951.

*Dr. Mark Cambron and Dr. Paul Ferguson. Dr. Cambron
conferred on Paul an honorary doctor's degree from
Florida Bible College in Kissimmee, FL.*

*McConnell Road Baptist Church - Paul Ferguson outside
church building, 1951*

Pine Set—A Big Harvest.

One of the meetings where I didn't see anybody saved turned out to be one of the best, long-term. Nobody was saved at that barren meeting, but some people came to hear me preach; and later I was invited to come to Pine Set for a meeting. At Pine Set, a large number of people were saved.

I preached at Pine Set recently, and many of them are still going strong for the Lord, the ones that are still alive. Of course, some have gone on to be with the Lord. Seven men were saved out of one family. Now, I never would have had that meeting if some people had not come to hear me preach at a little church where we didn't have anybody saved. So you can't always tell by the results of one meeting what God is going to use out of it.

I never did organize my meetings. A group in North Carolina, because I used so much Scripture in my preaching, offered to back me, and they said, "We'll make you bigger than Billy Graham." I don't always know how people feel about him. I don't have to give account for Billy Graham. A lot of people criticize him. I don't criticize any man that's preaching the gospel. We all make mistakes, and I've got to face my own record at the Judgment Seat of Christ.

But I turned down the North Carolina group that wanted to back me, because they didn't have the people in the group that I thought ought to be. I just decided that the Lord wanted me to go to individual churches. I never preached but one city-wide revival meeting. I know that God called me to preach in individual churches, and we saw some great meetings and some that were not so great.

Tulsa, Oklahoma—Shall We Visit or Pray?

A pastor in Tulsa, Oklahoma wrote me a letter. He had scheduled an evangelist from Salisbury, North Carolina, and had to cancel the meeting on him. The pastor had been divorced before he was saved, and several of the people in the church were divorced. I'll not tell what happened, but they cancelled the meeting.

> D.C.: *There would have been an unnecessary collision between the evangelist and the divorced people there who were trying to go on with their lives and live for the Lord.*

The preacher had seen my name in the *Sword of the Lord* and wrote me, explaining the situation, asking if I would come for a fourteen-day meeting. He said, "We'll visit about eight or nine hours every day, knock off an hour for lunch, and stop visiting at 5:00 o'clock; and that gives you time to get ready for the service." I wrote back and told him, "I'll accept the meeting. That's not usually the schedule I do, but I'll start it with you. I'm used to exercising, and I'll give out in the meeting if I don't play handball at least twice a week. I won't come unless you'll say I can have off those times to play handball. I can pray and visit some at other times, but I've got to play handball, if possible."

He wrote back and said I could play handball and told me where the YMCA was, so I went to Tulsa. When I got there, he said, "Now, we're going to visit. We'll start in the morning at eight o'clock and visit 'til twelve." I didn't play handball that day. So we went out and visited and visited and didn't have any results, and that night I preached on prayer and how important it was.

The next day we went out visiting. I had been praying all I could between visits and praying a whole lot at night. At the beginning he had said, "Visitation is the only thing. We don't need anything else." I didn't say anything. The next day we went to the first house and told the woman who we were. She cursed and slammed the door in our face. He said, "I never had that to happen before."

We went to the next place, and the next place, and the same thing happened. He said, "What on earth's the matter?" I said, "Preacher you didn't hear a word I preached Sunday night, did you?" He said, "Well, I don't think I can even remember what it was you preached on." I said, "I preached on prayer. The importance of prayer. And you're running this church without any prayer. You're running this church only on visitation, which I believe in; but you can go back to the disciples and apostles and you'll find out that they prayed hours and hours and hours. I know Pentecost was on God's schedule, but it couldn't have happened like it did without the praying. I believe that our trouble is that we're not praying. We need to pray.

He said, "We've got to do something. I don't know what it is." We went back to the church, and there was a whole group of people that had gone out on visitation. They had had doors slammed in their face and had been run off. They said, "Lord, there's nothing we can do but pray." We started praying.

That night I made a statement. I said, "People, if we pray like we ought to, God will send people here. Some of these people around here have rejected God and they may never get saved. They could, but they won't. God will send us some people if He has to send them all the way from Texas." That's the statement I made. I didn't mean to say it, but I said it anyway.

So we went on with the meeting, and people started getting saved. There was a grandmother that had four children in Texas. She went to Texas and brought them back. One man had been married before, and his wife had the four children in Texas; but the children were visiting with the father and they were visiting in the meeting. Another family had come from Texas and had brought some people from Texas with them to the meeting. On Sunday morning we had twenty-one people make a profession of faith, and twelve of them were from Texas. They couldn't believe it. I believe that in a meeting people should pray and then visit the people God lays on their heart.

Meetings and Prayer and Visitation.

We all agree that we should pray during the meeting, and we should visit people about the meeting; but visiting should be done mostly before the meeting. People of the church should be inviting others to the meeting before the meeting begins. Make a list of people to pray for, and then, during the meeting, pray for these people and visit the special ones God lays on the hearts of those praying. I believe this is the best plan.

Now, I didn't copy Billy Graham, but that's the way he does, or at least that's the way he did it for years. I don't know what he has done in recent years. People can witness as they come in contact with others, and God will make it special to them if you're praying right. I still hold to the way of the old time revivalists, and the main thing the preachers did in those meetings was praying. There's plenty of written record on what these men did in their meetings. Visiting should be done before the meeting - and some selective visiting during the meeting - but the main thing during the meeting is prayer.

Start praying ahead of time. However, I stopped urging people to get together to pray before the meetings because they came together and didn't pray. They would tell me they had prayer meetings, but actually they had social gatherings. They ate and talked for two hours and prayed for five minutes. Unless they have somebody to organize it and see that it's real praying, preceding prayer meetings don't do much good. Eating sandwiches won't bring down the power of God.

I saw on Signal Mountain one time where they had the right kind of visitation before, and the right kind of praying, and it brought unusual results. It was just a schoolhouse, a small place, and it was one of the most outstanding meetings I've ever been in. I've told some of the things about it already.

When we visit a little and we have a little sentence prayer – that's not the kind of prayer God answers. He'll answer agonizing, prevailing prayer. I'll say what E. M. Bounds said in his book, that if we could have a school of how to pray and set the people to praying, it would be better than all the theological schools in the world put together.

We've just lost out on praying – continued praying. We have our little sentence prayers. Here's something I think, something I know. Praying is not to persuade God. Prayer is to prepare our hearts to get where we can believe what God said and get ourselves out of the way and crucified – that we can have the real answer to prayer and real revival. It may never happen, but it could if people mean business. You know examples of that.

The least little thing happens and preachers say, "Well, people don't want meetings." They quit. Well, people may not want meetings, but God wants a meeting; and if a few people will earnestly meet with Him, He will meet with them. You don't have to have a majority of the people to pray and agonize and depend on the power of God. You know, in Highland Park Church of Chattanooga, Tennessee, formerly pastored by Dr. Lee Roberson, it's been noted through the years how much power they've had and how much they've done.

Did you know that it was only a relatively few people that prayed in that church? It was a few people, a small minority of people that witnessed. It wasn't the whole group. I guess with Brother Bouler (present pastor of Highland Park Baptist Church in Chattanooga), we have more people visiting and praying now than we used to. Brother Bouler is a praying man. I think the church is going to grow, because he prays and he insists on people praying. He believes in agonizing, prevailing prayer. He may not have practiced it over the years like he does now since he's been there. He had to.

> Dan: *Some would say, "When you pray, you should do no more than lay your needs out before the Lord. Just lay them out and say 'Lord here it is...this is what I understand the need to be and I'm depending on you to take care of it,' and then go on your way."*

> Paul: I've done that. That's fine for praying in public. In most of the better books on prayer, they say short praying publicly, and I believe that. A lot of preachers call on me to pray when I'm in the audience because they know I won't pray long. But most of them know that I pray for hours in private, and I'm not bragging on myself.

Jesus is the one who taught me to pray.

I learned how to pray from studying the life of Jesus – and from praying. From experience I learned that you have to pray long to get yourself out of the way so God can bless. And that's why we're not having any revival today. We're not having revival today because there's not much praying. Self is running everything.

> Dan: *So you don't believe, then, that if you keep on praying beyond the point of just laying out your need*

*before the Lord, that you are staying there, praying
further and longer, because you are unbelieving?*

Paul: No, I don't believe that. I believe it takes believing prayer to stay and pray. No, I got hooked with that for a while. I don't tell much about those meetings when we didn't have much happen. I listened to teachers and other people say that all you have to do is to pray in faith. I believe that. But <u>we don't pray in true faith until we get ourselves out of the way</u>. We have to get ourselves out of the way before we can really pray. You don't have to beg God. He's willing to help you. But He's got to get us at the place where we're willing and ready to receive.

How Do We Believe?

We can look at Matthew 21:22: *"And all things ye shall ask in prayer, believing, ye shall receive."* Fine. How do I believe? Do I talk myself into it? No. You pray yourself into it. It's really important for us to understand what's involved here. Preachers and other Christians have been taught carelessly, have lived carelessly, and we need to be brought back to the point of agonizing, prevailing prayer. You don't have to pray that way every time. But I don't think there's ever been anybody in the world that has had great meetings, like the Wesley's, for example, without agonizing, prevailing prayer.

I was saved in the Methodist Church. I don't go along with its founder, John Wesley, in believing you can lose your salvation, but I honor John Wesley and go along with him in prevailing prayer. He was a great man of God. According to the book records I have read, most of the people who have been used of God over the world believe you can't lose your salvation.

I don't guess a man has been used greater than Charles Finney, but I've read some of his older books where he said if you drink a cup of coffee or tea, you'll go to hell. Now, I don't believe that. I don't say it might not hurt your health, but it won't send you to hell, because not anything can send you to hell if you are born again.

There was one preacher that preached all the time on being born again, and some of the people went to him as a group and said, "Why don't you quit preaching on being born again?" He said, "When you people get born again, then I'll quit."

I told you earlier about Brother Kemp. He'd fill the room up with Dr. Peppers any time I was around Atlanta. He'd give me spending money, pay for my meals, and all kinds of things – anything he could do to help me. He gave me support money from his own pocket because he wanted me to be able to use the church offerings to pay my bills at home. There were women who followed Jesus and ministered to him with food and other basic necessities, and through the years, I've been blessed with people who helped me with personal needs that made a big difference.

Carthage, North Carolina—The Sucker Tale.

I had a meeting in Carthage, North Carolina. (I won't give the preacher's name.) His wife was quite a bit older than he was and they didn't have but one child, which was about seven or eight years old. I would give away suckers and different kinds of candy to the children every night. I've done that for years. I didn't think the children back then were spoiled and they needed a little treat, something from me, from my heart. So the first night I stood at the door with a sack of suckers.

The preacher's boy came by and said, "I want five suckers, and I want 'em right now." I said, "Well, I can't give them to you now, because I haven't given them to all the other children, and I don't know how many I'll have left. If I have some left, I'll give you four more. I'll give you one now."

He said, "If you don't give me those suckers now, I'll kick you on your old leg." I said, "Well, you shouldn't do that." But he kicked me anyway. After the service, I went by their house a minute and I gave him four suckers. The next night that little rascal came by again. He was the first one there about every night. He said, "I want five suckers and I want 'em right now." I handed him one and he kicked me on the leg again. After the service I gave him four more suckers.

The third night he came by and said, "I want my five suckers now or I'll kick you on the leg." I didn't give them to him and he kicked me on the leg. The same thing happened the fourth night, and he kicked me on the leg again. I said to the Lord,

"Well, I've got to do something. I'm going to stop that boy one way or the other." So he came by the fifth night. He said, "I want my suckers and I want 'em right now or I'll kick you on your old leg." I said, "Son, if you kick me I'm going to kick the living devil out of you. I'm going to kick you good."

His mother spoke up and said, "You won't kick my boy!" And boy he let me have it. So I kicked him on the leg and I brought the bark off of his leg. I mean I broke his leg open. I kicked him hard. He went to screaming. She said, "I'll bring my husband out here and he'll beat you to death." And I said, "If he steps out that door I'm going to knock him cold."

I meant it. I was going to knock him cold if he came out. I'd had all I could take. He didn't come out. I was standing there wondering whether I'd made a mistake or whether I should have waited a day or two, or what.

Just then a man came up and shook hands with me and said, "Brother, that's the best thing I've ever seen happen around here and I want to give you something." He had a bill and I stuck it in my pocket, but I didn't look at it. As the people came, by they gave me money. I believe it was four hundred and fifty dollars I had in my pocket. That was double what they gave me in the offering for the meeting, and that was a lot of money back then.

I said, "Lord have mercy! If I'd known that I was going to get that, I would have kicked the little devil every night." And I also said later, "Well, I don't know what happened to that boy, but if he turned out all right, I get the credit for kicking part of the devil out of him, because I gave him a good one that time."

Paul Ferguson the Fighter
Chapter 14

Middle Tennessee - Little Sammy.

I was preaching a revival in Middle Tennessee, and one night I preached on Hell. I hadn't intended to, but the Lord put it on my heart. We were taking people back to a little room on the side to deal with them. Eleven or twelve people came that night, and workers were there dealing with them.

A little five-year-old boy named Sammy came with them. They set him in a chair close to me, and he said he wanted to be saved. I had never seen a child saved that young, and I didn't think he knew what he was doing. So I was telling him some different things, just trying to comfort his mind because I didn't think he was lost. He was too young to be accountable to God for his sin, I thought.

He looked at me and said, "Preacher, I don't believe you believe what you preached." I said, "Why, Sammy?" He said, "You preached an hour and a half out there." (I didn't preach quite that long, though.) "You preached a hour and a half about hell, and if I die I'll go to hell, and I want to be saved. Will you show me how?" I said, "Yes sir, Sammy. I'll show you how to be saved."

I went over the Scripture in Romans 3:23, about all being sinners. He said, "I know I'm a sinner. I know that if I die I'd go to hell." And then I showed him some other Scripture about Jesus dying for our sins, and then I showed him Revelation 3:20: *"Behold I stand at the door and knock. If any man hear my voice and open the door I will come in to him and sup with him and he with me."*

After I prayed, I said, "Now, are you willing to ask Jesus to come into your heart?" He said, "I sure am." I said, "Well, do you want me to help you pray?" He said, "No. I know I'm a sinner." He started praying. He said, "Lord, I'm the worst sinner in all the world. And I want you to come into my heart and save me, Lord, because if I died, I'd go to hell. I don't want to go to hell. I want to really live for you and I accept you right now as my Savior. And thank you Lord for saving me."

I showed him two other Scriptures on the assurance of salvation. We went back in and presented Sam, and everybody seemed to be happy that he was saved. I use this story a lot of time when I'm preaching on fellowship. I think that Sammy was the greatest example of anybody in my life, in all my ministry of forty something years, of someone walking with the Lord.

As long as he lived, for two weeks after that, he had the greatest fellowship with the Lord I've ever seen. He'd just walk along and talk with the Lord. Also, that little fellow would just walk up to a sinner that had never been to church and say, "Mister, you're a sinner. You're going to hell. You need Jesus," and sinners would be saved.

During the rest of that meeting, most of the people that were saved were saved because of him. He'd just go around and talk to people. I believe if the Lord ever personally spoke through any person, it was him. I've never seen anything like it. The day before he died he walked up to the pastor and said, "Brother Pastor, I don't know the Bible like you do. I wish you would tell me some things about Heaven, because I'm going to die. Jesus told me I'd be in Heaven in a few days. I want to know a little about it before I get there.

The pastor said, "Sammy, you're not going to Heaven now. You're going to be one of the greatest pastors or evangelists or missionaries that's ever lived. Sam, you can't possibly go to Heaven now." Sammy said, "Brother Pastor, I love you, but Jesus knows more than you do, and He has told me I'm going to Heaven soon. Will you tell me about Heaven?"

The pastor took the Bible and talked to him about Heaven for awhile. In a little over two weeks after Sammy was saved, I stood behind the same pulpit where I had preached that revival and assisted in the funeral of little Sam, the little boy that I tried to discourage from being saved because I thought he was too young. When I looked into that casket and saw that little body, the Lord showed me what it really meant to let Christ live through you. I've never had daily, walk-around fellowship like that, and I've never seen anybody else that I thought lived close to Jesus like Sammy did.

That little boy just walked and talked with Jesus. He just walked around and talked with the Lord like He was standing there. He'd walk by a place and he'd say, "Now, Jesus, wait right here." And he'd do what he had to do and come back and start talking to Him. He'd just walk up to people, and they would just fall down and accept the Lord. Little Sammy had the power of God upon him. It was one of the greatest miracles!

Sammy got hold of some poison. I don't know what it was. His parents had left it where they shouldn't, and he drank it and died. That was the most unusual funeral I ever saw. The church building was not so big, and people came and stood around the outside. When the preacher told what Sammy had said when they were talking about Heaven, people came in from the outside to be saved.

People would go out to his grave and get saved for six or eight weeks after that. I have never in all my life seen or heard about an example like that. And I can show you where it is, the pastor, and many people know his name.

I use this illustration when I preach on fellowship, about letting the Lord live His life through us by the Holy Spirit. For years I used this illustration, and it was greatly used of God. People who wouldn't let their children be saved when they were young would change their mind. Grown men have heard it and gotten saved all over the country. This was in the early part of my ministry, and I've preached in forty-some states. God has used this story over and over again through the years.

A Little Revisit to My Earlier Years.

I was born in North Carolina and grew up on the farm. Some way I wanted to be a prize fighter and I did that, which I don't talk much about. I married Lena May Doggett – now she's Lena May Ferguson. The Yankees say "Dahgett," but I say "Dog-ett." We were married the week before I won the championship of North and South Carolina in professional boxing. I had been to King College in Bristol, Virginia and boxed there. I won the golden gloves and went to the National Championship and broke my hand. I'll not tell any more about that here.

Lena May and I were married on July 19, 1939. Our oldest son, John Paul, was born in South Carolina on June 18, 1944 at 2:17 p.m. I always called John Paul a "sandlapper." Timothy Andrew was born in North Carolina – a "tar heel" – after I

177

was called to preach. Mark Thomas was born in Tennessee - a "volunteer" - after I was at Tennessee Temple School in Chattanooga. John is a Baptist preacher now, Tim teaches in a Christian school, and Mark works at Acheson Foundry in Chattanooga, and teaches Sunday school.

John was saved when he was seven years old. Tim was saved when he was about three and a half. And Mark was about four and a half when he was saved. They've all got good wives, and I'm glad to say that.

Fighting Again At 56.

I started boxing when I was real young, and I don't talk too much about boxing unless I tell my life's story. I spent twenty years in amateur and professional boxing, so it left a thumb print on my life. Charlie Marshall, a Temple graduate, traveled with me a lot. He's now a good young-people evangelist, doing a great work. He travels around over the country. For a while he was head of the youth at Jack Hudson's church at Northside Baptist Church in Charlotte, NC. He asked me if I would come there and put on a fight. He believed that would draw a lot of young people and maybe we would have quite a few saved.

Charlie found a fellow there that had been a golden glove champion. I was fifty-six and he was twenty-two or twenty-three. The fight was planned. We didn't want anybody to get hurt. I played handball regularly and ran regularly and punched the punching bags when I was at home. I had a heavy bag and a light bag. I jumped the rope and was in pretty good shape. I've always tried to keep in fair shape. I'm seventy-six now, and I still play handball.

Well, Charlie made the arrangements, fixed the ring out in front of the church. They were gonna bring the young people around, but it started raining about a week before that and rained all the time. When I got to Charlotte, it was still raining, even on that Sunday morning, so they saw they couldn't use that even if it quit raining. Charlie called the wrestling arena, and they didn't have anything scheduled for that Sunday morning. So we had the fight there. Charlie got the figures together and said there were between seventeen and eighteen hundred young people there for that fight.

178

When I got to the arena, Charlie said, "This fellow is young and you're a little over twice as old as he is. He plans to try to just box around and take a dive in the third round." But the boxer said to himself, "I'm not going to let no fifty or sixty year old man show me up, so I'm going to knock him down a couple of times. Then I'll go ahead and let him knock me out in the third round - but I'm going to show him up."

Well, I don't think that would have caused me to look bad since I'd fought so many years and I was getting up in years. The fight was ready, all geared up, and my opponent was dressed up like a devil. Two fellows were over in his corner dressed like demons.

The plan was that, when I knocked out the devil, the demons would run over to the devil and I would knock both of them out. I was watching my opponent, and when he came in he threw a right hand just as hard as he could. I just let it pass me over the shoulder. I guess I forgot, but I hit him with a left hook.

When he fell, this was fortunate for the fight, because he fell on my shoulder, on my breast, and he was knocked cold. Now, this was when the fight first opened. He just came out and the first thing he did was to throw that hard right punch at me. I let him miss and hit him with my hardest punch, which was a left hook. My left hand was stronger than my right hand.

It was the first thing in the fight. He was out cold. I was having to hold him up with my right hand, so I made out like I was hitting him with my right. I was banging on him but wasn't hurting him. He wouldn't have known it anyway, 'cause he was out. He came to just before the first round was over and went back to the corner.

He told his helper in the corner, "That man hits harder than a mule a kickin'." He said, "I've been in the country when I was a boy and got kicked with a mule once, and it didn't hurt me as bad as that." Then he said, "The first time he hits me again, I'm going out of there before he kills me. It's over with."

So I came out the next round and hit him just a light punch, and he fell out on the floor and quit. The two demons came running out and I hit one of them a little hard, and the other one fell before the punch got to him. The young people liked it good. They didn't mind it being so short. The young people were screaming and hollering.

We were boxing in the wrestling arena and one of the wrestlers was watching. He came up and said, "That was the best acting I've ever seen of somebody being knocked out. When he hit him that one time and he went out, boy, that was good acting!" It wasn't acting. That was reality. He was out cold.

Northside Baptist Church had sponsored the fight to draw in young people to hear the Gospel. Pastor Jack Hudson, who has now gone on to be with the Lord, watched the fight before he preached that morning. Charlie Marshall told me that between eighty-five and a hundred young people accepted Christ at the service following the fight (that is they professed faith in Christ.).

No children were in that number. They were all in their teens and up. After the fight I preached a message in the wrestling arena, *Who Is the Greatest Heavyweight Champion in the World?* I used the boxing theme for it and, of course, Christ is the greatest champion of all.

Sunday night I was with Pastor Charles Foshee at the Ridgeview Baptist Church in Charlotte. His song leader had been one of the demons in the fight that morning. He told everybody about the fight and how hard I could hit.

Charlie Marshall told me later that, for six months following the fight, they had people coming to the church to be saved. The young people who were saved at the fight, and the morning service following, went out of the meeting witnessing to their friends and kept bringing them to church with them to try to get them saved. He said that was the greatest soul-winning effort he had seen in a long time in Charlotte, North Carolina. He had seen some big-name preachers come for meetings, but not with the same results.

Now, let me say this. I don't believe it's wrong to put on things like that to draw young people to try to get them saved. A lot of people came to see the fight that never went to a church anywhere. More than young people came. Some older people were there too. But it still takes prayer and the Holy Spirit to work to get people saved.

Sometimes you won't get them in, otherwise. But if you put on these various programs and don't pray, it's just sounding brass and tinkling cymbals. But if people have spent ample time in prayer, like the time they spent in promoting the activity, there'll always be good results.

Graduation from Tennessee Temple.

I graduated from the four-year Bible School at Tennessee Temple, and then from the four-year college – but I did both of them combined in four years.

> D.C.: *What he is not telling here is that he was the Bible School Salutatorian. I was there and heard his salutatorian speech.*

Second Meeting after Graduation.

The second meeting I held after graduation was with Lee Zane Lambertson, at the Westside Baptist Church in West Palm Beach, Florida. (I had fought my first professional fight as a prize-fighter in West Palm Beach, Florida.) Brother Lambertson was a good man of God, and he knew I hadn't been preaching long – hadn't been out of school long – so he wanted to encourage me.

He told me this. He said, "We've had Dr. Lee Roberson, Dr. John Rice, Oliver Greene," and he went on and named eight or ten or more outstanding evangelists that had been in that church and said, "They had never had very many people saved." Well, that was the best thing he ever told me, because I went to the motel where I was staying and spent hours in prayer. So what he told me really helped me. But during the meeting, he said, "We will not allow anybody to go to anybody during the service and ask them about being saved." I said, "Well, Brother Lambertson, I can't preach the meeting then." He said, "Why? I have advertising up! You have to preach!"

I said, "I don't <u>have</u> to do anything." I said, "I respect you, I've heard of you and know you're a man of God, but you tell me that I can't – if the Holy Spirit tells me to go and leads me to go – and you tell me I can't go, I won't preach for you." He said, "You've got to because I've got the advertising up." I said, "No, I'll leave right now." (Chuckle.) He didn't know I didn't have any money. I would have had to hitch-hike back home. I had to hitch-hike down there. I caught a ride all the way from Chattanooga to West Palm Beach and I didn't have any money. But I would have left. He said, "All right. I see you mean it, that you're not going to preach if I don't tell you that you have freedom to do what the Lord leads you to do." I said, "Yes sir, that's right. And I'll preach the meeting if you'll go ahead."

Well, we had some people coming forward in the meeting to be saved. We started on Sunday morning and went through the next Sunday night – an eight-day meeting – and people being saved right from the first day.

Judy Is the Key.

On Tuesday night a different thing happened. A teen-age girl named Judy had been coming every night. You could tell from her actions that she was under conviction. Now, I don't go to people in the audience just because of that, but the Lord definitely laid it on my heart to go and talk to her. I knew how the preacher felt about it, so I thought I would pray a little harder and we'd get her saved anyway, so I didn't go to her during the invitation.

The next night, Wednesday, the Lord laid it on my heart again to go to her, and I didn't go. On Thursday night we were still having people saved, but I still wasn't doing what the Lord wanted me to. I thought I would outsmart the Lord. (We know when we're trying to get out of doing what the Lord has told directly to do.) The pastor had thought that since I was fresh out of school, he would help me by telling me not to go to anyone during the invitation.

> D.C.: *In some churches where going to people during the invitation becomes a regular thing, lost people refuse to go to church because they don't want to be dragged down to the front to be embarrassed. Some go to the altar just to get the personal worker off their neck, and thus they make a false profession of faith.*

I had watched what bus Judy rode on, and on Thursday night I was going across the parking lot to get to her just when she got off the bus. I stepped in a hole and like to have broken my crazy neck, and I didn't get to talk to Judy at the bus; but that night after I preached, the Lord put it on my heart again, so I told Brother Lambert, "I've got to go talk to that girl. The Lord has put it on my heart three nights and I haven't gone. I've got to go now." He said, "Go ahead."

I walked up to her. I said, "Judy, would you like to go to Hell?" She said, "Go to Hell? I can't be saved." I said, "Why not?" She said, "My mother's not here." I said, "Little lady, if you died right now would your mother keep you out of hell?" She said, "I'll go." When she came, six other young people followed her, and then others came to be saved beside that.

After Judy accepted the Lord, on Friday night, Saturday night, Sunday morning, and Sunday night, Judy brought either twenty-three or twenty-six teen-agers to the meeting that were saved. I don't know just how many were saved, but we had a large number of people saved in that revival. I was back with him at least three other times and never did go with him that we didn't have a good meeting. The second time there, my wife and boy went with me. Brother Lambertson has since gone on to be with the Lord. He was a great man of God.

Going to Another Person During the Invitation.

I've gone to people during the invitation many, many times. In a meeting in South Carolina, I preached the message, *The Last Train to Heaven*. This message usually stirred people more than my other messages. I saw a man standing during the invitation, holding to the seat. He was about to fall. I asked the Lord what to do, and He put it on my heart to go to him. I went back to ask him if he would go forward for counseling. He said he would gladly go, but that he couldn't go until "You came to me."

He said, "I had always said that if anybody ever came to me I would hit them. So when you were walking back here to me, I drew my fist back. God then hit me so hard that I know I'm going to die if I don't get saved." So he accepted the Lord and was saved. About eight or ten others were saved. I've told already about several others who said they wouldn't be saved. Over at Stevenson, Alabama, a woman said she wouldn't go forward to be saved, and she didn't go; she couldn't go until somebody came to her. I think it's a great thing that the Lord will use anybody that's willing to be used.

There used to be more conviction during the invitation part of the services when people would hold on to the bench or pew, sometimes until their knuckles would turn white. Some of them would weep until the floor would be wet with their tears. There's not as much of that now, but I still see it happen. Those people are not quite willing to be saved. God has to hit them with a special power of the Holy Spirit to break their will. Sometimes God wants so strongly for some people to be saved that He has to break their will. Some people are stubborn like that.

Some of these people have told me after they were saved that they had had a bad experience with other preachers. A man told me in South Carolina that the reason he would never accept the Lord was because they would take the visiting preacher home with them for dinner, and the children would be put out on the porch while the preacher and grownups ate.

This man said there was a particular time when he and his brother were on the porch watching from a distance. He told his brother, "That so-and-so got the last piece of chicken and we won't get any." I chuckled and said, "Well, you couldn't be mad at me because I don't even eat chicken." That guy got tickled at me when I told him that. He laughed and laughed. He said, "Fellow, I believe I will let you talk to me."

I let him talk for about thirty minutes. You have to do that with some people to let them get loosened up. Sometimes we get on them too quick. So he was telling me all the things about his bad experiences with preachers. He accepted the Lord, went to church that night and was baptized. The last time I heard about him, he was still living for the Lord.

Approaching People for Witnessing to Them.

In approaching people to witness to them, I may open the subject by telling them I'm a Baptist preacher, or that I'm the preacher holding the meeting down the street, or ask them if they died today would they go to Heaven. Now, some preachers hold to the idea that you ought to witness to everybody you meet whether the Lord leads you to do it or not. I don't go along with that.

When I was younger, I went to people and began witnessing to them when I should have taken the time to get acquainted with them. Now, there are experiences where you have to talk to them about salvation right away or you never can talk to them. You may never see them again. I rely heavily on the Lord to guide me in talking to people. I don't try to use psychology on them.

There are special cases where I let a person talk all they want to and then I get around to talking about salvation. Sometimes there are cases where you have to be bold with them. If you play around with them, hint around with them, they'll run you off. There was the case of "Wild Bill" that I've told about. He actually wanted somebody to stand up to him.

There's no book anywhere you can read that will tell you who wants you to be bold and who does not. There's no book to tell you who to be easy with and let them talk around the world first. I just lack three semester hours having a major in psychology and philosophy, but you can't go by psychology. You have to go by the leading of the Lord.

Paul Ferguson the Fighter
Chapter 15

How to Talk.

In James 4:15 we read, *"...If the Lord will, we shall live, and do this, or that."* Some people think that if you are saved and you say, "If it's the Lord's will, I'll live," that is a lack of faith. But James 4:15 says, *"...ye ought to say, if the Lord will, we shall live, and do this, or that."* "YE OUGHT TO SAY!" This is how we ought to talk.

That reminds me of a story of two farmers. One was Mr. Jones and one was Mr. Brown. Brown was out plowing his field and Jones came up the road. Brown looked up and called out to Jones, "Where are you going?" Jones replied, "I'm going over to Farmer Smith's to buy a cow." Brown said, "Wait a minute there, Brother Jones, you ought to say, 'If it's the Lord's will that I live to go over there and back.'"

Jones said, "Now, Farmer Brown, I don't have to say 'The Lord's will.' Farmer Smith has a cow and I have the money, and I'm going over there to buy the cow - and in about a half-hour I'll come back leading the cow, and I'll show you that you don't have to say 'The Lord's will.'"

Farmer Jones went on up the road and he was gone about a half-hour; and so he came back, and Farmer Brown looked and there he was. His hat was torn to pieces. His clothes were ragged and he was bloody all over. Farmer Brown said, "Farmer Jones, what on earth has happened to you?" He said, "Well, I was going up the road and a bunch of robbers jumped out of the trees and liked to have beat me to death and took all my money, and I'm going home....the Lord willing."

Chattanooga, - Shoaler Avenue Baptist Church.

I was at Shoaler Avenue Baptist Church under I don't know how many pastors - Bob Burnett, Hank Beckter. Hank wanted me to go over to a woman's house. Some of the children had come to the church and accepted the Lord. Hank went over to the house to talk to the woman about the children being baptized. He showed her the verse in Matthew 18:6: *"...whoso shall offend one of these little ones which believe in me, it were better for him that a millstone were hanged about his neck, and that he were drowned in the depth of the sea."*

She threatened him and said that if he ever came back she would kill him. But we were in the meeting and he said, "Brother Ferguson, I want you to go with me over there. I've got to talk to that woman again. The Lord told me to go, and I'm going." I said, "All right, I'll go." We went over and he knocked on the door, and this woman came out.

Now, she wasn't ambidextrous like I am, able to throw with both hands. But there was a whole line of flower pots of several inches around that you could pick up with one hand. There were rows of flower pots all over the porch, and she ran out and started cursing the preacher and grabbed those flower pots and throwing them at him. She grabbed up one pot after another with the right hand and with the left hand and started throwing flower pots as fast as she could.

He was a big, tall, slim fellow, and when he ducked down, one pot hit me on the leg. I said, "That woman can go to Hell if she wants to. I'm getting out of this place." And I left. It's amazing what preachers go through with sometimes in going to different places. Bob Burnett was pastor there while he was also teaching at Tennessee Temple Schools, and I was at the church with him. We had a good time.

Sumpter, South Carolina—Eating Chicken.

I was with Presley Morris twice. He went to one of Billy Graham's services just to see what it was like. He then went a couple of times to an Oral Roberts meeting and got under conviction and was saved. Presley became a Baptist preacher; he's been a good preacher, a real man of God and faithful through all the years.

We had real good meetings with Presley both times. The second time, my wife and Mark and Tim went with me, and we stayed in a furnished house to ourselves. In those days, I didn't eat chicken at all. My mother raised chickens back in the depression days. She raised chickens and sold them and made some good money to help our family in those depression years. I got to where I didn't like chicken like I did when I was young.

187

One man I talked about earlier had said that if he ever met a preacher that didn't eat chicken, he'd get saved. Well, he met me and he did get saved.

One of the women in the church brought us one of those barbecued chickens. When it was time for lunch, the main thing they had was the chicken, so I ate some. My wife and the two boys ate it. I found that I liked it and I ate a big portion, but I didn't like other chicken for several years. Today I'll eat it, but I'm not crazy about it.

Atlanta, Georgia—Mt. Olive Baptist Church.

Just bringing boys to church meetings doesn't really impress a lot of people, even Christians. But no greater work will ever be done than caring for boys and girls and teenagers. Caron Jernigan was the pastor at Mt. Olive Baptist Church. I had been in other churches in the Atlanta area. Jim Finley was the Sunday School teacher of the junior boys. He said to me, "Brother Ferguson, I've got a whole class of about sixteen junior-age boys, and not any of them have accepted the Lord. I've talked to them, but they won't accept the Lord. If you'll tell me, what can I do?" I said, "Have them there the night I preach *The Last Train To Heaven.* I preached this special message in many meetings.

He did something special for them on the condition that all of them are there for that meeting. The boys brought some others, a total of about twenty junior boys. All twenty of them accepted the Lord that night. Jim Finley started liking me then, and it turned into a long-term relationship.

He went to Tennessee Temple Schools and graduated. He had me to preach in his church at Trion, Georgia and in two other churches in Georgia - and also in Missouri - and we always had good meetings, with professions of faith. He and his wife have moved back into this area while their youngest daughter is going through Tennessee Temple, and he is pastoring a chapel of Tennessee Temple. Jim Finley has been a real friend to me, a real man of God.

Greensboro, North Carolina—My Headquarters for Boxing.

My headquarters for boxing was finally located in Greensboro, North Carolina. Before that, I had fought a long time as a professional, and before that as an amateur. In Greensboro, I fought an older fellow from Chicago named Eddy Burgess. Burgess had been a good fighter in his day and was a real hard puncher, but he had gotten fat.

We were fighting a ten-round main event. Nobody saw him, but while the other fights were going on he came into the dressing room and talked to me. He told me, "Ferguson, I know you can beat me. But the thing I want you to do, a favor, is to not hit me hard with that left hook of yours, because you have one of the best left hooks I've ever seen, and I've been fighting for years. I want you to promise me that you won't hit me in the stomach hard, and I'll promise you that I won't take advantage and clip you."

You see, it's easy to get hit when you're trying not to hit somebody in a certain place. A clip is a punch that you're not expecting. It can knock you out. So I told him, "OK, I'll do that. I won't let you beat me, but I won't hit you in the stomach." If you're a good boxer, you're never hurt by a punch you can see.

Fighting by Instinct for Eight Rounds.

So the fight started, and the first round I won easy. I didn't hit him in the stomach. The second round started, and he hit me with his right hand. I remember him hitting me, my falling on the floor, and them dragging me to the corner - and that's all I remember.

But that's not what happened. When he hit me, he said my knees sagged just a little and I boxed better than I did before. I didn't know a thing about it, didn't know I was fighting on instinct. People who know boxing talk about fighting on instinct, and that's what I was doing. I went on and fought the rest of the ten rounds. Eight rounds, I fought - and didn't know where I was. I won the decision and fought every round in the fight. I still didn't hit him in the stomach.

So the fight was over and, in the dressing room, I came to and was apologizing for losing. They said, "Why, you're crazy! You won every round in the fight." I didn't believe it, really, 'til the next day I read it in the paper. I went ahead and accepted it, but I didn't really believe it 'til I saw in the paper that I had won the ten-round decision.

Training for Revenge.

It was such a good fight that they scheduled us right then to come back the next year. After that, I wanted to fight that fellow again. I put his stomach on my punching bag - the big bag - and I practiced and practiced. Every fellow I fought from that time 'til the next year, I saw his stomach on every fighter.

By the next year, I had improved and he had gotten a year older, in his thirties. When you get older like that you don't improve much. Some fighters do, but not many when they're that old, 36-38 years old. I was a little younger than 22, just starting out real good as a pro. As I said, I saw his stomach on every fighter and on my big punching bag the whole year.

He came into the dressing room again and said, "Well, Ferguson, we'll do just like last year." I said, "Yes sir. We'll do just like last year." We came out, and in the first round I jabbed him a couple of times and hit him with my left hook to the stomach as hard as I could. He fell into the ropes, and I held him up to beat him in the stomach. I really did. I belonged to a Methodist church, but the Baptist was coming out in me. I was going to get even with him. That's the way they do the preacher when he makes them mad by saying something to them.

I knocked him out. I don't remember hitting him in the ribs, but I broke two or three of his ribs. And it might have been that, when he fell, he broke his back. Not a serious back injury, though they thought at first that it was a serious injury. We thought at first that he was going to die. I went and apologized to him. He came back and fought again after that. I didn't hit him as hard in the last fight. I knocked him out without hitting him so hard in the stomach. He had been a real good fighter over the years.

My Youngest Sister— Margaret (Ferguson) Crawford.

When Margaret was born, I was nine years old, and I was a pretty big baby about my daddy. I was afraid she would be a boy and then I wouldn't be the baby boy. It was a big relief to find out Margaret was a girl. After she got to be seven or eight years old, I began to teach her all kinds of things about athletics. She became a track star. I had taught her a lot about track and she won several championships. I know she won the county championship, but after all these years I'm not sure about the state championship.

I also taught her about fighting. She had a left hook, a left jab, and a left upper cut and a right upper cut. She knew defense. I had taught her all of that. She had the best hand of nearly anybody I've ever seen. She could punch like a mule a kickin' with that right hand. After she was thirteen, Mother wouldn't let her box any more. I've seen her hit boys seventeen, eighteen years old, when she wasn't but ten or eleven, and knock 'em cold with one punch. Man, she could hit! And she can hit today. I've got several stories I can tell about her. She's a good Christian, loves the Lord, but she doesn't take too much off of people today.

After I had won the North and South Carolina Welter Weight Championship, the night before I came home, I was feeling pretty good about it. She said, "I can whip you." I said, "OK." I was playing around, not trying to keep her from hitting me. She was sixteen or seventeen then. She clipped me on the chin with the right hand. I saw the stars and the planets and two or three trees fell on me. I went down to my knees and grabbed her around the body and was playing like I wasn't hurt. But I was hurt! I was almost out!

I held to her until I got up. I never told her about that until I was a preacher. I owed it to her to set it right with her. But she really clipped me. That was the punch that hurt me the worst. Now, when Burgess hit me, it didn't hurt me because I was out and didn't know where I was, but when she hit me it hurt. That was the hardest punch I ever took, and it hurt me the worst of any punch—and it was from my baby sister.

Pastors' Wives - Evangelists' Wives.

I've been in a lot of churches, and I've told stories about pastors having a hard time. One pastor had flower pots thrown at him – and, Dan, you had steel lawn chairs thrown at you from the porch and got hosed down. Sometimes the churches are hard on the pastors, but I think that being a pastor's wife is one of the hardest jobs.

An evangelist's wife gets rid of him for a while. She'll miss him some, but she has the responsibility of running the whole house while her husband is away. Sometimes it's harder financially for

191

the evangelist and for the evangelist's wife. The evangelist may make a lot in one meeting and then not have any income for a long time. Any income difficulties are going to be a problem for the wife. Her sense of security is tied to that.

If the pastor knows how to control his budget, the pastor can fare a little better than the evangelist because he has a steady income. The pastor's wife, though, really has it hard because she has her own family to look after – and then all the women of the church tend to be critical of the pastor's wife.

In one church in Illinois, the women of the church went over to inspect the pastor's parsonage to see if it was clean. If it didn't meet their approval, they would bawl the pastor's wife out. I would have run them off if it had been me. I would have been mean then. I would have been as mean as I was to that Burgess guy I was fighting. If anybody would bother my wife, I would get on them in a hurry! Like Festus says on Gunsmoke, "like ugly on an ape."

But it's really hard on pastors' wives. I began to notice that after a few years. When I could, I tried to help them by talking to them and encouraging them. That's the only way I could help them. I've had wives to tell me they appreciated me talking to them and encouraging them. I'm not talking about a romantic thing – I'm talking about meeting a need in their life for encouragement. They would be despondent and down. It's easy to get that way. Their husbands are gone a lot with long days and sometimes out of town and everybody criticizing him. It's not that way in every church, but it's more that way than we realize. I think that pastors' wives ought to be prayed for, ought to be encouraged, and ought to be helped just as much as the preacher.

I never found in forty years over eight or ten pastors' wives who were not good women – honorable, kind, and who really loved the Lord. The majority of them have been good, have backed their husbands, and have stood behind them. If their husbands were wrong, they told them sweetly and tried to help and encourage them. I have met one or two pastors' wives that criticized everything their husband would say, in the pulpit and out of the pulpit. If I had been married to them, I believe I would have broken their necks, but most of the women have been understanding toward their husbands.

Occasionally a pastor's wife comes to the end of herself. She just can't take it anymore. She may leave with the children, or she may leave without the children. Or she stays and begins to fight back in different ways. Some pastors are mean to their wives. Some pastors are crooked. After the first year or two, I had been with nearly all good pastors, and then I began to be with some of the other kind.

In summary, the majority of the preachers and their wives I have been with through the years have been outstanding, good people. Most of the pastors I have been with were publicly kind to their wives and treated them with due respect.

Preachers' Children.

It's also hard on the children. They catch it too. I'm an evangelist and not a pastor, but my children were picked on. The children would pick on them and say, "You can't do so and so." They do a little something and the children, even in the church, would tell them they couldn't do this or that because their daddy was a preacher. Sometimes the children may do something they shouldn't do just to show the other children they can. That makes it harder. My boys all turned out good, and nothing can be said about that.

My Good Wife.

There's never been a better person than my wife. I'm glad she didn't have to go through what some have. It is harder on the woman than it is the man. In I Peter 3:7 the Bible says *"...giving honour unto the wife, as unto the weaker vessel..."* In some ways women have more intelligence and the like, but physically and emotionally they are not. And it's harder on the woman than it is the man to take some of the abuse they take in the church. I have learned to pray for the pastors' wives and to try to help them any way I could over the years.

Paul Ferguson the Fighter
Chapter 16

Revival and Attitude.

I used to go to meetings and the people would say, "We don't have any problems, everything is all settled. We're all in one accord." Most of the time they're in one accord in not doing anything. You go in and preach and pray and don't see much. I've never been in many meetings that I didn't have somebody saved, but in these places we wouldn't have the real moving of the power of God.

Then I go into some other meetings where half of the people would be for the pastor and half against him—real division in the church—but I didn't let anybody tell me about it. I didn't talk about it. What the Lord led me to do was to preach, and He always leads me in the direction of how to preach. These people get stirred up and get burdened because they realize they were not good enough. When you get people that think they're good enough, they won't pray. They won't be concerned about souls.

That leads me to say this: "It's not us. It's the Lord." When we think we've arrived and we don't need any thing else, that's when we're in a bad condition. When we see the need of having more of the power of God and spend time in prayer, then we can see a manifestation of the power of God. Some preachers say today that it's not possible to have revival today, and the way we're going into these "mini-skirt meetings," we have two or three days. No, we can't have revival with that. When we get concerned, we can still have revival today.

New London, Ohio—Big Snow—Bobby Murrow.

Bobby Murrow was one of the best basketball players Tennessee Temple ever had. We were friends, and I was scheduled to be with him in February in New London, Ohio. In January, there was a big snow storm across that whole region, and one man was covered up in his truck for ten days—and survived.

When I was there in February, there was still six or seven feet of snow on the ground, and snow drifts much higher. People came to the meeting with that snow on the ground, and we had people saved in the meeting. We couldn't do much visiting because we couldn't get into the houses off the streets, but they would somehow come out of their houses and get to the meeting.

John Brown—Georgia—Men Stay Outside.

I didn't give any invitations for a while at this place. Some men were outside listening, and I began giving short invitations to them and was giving it a little hard. I talked to the Lord about this and He was directing me. They came to the church house, but stayed outside. They said the pastor had been preaching on Hell but had not been giving an invitation. They said, "We're lost and if we die we'll go to Hell so, we decided to go to the meeting and get saved." Four or five of them came inside and were saved.

Arthur Estes—Chattanooga—Lonnng Singing!

I was with Arthur Estes while I was still in school. It was a good meeting. Most of the noticeable things happened at the end of the meeting. We had a group of singers to come for the meeting. In every church there'll be somebody that has some singers that want to come in. Arthur was a little concerned about having these singers, but he went ahead with it. He figured that unless the Lord gives an outpouring of His Spirit, it's best not to hold people long.

So he told those singers he would give them time for seven or eight songs. They got up and started, and each singer would bless us out between songs because we were trying to follow a schedule and not giving the Holy Spirit time to lead them. Now, I think it was not the Holy Spirit leading them. I think it was their selfish spirit wanting to show off. If it was going to be better for the service for me not to preach, I'd rather not even say a word, but God doesn't get people saved by "the foolishness of singing," but by "the foolishness of preaching."

"Just for the record, I saw one time in Florida where we began the invitation at twelve o'clock noon and we were still going until 2:30 in the afternoon, and people were still being saved. But if you keep people too long when the Lord is not working, it hurts the meeting. More about this service in a few minutes.

But in this meeting, these five or six people got up to sing. They took turns talking between the songs. One would talk at least ten minutes after a song, and after the next song another one would talk a long time. So they took up a good hour with this procedure. We didn't have a thing to happen in the service. I really believe that singers that have been invited in to sing should sing and shut their mouth and get out of the way. I know that good singing will bless the service, but these people had that wild kind of singing.

Some people don't especially care for the singing at Highland Park Baptist Church in Chattanooga, Tennessee, but I'll tell you one thing—they don't let the singers get up there and talk a half-hour. They come out and sing. Sometime they tell their name and sometimes they don't. They get on with the singing and get it over with, and that way, you can have a lot more singing. If you get singers in that tire out the people with their singing, they'll be dead when the preacher gets up to preach. That's the thing I've experienced over the years.

Florida—Long Singing—Short Singing—Revival!

In another meeting in Florida, the singers would come in and sing as much as an hour and a half. The preacher asked me why we weren't having any results. I said, "Well, they're singing an hour or an hour and a half. On Sunday morning we ought to have a break from all that singing. Let them sing and let me preach, and let's get it over with." They did, and on that morning we had six people come forward to be saved.

The invitation was over and we dismissed. A man jumped up and said, "I'm going to Hell! I want to be saved." They started to sing an invitation song, and people kept coming and kept coming. After a while they dismissed the service. Another man jumped up and said, "I'm unsaved and I'm going to Hell." We continued to sing invitation songs. When we finally finished, it was between 2:30 and 3:00 o'clock in the afternoon.

But this meeting didn't wear the people out. The Spirit of God was moving. In this meeting a large number of people were saved and about ninety-five people came for rededication. That revival went on for the rest of the week – people being saved

196

every single night. After that Sunday afternoon, the song leader never again tried to have a long song service.

It's important to realize here that we're not talking about what *human thing* will produce results and what *human thing* will not produce results. We're talking about what God has chosen to use. God has chosen to use God-called preachers to do God-anointed preaching to bring about conviction of the Holy Spirit in the hearts of people. Great singing, even simple singing, has an important place in the service of the Lord. God has ordained it to be so. But even the best of singing rarely convicts of sin, righteousness, and judgment necessary for a person to be saved.

So many people in revival meetings want an hour or more of singing. I went to a place in the mountains of Georgia, and they started at 6:30 p.m. It was 10:30 p.m. before I ever got to preach. I have to say that the *old man* came out in me. I preached an hour just to spite 'em. I got through preaching at about 11:30, and I've never been back there since. I'm not exaggerating this a bit – it happened.

What Does God Use?

What should men and women, boys and girls look at today? What can we expect God to use? When are we just spinning our wheels and beatin' our gums together? When are we just wasting our time and energy and money? I don't have the precision answer for these questions. We read in Galations 6:9: *"...in due season we shall reap, if we faint not."* God uses the Word of God. He uses singing. But the most-needed thing today in all the revival efforts is more praying. We need the special meetings to be longer than they are today, two weeks at least.

I once went to a church where they had *"prayer meetings"* before we began the revival services. They'd have forty minutes of gossip, and after they got through with their gossiping, then they'd eat. That's the wrong time for anybody to try to pray, after you've eaten a whole lot. I couldn't pray for an hour to save my life if I had just eaten a big meal.

But these people would eat and feast for two hours and then have a little sentence prayer, a short, minute-or-two prayer. They weren't praying. That's more of a mockery than anything. The best preachers, the best people do not get rid of our *selves* in a short prayer. Self is the biggest enemy of all of us. We think so much of our selves that we don't give up all of self in prayer in two minutes. That's why in revival efforts we need continual praying.

God Uses Death to Self.

Much praying gets our self out of the way so the Holy Spirit can work through us. The prevailing idea today is not that the Holy Spirit works through us, but that we are doing the work, and we need the Lord help us do what WE are doing. Christ lives His life through us by the Holy Spirit. When we get ourselves out of the way, God will work. In meetings where there were outstanding results, I didn't have the results—the Lord brought the results.

In most of the meetings where I ever had good results, it was when I had gotten alone with somebody or by myself in agonizing prayer. The more people that prayed, the more God blessed. If you get a whole church praying, and I mean really praying, it's untelling what God will do. In some of the places I have been, the people would pray hours and hours, and there would be a large number of people saved. The meeting would last and the people would go on for a long period of time after I left. Sometimes I've seen more people saved after I left than while I was there.

In studying the lives of a lot of the outstanding men of the past, you find that most of them went through some hardship. Philippians 1:29 says, *"For unto you it is given in the behalf of Christ, not only to believe on him, but also to suffer for his sake."* In this day people think they're suffering if they go to a service for four or five nights. They think they're suffering for the Lord. That's not suffering for the Lord! I don't know why there must be suffering, but that's the way it works.

God Uses Surrender.

The average person doesn't know where it may lead if they say they surrender everything to the Lord. And here's the big question: Are they surrendering the "old man" or the "new man?"

198

We have both. The old man was crucified on the cross, but we don't recognize that. We don't recognize that surrendering to God is really just saying that the new man is going to rule. The new man is the one that the Holy Spirit can guide. The new man is the ONLY one that the Holy Spirit can guide. The "old man" is part of: *"....But now we see not yet all things put under him"* (Heb. 2:8).

There's not any way that God can use the "old man" that's in us. It's all the "new man." It doesn't help anything to perfume and dress up the "old man." But that's what's happening in this day. It's so much the "old man" and hardly any of the "new man." A lot of churches will run you out if you preach about the Holy Spirit. It's the Holy Spirit that lives Christ's life through us. And it's Christ's faith operating in us, and not our faith, that's operating in doing God's work. There's something else about this . We don't get there in two days. We may not get there in two weeks. Today, churches will advertise weekend revivals – a meeting on Saturday night and two services on Sunday, and they call it a revival. With God it just does not work that way, not one time in a thousand.

I know a man – he's already gone to be with the Lord – he went to a meeting (I heard tales in North Carolina when I was a boy of this kind of thing happening) and was preaching, and the people wouldn't be stirred. He stopped preaching and told the people there was no need for him to preach until some serious praying was done. He said that the preacher and some others had been praying for hours.

God Uses Unusual Things.
While this group was praying, a ball of fire came down and rolled out across the church and rolled out the front door. This was a good man, a graduate of Tennessee Temple, Wally Jonas. I believe him. It stirred them up. They had over sixty or seventy to accept Christ as Savior. God knew what it would take to stir this church and He sent it – a ball of fire. The fire came out from the pulpit and rolled down the aisle.

Now, I've never had fire to come out of the pulpit, but the thing that happened at the pulpit in Stevenson, Alabama at the Centennial Baptist Church was a manifestation of the power of God. That was an unusual case. At the meeting above with Arthur Estes, the Lord put it on my heart to fast. You don't have to fast every time, but the Lord put it on my heart to fast; and I said, "Lord, I'm going to fast until this meeting breaks." Today, I would modify what I would say to the Lord about that. Today, I would say, "Lord I'm going to fast as long as you lead me to fast."

God Uses Children.

But back then I said, "I'm going to fast until this meeting breaks." Well, we didn't have anybody saved for two weeks, not until the last Saturday night. A little boy, seven or eight years old, came and accepted the Lord. I ate then. This boy went home on Saturday night and told his daddy that he (his daddy) was going to Hell. So his daddy, mother, and the whole family came the next day, and they were all saved. That meeting went on and on for weeks after those people were saved. I can tell of many other places where they had more saved after the meeting was over than were saved while the meeting was going on.

On that Sunday the meeting broke out, and there were thirty to forty people saved in one day. The preacher, Arthur Estes, had said, "I can't go very long without eating and I can't fast." He was frying him some eggs and bacon and God told him, "You haven't fasted long enough. If you eat those I'll choke you to death." That's what the preacher told.

> D.C.: *I knew Arthur Estes as a Temple student and as a pastor in Jacksonville, Florida.*

God Uses Fasting.

I believe there are times when we should fast. I don't fast as much as I used to. We don't buy anything from God by fasting – I believe the Bible teaches it. Some say that in this dispensation, this period of time, you don't have to fast. The reason I'm for fasting is that in fasting we give up something. It lets us go through a little hardship, helps to put us in line with some things Jesus went through. It's just doing without.

We identify fasting as entering into the suffering of Jesus Christ. It's not necessary in every situation. I used to think that if the Lord led you to preach on it, that I would have to fast, but I don't believe that now. If God wants you to fast, He'll let you know if you're willing to be led. Fasting reminds us to pray as we realize we are hungry. Fasting reminds us of our decision to seek the Lord for that day. We don't fast so God will feel sorry for us and give us what we want just because we are going without food. We are not to fast as the Pharisees did in their pride. We are to fast with thanksgiving.

South Dakota—Several Times.

In one town, I was told that there was no handball court in town, but the local school coach let me use the gym to jump rope and work out. I asked the coach to come to the meeting and he said he would come. I asked him if he was saved and he said, "No." I talked to him a little. He came to the meeting, and the first meeting he came forward and accepted the Lord.

He then brought several of his high school ball players—basketball, football, baseball. Many of his students were saved through his invitation to them to come to the meeting. Some of the people of the church wrote me later about him going on in his Christian life, still witnessing and winning people to the Lord for a long time. The people in North Dakota don't get fired up so fast, but when they do get saved, they tend to continue on. In South Dakota, we didn't have as many people saved during the meetings as in other places, but they had more saved afterward.

Humor—How Much?

I don't believe there can be any set standard as to how much humor a preacher should use. Now, with me, I guess I'm funny to look at anyway. I've always told people that they don't laugh at what I tell. They just wanted to laugh, and when I tell a joke they laugh at me and not at the joke. I used jokes to help people settle down. They come into the meeting a little nervous, and a funny story helps them to relax and get their mind on the meeting. I don't believe in telling anything shady. I've stopped preachers from telling jokes or stories when they were the least bit shady.

When I first started preaching, I told humorous things before

I preached, and sometimes I'd have people to get up and leave. Some people would say that I ran the Holy Spirit off because I told a joke; so I prayed about it, and the Lord put it on my heart to use humor. Since I prayed about it, I began putting humor into the messages.

When I first started doing this, it would be mostly young people that would listen to it and come back because of it. Some people even told me that they came just to hear the funny stories. As they came, God convicted them and they were saved. They told me this after they were saved. God says that it's by the foolishness of preaching - *not foolish preaching* - but by the foolishness *of* preaching that people are saved.

Now, some people can't tell funny things. Others can. I have been told that I have a gift of it. It makes it easy and goes with what I say. I know other preachers that, if they try to tell something funny, it goes flat and hurts the whole service. They shouldn't tell jokes. I think preachers ought to be directed what to do about humor. Telling a funny story doesn't show irreverence, I don't think - and especially the day we're living in now. Anymore, I don't hear about any complaints against humor like I used to when I first started.

In the south, they didn't like me at all. In Ohio, Indiana, Illinois and all the midwestern states, out west, in New York and that area - they liked it. But in the south they didn't like it. In my early years of preaching, I didn't have half as many meetings in the south as I did in the midwest and the north. The reason is that the southern people didn't like for me to tell jokes.

Well, I'm a southerner, southern-bred, southern-born, and when I die I'll be southern-dead. I'm a southerner, and I don't try to put on an act like I'm a Yankee. That's what they liked. I don't think it's wrong to use humor in preaching. Now, I didn't go to these places as an entertainer. I went as a preacher. But when the Lord showed me to use it, I did. If you mean business for God you never go anywhere as an entertainer. But, as you go, you do different things as God leads you that get the attention of the people.

I've told this story earlier. In Florida a man told me he wouldn't have come to the meetings at all except for the funny stories. He said he was so tied up and tense from the strain he lived in all day at work that when he came to the meetings it relaxed him. The meetings changed his life with the Lord. God used the humor. It wasn't me. It was the Lord.

How Much Are We To Be Like Somebody Else?

God makes each one of us different. We can get into trouble trying to be exactly like somebody else, even somebody in the Bible. For example, the Apostle Paul said, *"...I have great heaviness and continual sorrow in my heart"* (Rom. 9:2). God didn't make everybody to have the same emotions and mindset as the Apostle Paul.

Of Jeremiah, the Bible says: *"Oh that my head were waters, and mine eyes a fountain of tears, that I might weep day and night for the slain of the daughter of my people!"* (Jeremiah 9:1). Jeremiah was different.

> D.C.: *God took Ezekiel's wife (Ezek. 24:15-27) and did not allow Ezekiel to weep over her. This was a sign to all Israel of what was coming upon them; but God doesn't take everybody's wife and forbid them to weep and mourn as He commanded Ezekiel.*

God appoints each of us our particular role, gives each of us our particular gift. Every one of the prophets was different and they approached their work differently. I don't want anybody else to be like me. Our oldest boy is a preacher, and he's not like me. He's altogether different. The youngest boy preaches some, and he's different. Tim is teaching school, and he's different. We should all try to be ourselves, directed and led by the Spirit of God. God leads different people in different ways.

We have a tendency, in the day in which we live, that if you don't do just like me and my little group, then the Lord is not in it—and that's not true. God leads people in different ways. We feel safe and secure in following some kind of a human pattern, and that can be good up to a point; but if you follow a human pattern, you don't have to depend as much on the Lord.

Sometimes it takes men a long time to realize that God didn't call them to be like somebody else. We may be under the strong influence of great, Godly leaders, successful men. We can get the idea that success is being like those people that we admire, being like those people God made a certain way. But serving God in the way God intends doesn't mean that we copy other people in the way they dress or speak. That's not where the power lies in these great people. The power lies in the Holy Spirit working through us. Christ's life working through us by the Holy Spirit is where the power is.

We can learn from other people, but we can't get the power of God from them. All young people tend to mimic somebody for a while. They used to accuse me of holding my neck like John Rice. I didn't hold my neck like John Rice! I did that because for twenty-something years I had held my neck like that in boxing. I don't do it as much now, but it was because of that and not because I was trying to hold my neck like John Rice. I liked John Rice, but I never tried to mimic him.

I never mimicked Dr. Lee Roberson. I'll tell you something I learned from Dr. Roberson that really helped me. If you preach on Sunday morning, quit at twelve o'clock; and that's something most preachers don't learn. I learned that right away from him.

A few times, I've had a hard time doing it when the song service runs a long time. I have gotten up at ten minutes before twelve, gave the plan of salvation, and didn't preach. Now, if the power of God is there like I told about a while ago, like the time in Florida, I went past twelve. Not one person complained, and we didn't get out 'til 2:30 or 3:00. But the power of God was on the place and people were getting saved, and we dismissed seven times before we stayed dismissed.

You don't work those things up. You don't copy those things. What we need to learn is that the Holy Spirit lives the life of Christ through us as much as possible with the condition we're in – but we are to be ourselves. I'd tell all young preachers and everybody, just be yourself. Learn to improve what you can, but the main thing is not in improving the fleshly faults. The main thing is learning to let Christ live through us, as we find in Galatians 2:2: *"I am crucified with Christ: nevertheless I live; yet not I, but Christ liveth in me: and the life which I now live in the flesh I live by the faith of the Son of God, who loved me, and gave himself for me."*

The crucified life comes only by faith. It doesn't come by

working. That's like the fruit of the Spirit. The fruit of the Spirit is not produced by the flesh but by the Holy Spirit. It's all the life of Christ working in us by the Holy Spirit who lives in our bodies. A rabbit would be a terrible flop if he tried to fly like a bird. A rabbit needs to do what God made him to do. There's great liberty and freedom in realizing that God has a plan for each one of us.

Personal Witnessing.

Throughout these days of discussions, we've touched on witnessing to individuals scattered here and there. The main thing in witnessing is to ask the Holy Spirit of God to lead you in what approach to use. If you do that before you talk to someone, you will do much better, because you don't approach everybody alike. Some people you go to, you need to find out what they do and if you have any things in common with what they do. Find out what they're interested in. Get their attention – that's my general approach. That's the way I usually approach a lost person unless the Lord is using me different.

I've always picked up hitch-hikers. Since I was up here (Flat Rock) the last time, I've led a hitch-hiker to the Lord. I was going to Cleveland, Tennessee to play handball, and this man was beside the road. He got in the car and put a few things in. He said he was going over to Asheville, North Carolina to the Veteran's hospital. I talked to him a few minutes and asked him if he knew the Lord as his Savior and if he died would he go to Heaven. He said he didn't know that. I said, "Well, would you like to know? I'll stop the car up here and show you how to be saved, how to know you're saved by the Bible." He said, "Fine."

Explaining the Gospel.

We went on to this stopping place where I had led a man to the Lord two years ago when I was going to play handball at Cleveland. We stopped and I showed him Romans 5:12: *"Wherefore as by one man* [Adam] *sin entered into the world, and death by sin; and so death passed upon all men, for that all have sinned…"* I showed him Romans 3:9-12: *"There is none righteous, no, not one…"* (v.10), and Romans 3:22, 23: *"…all have sinned and come short of the glory of God"* (v.23). I showed him the verses that showed him that he was a sinner.

Then I showed him II Corinthians 5:21: *"For he hath made him to be sin for us, who knew no sin; that we might be made the righteousness of God in him."* Then I showed him Acts 20:21: *"Testifying both to the Jews, and also to the Greeks, repentance toward God, and faith toward our Lord Jesus Christ."*

Really, repentance is just coming to the end of self and becoming willing to put your dependence wholly in the Lord. After a man sees his need, I show him Romans 5:21: *"That as sin hath reigned unto death, even so might grace reign through righteousness unto eternal life by Jesus Christ our Lord."*

I show a person that when he accepts Christ he becomes a child of God. I show him John 1:12: *"But as many as received him, to them gave he power to become the sons of God, even to them that believe on his name..."*

When you receive Christ, the righteousness of Christ is put over into our account in Heaven, just the same as our sins were put on Christ on the cross. I Peter 2:24: *"Who his own self bare our sins in his own body on the tree, that we, being dead to sins, should live unto righteousness: by whose stripes ye were healed."*

Our sins have already been placed on Christ on the cross, and His righteousness has been put over into our personal account in Heaven. These two things have already happened in time; but we don't become a partaker of our sins being placed on Christ on the cross, nor do we receive the righteousness of Christ into our account into Heaven until we receive Christ as our Savior. Another word for this is "appropriate." We do not appropriate for ourselves the death of Christ on the cross; we do not appropriate for ourselves His righteousness into our personal account until we receive Christ by faith into our hearts as Savior and Lord.

Then, we become the children of God. I use Revelation 3:20: *"Behold, I stand at the door, and knock: if any man hear my voice, and open the door, I will come in to him, and will sup with him, and he with me."* That's Christ talking. Christ comes into our hearts to abide by the Holy Spirit, and to live in our hearts. Romans 10:13: *"For whosoever shall call upon the name of the Lord shall be saved."*

Not Under Conviction.

When I am dealing with people who are NOT under much conviction, who have NOT been dealt with much – especially grown people – I usually use quite a few scriptures. Otherwise, they'll think, "Well, he's just picking out one point." But if you show them from several different places that it's just Christ alone that saves and keeps you saved, then they're more likely to accept Christ.

Sometimes people are not ready. Now, the man I picked up on the way to Cleveland to play handball, he was ready to be saved. He was happy and went away rejoicing, thanking me— not for picking him up, but for talking to him about Christ. The Lord had already worked on his heart and had him prepared.

Sometimes God uses us to prepare hearts for other people to reap the results. The Apostle talks about this in I Corinthians 3:6: *"I have planted, Apollos watered; but God gave the increase."* In John 4:38, Jesus said, *"I sent you to reap that whereon ye bestowed no labour: other men laboured, and ye are entered into their labours."* Many times I've talked with people and they didn't get saved, but later I found out that somebody else had led them to the Lord. I've had people tell me that.

A young preacher was preaching, and a man came forward and was saved. The young preacher was so proud about this man coming to be saved. He was one of the hardest men in the community and nobody could do anything with him. Here, he preached just one sermon and this hard-hearted fellow gets saved.

The preacher asked him, "Mr., I want to know what it was that I said that caused you to be saved." The man replied, "Son, I never heard a word you said. Forty years ago I heard Billy Sunday preach, and he said something that I've not been able to get off of my heart in forty years – and I've come today to be saved." That ought to illustrate what I'm talking about, that we witness to somebody and another person will reap. That's Scriptural.

It's like I said earlier, there are different approaches to witnessing. You just can't say there's a standard approach that works for everybody.

Paul Ferguson the Fighter
Chapter 17

Problems with Pastors.

Sometimes I had problems with the pastors of the churches where I held meetings. One time, after I had been preaching about two years, I was with so many men that were aggravating and mean and hard to deal with that I told God that if He didn't give me some good ones, I was going to quit. I won't tell any of their names. That's the truth. I said, "If I don't get some good people...soon...I just can't go on like this." From then on, I got about one bad one to about twenty-two to twenty-five good ones. It was right the opposite in the first part of my ministry.

> D.C.: *This paragraph does not contradict his earlier summary of the high number of good pastors, but merely focuses on a particular time in his ministry. Overall, the pastors and their wives were good to work with.*

From my days of boxing I had formed some habits that I carried out before the fight. I needed to go into the ring as relaxed as I could so I could focus on the fight. In preaching, I preferred to stay in the back of the auditorium or sit on the front row of the audience. In the early days I was in a meeting in Missouri, and the pastor wanted me to sit on the platform, so I came on up to the platform and sat with the pastor.

Preaching on the Family.

In one church, I preached a message on the family and was talking about the different responsibilities in the family. The preacher had done a lot of things in his family that the people knew about. I was staying with this widow woman in her home. The next morning after I had preached on the family, this widow woman commented on the different ways my wife and I contacted each other and different things about our relationship.

She said, "Who told you about our preacher?" I said, "Not anyone. I don't know what you mean, lady. I don't know what you're talking about." She said, "Well, you drew his picture last night. You painted his mustache and his beard. Of course, the preacher didn't have a mustache and beard, but she was giving the description of the way I had drawn his picture and about things in the church. I had a hard time convincing her that I didn't know anything about the preacher, but after a while she believed it.

The preacher thought I was preaching to him, that somebody had told me about him. I told him that I didn't know a thing. I just preached the message the Lord laid on my heart to preach. I already had it prepared and I just preached it. It wasn't made for anybody especially, just anybody it hit. He was mad at me.

The next night he said, "I think we had better go to pray." So we went to a place to pray. He said, "Lord, you tell Brother Paul that I don't beat my family. You tell Brother Paul that I don't mistreat my family." And he went on for about fifteen or twenty minutes telling the Lord to tell me the things he hadn't done and what he wasn't, and all of that.

After about twenty minutes, I got tired of it. I went over and patted him on the back and said, "Now listen brother, if you've got something to tell me, I'd rather you come direct to me and not go all the way to the Lord and come back to me, because I can hear everything you say. Why don't you just tell me about it?"

He jumped up and threw his hands in the air and ran out of the room screaming to the top of his voice. I thought he was mental, and maybe he was a little. The meeting went on and we had some people to come. We had agreed before the meeting started that we'd take them back in the prayer room, but because he was mad at me, he wouldn't take people back to the room. He would deal with them down at the front. A lot of the women told me some of the things he had done. He beat his wife, went out of town. I'll not tell the worst part, worse than that.

He went to a meeting in another state by himself, and his boy got hurt while he was gone. His wife didn't even know what state he was in. That's the way he left his family, didn't tell them anything. She couldn't get in touch with him, and the deacons had to sign for the boy to go into the hospital. These were just minor things with this man. I'll not tell the others, but it illustrates hindering difficulties I sometimes encountered.

Visiting a Mean Man.

He [the preacher above] and I went out to see a man in the community that was supposed to be mean. He would run preachers off. Actually, he was a good, moral man and helped people in the community and was respected, but he was mean to preachers. I talked with the man a while and tried to find out what he liked, and we talked about different things. After a while the man said, "I like you. I know what you came for. You came to talk to me about the Lord, and I'll let you. You don't even have to ask me. Take the Bible and show me how to be saved."

I went through the plan of salvation, showing him he was a sinner and that he had to accept Christ. I'll not give all the Scriptures. After anybody shows somebody how to be saved, I believe they ought to pray. Now, this is a standard thing that I think ought to be done. If you pray with them, they'll come nearer coming under conviction of the Holy Spirit if you pray with them after you show them how to be saved.

The Pastor Says I'm The Stupidest Preacher.

I said, "Will you accept the Lord as your Savior?" He said, "Yes I will. Tell me what to do and I'll accept Him right now. I know I'm a sinner and I want to be saved." This preacher jumped up right then and said to me, "You're the stupidest preacher I've ever seen. You've made the biggest mess out of showing this man how to get saved!"

He had seen this man repeatedly and knew he had never been saved. He knew he was mean and ran preachers off. The preacher was mad at me and took me over there to see this man thinking that he would kill me. And now that the man was getting saved, he thought that I would get the credit for leading the man to the Lord and he wouldn't get it. So he was going to show this man that he was the one that would get him saved. The man had always run him off before.

The man didn't get saved. He jumped up and picked up a gun. He said to me, "I like you. I was intending to be saved, but I'll never be saved when this (bad word) is around. Don't come back if you're preaching for him. Now, if you're preaching somewhere else I'll come. But as long as you're in his church don't come back here, and if you do, I'll shoot you." And I didn't go back, I'll tell you that!

We got out to the car and the preacher said, "Boy, you made the awfullest mess I've ever seen in my life. It's a disgrace the way you talked with that man." I have to admit I didn't like it, so I told him that if he batted his eye I would hit him – and I would have. I told him to take me back where I was staying and told him, "I'll not go out with you anymore." And I didn't.

Pastor Sticks His Tongue Out Every Night.

After that, every night he led the singing. (He was a good song leader.) I didn't always come up on the platform, but when I did, he'd turn around and stick his tongue out at me! That's no exaggeration or made-up stuff. Every single night from then on he stuck his tongue out at me. He'd even do it during the invitation time if I was behind him. He wouldn't do it otherwise. The choir was on the side, so there was nobody behind me to see him do it.

Many of the ladies told me that they had talked to their husbands about being saved, but none of their husbands would let this man talk to them. They said, "Will you come over and talk to my husband?" I went over to a house the first afternoon. Now, I want to make this statement of fact – I never went against the pastor. But this was one exception and the only time that anything like this ever happened. When there was trouble with the pastor, I talked with him in private and tried to get things worked out to work together.

But not with this guy. He was crazy! The first night three people came forward that I had talked to in the home. He'd run down and say, "Oh, you came to be saved." Every one of them said, "No, I didn't come to be saved. Brother Paul led me to the Lord today, and I'm coming to be baptized and join the church." He got madder and madder about that.

I don't remember the exact number, but I believe there were between twenty-five and thirty men that I personally led to the Lord in the afternoons and sometimes at night after the service. I couldn't take the preacher with me to make those visits. The lost men wouldn't let him talk to them. (I wouldn't have taken him anyway.) Every one of these men then came to church and was baptized and joined the church. We had a large number of

211

men saved.

Do you know what that man had the nerve to ask me? He asked me if I would write a letter to Dr. Lee Roberson and to John Rice and tell them what a great preacher he was and what a man of God he was. I said, "No, I won't, because you're crazy. I won't do it." And I didn't.

I wasn't going to tell this, but maybe I ought to. One of the things this crazy preacher did to make this unsaved man mad at him was the sham stuff the preacher had pulled off. One Sunday morning, the preacher stayed home from church and sent his boy on to Sunday School to tell the people his daddy was sick and wouldn't be there. This man in the neighborhood – a good, moral man – was good to help everybody. He just didn't like preachers and was mean to them. He did more to help people than most Christians, more than most preachers. He went down to the preacher's house to help him out.

When he arrived at the preacher's house, he knocked on the door and nobody answered. He just opened the door and walked in, thinking that the preacher was sick in bed. Here stood the preacher in the living room with only his shorts on, cursing his wife. He wasn't just saying bedtime stories. He was cursing.

The man came a time or two to the meeting because he wanted to hear what a prize fighter would have to say since he kept up with boxing, but after the pastor and I visited in his home he stopped coming to the meeting. He sent me a note by his wife that if I'd come over to their house and eat dinner with them, he'd accept the Lord. The preacher told me not to go. I had been in so many battles with the preacher during the meeting that I didn't go. I made a mistake. I was wrong. The man got saved later, but I would have had the privilege of leading him to the Lord. I've always been sorry I didn't go. Another Baptist preacher came by his house and led him to the Lord. He was baptized and joined another church. I think he moved his letter back to his wife's church after the pastor left.

That pastor didn't stay at the church very long after the meeting. He made out to me that he was a great student of psychology. I had studied psychology. *[He lacked just a few semester hours having a second major in psychology and philosophy. dc]* He didn't need psychology. He needed the power of the Lord to change his life.

We always consider that the church in unity can do a whole lot; but this experience proves that, although this preacher was like this, these church people, these women, were burdened over their husbands. They had been praying, and God honored it and blessed many of these people in spite of the preacher.

I've always said, when we would have a lot of people saved in a meeting, that God did it *in spite of* me. He has to do a lot *in spite of* us. It's His greatness and His goodness and His power and His grace that does the work. He allows things like this to happen. We know it is good if everybody in the church would be burdened, if everybody would be concerned, including the pastor and all of us.

The Small Number Always Carries the Load.

But usually in the normal church of two to three hundred, and even in larger churches, there's a small amount of people that want to be filled with the Spirit and be soul winners. There's just a very few, actually. I hear people say, "This man's a soul winner." Not anybody is a soul winner. The Holy Spirit is the soul winner, and we have to let the Holy Spirit work through us before people really get saved.

People may make a profession of faith, but they will *NOT* be saved without the conviction of the Holy Spirit. The Bible says in John 6:44, *"No man can come to me, except the Father which hath sent me draw him; and I will raise him up at the last day."* So there's a need in the churches today, not for greater preaching, but greater praying. Greater praying will bring the power we need. It's not more ability, not more methods, but the power of the Holy Spirit. There are so few that understand this – so few that practice this – that it's a great opportunity for those who want to. All you have to do to take advantage of this great opportunity is to be willing to do it. We tell people, "If you're willing to be saved, you can be saved." We believe that. It's also equally true that if people are willing to be used of God, He'll use them.

God Uses Determined, Surrendered People.

I want to tell about a story I read in a book. A woman that

lived way out on a farm went to a meeting where the preacher preached on the Holy Spirit. He said, "If you'll accept the Holy Spirit by faith, you can go out and win people to the Lord." She had a burden and concern about leading people to the Lord. She started praying that God would send somebody to her house.

A business man was traveling through the country and stopped by her house to ask directions on where to find another place. The woman led him to the Lord. That shows how willing God is to use us if we're willing to be used. Being used of God does not begin by getting a lot of technical knowledge. I'm not talking against knowledge. I'm not against knowledge, but knowledge is not enough within itself.

Diplomacy in approaching a lost person is good, but not everything. A friend of mine – I won't give his first name, but his last name was Morgan – was the poorest witness I ever saw. I was in a meeting in South Carolina, and this man was the poorest witness in knowing how to deal with anybody that I ever saw. He talked about the Second Coming and the Rapture and the Tribulation and everything else, and never did get around to showing anybody how to be saved.

One night in the meeting, a young lady in her middle twenties came forward to be saved. She was willing to be saved and accepted the Lord. The preacher asked her, "Why did you come? You've always been so hard to deal with and didn't care anything about the Lord. Why did you come?" She said, "Well, when Brother Morgan came over by my house and talked to me about all those things, ever since that I've not been able to sleep day or night. I just couldn't stand it any longer. I had to come and be saved."

It wasn't my preaching. People were praying. This man had witnessed to her, and it was just as bad a witness as I ever heard to an unsaved person, and yet God used it – showing that the technical aspect of a Gospel presentation doesn't always turn out to be the thing that touches people.

Just a Simple Minded Boy.

I read of a boy that was·a little simple in his mind. In the same community there was a man that ran everybody off when

214

they tried to talk to him about the Lord. This boy got burdened for him. He walked up to the man and asked him about being saved. The man just blessed him out. The boy said, "All right, I don't care. You can go to Hell if you want to." That's not always the right way to approach people, but that's what he said, and walked away. The man got to thinking, "Good night! Maybe God might do me that way if I don't go and get saved." He went to the meeting and was saved.

Now, the boy didn't know a thing about the right technique about presenting the Gospel, but God used what the boy said to bring this hardened sinner to the Lord. Now, I don't say that this means we shouldn't study. We should use the best technique, we should use diplomacy, but let the Holy Spirit lead us at the time to show us what we ought to use. Some of the things I've told, I never did it but one time, but it worked for that particular time. The Lord led in it for that time. I told about the unusual things in Brother Lamison's church, and I said at the time, "Don't try this." The young people went out and tried it, and the people ran them off. Don't do something unusual in witnessing just because somebody else did it. Do it because the Lord directs you to do it. He'll let you know.

Returning To the Early Years.

I was born in North Carolina near Wilkesboro at a little place called Goshen. At the time, I didn't know that was a Biblical name. Goshen was in Egypt where the children of Israel lived. My father was Bob Ferguson and his wife was Rosalie Ferguson. My father was a farmer. In those days a farmer profited by having more children. The children could help earn their own keep by working in the family farm; all of us worked on the farm. My father was not pleased with my wanting to be a prize fighter, but he never tried to stop me.

My Daddy sent me out to replant corn, and I dug a hole and put all the seed corn in the hole and covered it up. Daddy was wondering why the corn didn't come up and, all at once, it all came up together in one spot. He used the board of education on the seat of knowledge for me. That's like Numbers 32:23: *"Be sure that your sins will find you out."*

Mr. Doggett was a school teacher, and Mrs. Doggett was

an expert seamstress. She sewed for many people and made pretty good money for that day. She had one of the old Singer machines with the foot treadle. My wife, Lena May, was the oldest girl in her family. She had a twin brother who was older than her. My mother was one of nine children, and there were nine of us. People kidded my parents that there would probably be eighteen of us.

My oldest sister's name was Pansy Ferguson; she taught school some. My oldest brother was Willard Winfield Ferguson. Then there was Howard, Ervy, and Erby. Erby became a school teacher. Two of my other sisters were teachers at times. Mary was a school teacher and died with leukemia at 47, the first one of us to die. Then came Winifred, and I came along as number seven. Seven is the perfect number. I used to tell my two younger sisters that our father and mother should have quit with seven since seven is the perfect number.

But my next sister, Verna, learned from some books I gave her that number eight is the number of resurrection, and she reminded me about that. Margaret was the youngest and the last one. She's the one I didn't want to be a boy. But after she was born and I got a little older, I wish she had been a boy.

Playing Football in High School.
When I went to Greensboro, I played football, the only sport I played. The quarterback was the only player that was smaller than me. I played left guard and weighed 146 with my uniform on, but my main interest then was boxing. I ran some in track, but they didn't do much in that sport. When I was training for boxing, I used to run 20-25 miles in a day.

In football I played against a fellow from a mountain section close to Boone, North Carolina. He weighed about three hundred pounds. Every time he'd come through he hit me with his fist. He didn't know I was a boxer. I told him, "If you do that again I'm gonna let you have it." He did it again and I knocked him out. I hit him in the stomach with a left hook. He never bothered me again.

They penalized him and not me. Nobody saw it. They thought he fell – and he did! He was swinging at me when I hit him. They could see him swing, but they couldn't see me down underneath. When I was fighting I could knock anybody down and break his ribs and his back with less than a six-inch punch. Course, I was younger when this happened. I'm telling this to show how much power you can have with a punch like that and especially in my left hand.

Lena Was Riding a Bicycle.

I saw my wife riding down the road on a bicycle one day. I'd never seen her before, didn't know her name or anything. I said to myself, "I'm gonna marry that girl," but I didn't tell anybody else. I was twenty-one and she was sixteen.

She came down to see my aunt, and I met her. Her name was Lena May Doggett. My aunt went to a Presbyterian church, and they were having a revival. I went to church with my aunt. About a week later, I asked Lena May to go to a prize fight with me. That's the first time we went out by ourselves together. On July 19, 1939, we were married in Mountain City, Tennessee. I was twenty three and she was eighteen.

> D.C.: *This is the same town where I got saved, in the fall of 1944, in a revival meeting held in a bean market.*

On July 18, 1944, at 2:17 p.m., our oldest boy was born at the Naval Hospital in Charleston, South Carolina. Before we were married, I told my wife that the first child would be a boy and we would name him John Paul – so, he was named before we were married. Tim was born in Greensboro, North Carolina in 1951. Tim wasn't much over two weeks old when I started school at Tennessee Temple in Chattanooga, Tennessee.

Mark was born in Chattanooga, Tennessee in 1963. They're all good boys. John was saved when he was seven and is a preacher. Tim was saved when he was three and a half and is a school teacher. Mark was saved when he was four and a half and works at a steel plant and teaches Sunday School.

Before Mark was saved, I had preached about children being left behind at the coming of the Lord if they were old enough to know right from wrong. The Lord put it on my heart about Mark. He got real sick and I talked to him about the Lord. He accepted the Lord and got well right then, immediately – just like you snap your fingers. He was healed that quick! He must have been under conviction along with it.

John Paul and his wife, Brenda (Christ), have a girl named Pam. Their son is John Paul II. Pam has two boys, John and Dave. Tim's wife is Kathy (Franz). They had three children. Tiffany died when she was about eight years old. She was born with a disease that cut her life short. Their other little girl is Trisha. The boy's name is TJ. (That's his name, not initials.) Mark's wife is Charlotte (Hardy). Her daddy was a preacher, originally from Alabama. They have two boys, Tommy and Johnny.

I Don't Consider Myself a "Prayer Warrior."

I never considered myself to be a real prayer warrior. Today, if you pray all night two or three times, people will think you're crazy. If you pray three or four hours a day, people will think you're crazy. The only reason I prayed was that God showed me I needed to pray – it's in the Bible. Of course, we don't take everything the Bible says, but there's strong teaching on prayer throughout the Bible. It was God that caused me to pray and spend time in prayer. I've prayed over the years and tried to get other people to pray.

It's not to our glory to pray, but He has promised that if we pray He will answer. It's not that we do something big. When we pray we're just doing what He said, and He answers because He has promised. It's all of Him – *everything!* All the glory, all the praise goes to Christ.

Some preachers – I know many – think that because they're gifted in a certain way – a great personality – that God will bless them because of that. Well, personality is not always of God. That's an earthly thing and fleshly, and God doesn't bless that. Now, it doesn't hurt to have that if a man will let the Lord use it, but if you try to go on personality and things that are from man, then those things are not acceptable in the sight of God.

I want to make it very clear that I am not against schools, but we have to remember what God said in I Samuel 16:7: *"But the Lord said unto Samuel, Look not on his countenance, or on the height of his stature, because I have refused him, for the Lord seeth not as man seeth; for man looketh on the outward*

appearance, but the Lord looketh on the heart."
Sometimes in theological schools today, the idea comes across that if you prepare enough and do all the school-recommended things, that those are the main things acceptable to God – your basic, essential training for ministry. But it isn't. If anything is not directed by God and the power of the Holy Spirit, it's accepted by God only as a work of the flesh. If it's motivated by flesh and not by the Holy Spirit, then the Spirit will not endorse it. Learning is good, but it is not the instrument for the power of God. That's the secret for today.

The emphasis should not be so much on schooling as the essential thing. And remember, I earned two degrees that normally require a total of eight years of schooling, but that's not what counts. The thing that counts is when God works through the power of the Holy Spirit. The Holy Spirit is the only one that gives power.

Paul Ferguson the Fighter
Chapter 18

Will God Work in Divided Churches?

In Gainesville, Florida, I held a meeting for Pastor Mack Richardson. Half of the church sat on one side and the other half sat on the other side. The building was filled all the time. Half of them were against the pastor and half were for him. They were against each other. I was there for twelve days, Wednesday through Sunday week. Over sixty people made a profession of faith with the church divided like that.

I was with Charles Betting in Charleston, South Carolina. The biggest majority of the people were against the pastor and still we had a large number of people to make a profession of faith in the meeting. It is unusual for God to bless a meeting with such a number of professions of faith and the church divided.

But I think it happened in both of these places because the people realized they needed to pray. Both sides began to pray. I started the meetings by preaching on prayer and revival, and I spent a lot of time in prayer. The people from one side of the church would gather on one side and pray. The people from the other side would gather on the other side and pray.

After the meeting in Gainesville, Pastor Mack Richardson stayed on for a good long while, whereas Pastor Charles Betting in Charleston, South Carolina left the church. Even after the meeting, Pastor Betting could not get the backing he needed to stay as pastor.

I cannot understand the above church situations of division, and yet God moved in conviction upon the hearts of lost people. It usually doesn't happen that way. We've heard the old saying that God moves in mysterious ways, and that is what happened in these two churches.

Get Your Crutches Out of the Car.

Pastor George Cleansing at Dart Gospel Church in Dart, Ohio, was a great big man, about 250 pounds or more. Glen Saunders worked with him as an associate. Somehow, Glen got it in his head before I arrived for the meeting that I was crippled and on crutches. I felt like I was crippled by the time I got to the pastor's house after driving some seven hundred miles. I had delayed leaving home because I wanted to stay with my family as long as I could. As I got out of the car my legs were tired and stiff. Pastor George grabbed me and started to help me inside. He said, "Get your crutches and bring them along." I pushed him out of the way and said, "Are you crazy? What's wrong with you?" And then I found out the other preacher had told him I was crippled. I said, "Well, I'm not crippled now...." And that's been about twenty years ago. This was also an unusual meeting with many professions of faith.

Some Meetings Plow up the Hard Ground.

I had many meetings where we didn't have a great number of people saved. But as I have already told, I had many meetings where more people would be saved after I left than were saved during the meeting. It would go on for some time after I left with people continuing to be saved.

Sometimes people are not ready to be saved. You do a lot of praying and still you don't have many saved, but after I left there would be more people saved. God has a purpose in that. I can't explain it. We had three meetings in all the time of my preaching when we didn't have anybody to make a profession of faith in the meeting.

Riverview, Michigan—Wayne Dunn.

The Ford place was closed down, and it was a bad time for the economy. Everybody in the church was out of work. The meeting had already been scheduled and, instead of canceling the meeting, they went to the bank and borrowed enough money to pay my expenses and to give me a good offering. They had the faith to do that, saying, "God will supply." We had over fifty people saved, and it was not a big church.

Right after the meeting was over, some wealthy man in the church donated about two thousand dollars to the church – over three times as much as they had borrowed for me. They paid my bus fair round-trip and several hundred dollars as an offering. They said they couldn't have an evangelist come without paying him, because that's the only way an evangelist has of getting any money. So they borrowed the money for the evangelist, and then they more than tripled into the church treasury what they had borrowed by faith. That just shows how the Lord blesses when people trust Him.

I've had so many people say, "Well, we can't have a meeting because we don't have the money." But these people went and borrowed the money by faith, believing that God would supply the money that was needed. I believe that's why God honored them and let some man donate the money. Now, most of the time in churches, they don't usually get money from wealthy people.

I was in a meeting in Ohio and there was a wealthy woman there - a *very wealthy* woman. I have reason to believe that she was a billionaire or close to it. She gave the pastor and me a special present of ten dollars a piece, and she gave five dollars in every offering. That's all she gave. The reason I tell that story is because people think you have to get big offerings from wealthy people to get along in church, and it usually doesn't happen that way. It's just ordinary people that give the most. This lady (above) came to all the prayer meetings. She was there every time. But she never gave anybody over ten dollars at a time. I guess that's the reason she was so rich and we're so poor (chuckle).

Sour Preachers.

A certain preacher was a good friend of mine, and I was with him in meetings in South Carolina and again in Alabama. I hate to say this, but this preacher and another preacher in Georgia were the two most critical preachers I've ever met in my whole life. I don't care if you put their names in there. [Note: *I have withheld the names and their towns. dc*] Some preachers get old and critical and cranky, but these two preachers were young men. They were critical and criticized everybody. These preachers were my friends, but they had a sour tongue.

I believe that it ought to be told that a critical person doesn't have faith. They don't believe God. They're trying to build themselves up to be equal with everybody else. Now, there are times to stand against sin; there are times to be against wrong. But I believe a critical attitude is a sign of a lack of faith and a lack of thinking that they are a capable person.

You've heard me say that I've never drunk any whiskey in my life, and I grew up in a whiskey section of the country. But I don't think that anybody that got drunk would be any worse than a person with a critical attitude. That's a hard statement to make, but I believe it. I'm not going to take it back, because it's true. I believe God can forgive it. My pastor, Brother Ellis, used to preach on this, and I've said a lot about him – one of the greatest preachers I've ever met, J. T. Ellis at McConnell Road Baptist Church in Greensboro, North Carolina.

Brother Ellis used to use the following illustration. A man used to come and criticize the preacher, and one day he came to the preacher and asked him to forgive him. The preacher said, "I'll forgive you, but I will you do me a favor?" The man said, "I'll do anything. I was wrong. I've been talking about you for a long time. I've done a horrible thing. I'll do anything you say." The preacher said, "Go get me one of those old feather pillows." The man brought the preacher a feather pillow. The preacher said, "Tear it open." He tore it open. The preacher said, "Now go outside and scatter it." The man went outside and scattered the feathers everywhere and the strong wind carried the feathers away in every direction. The preacher said: "Go pick them up." The man said, "I can't pick those feathers up! Man! I'd never find them." The preacher said, "That's right. That's the way your critical attitude and your critical talk are. The wind has scattered your talk everywhere, and different people have repeated it and added stories to it." And that's the danger of a critical attitude. That helped me! That helped me a whole lot about not having a critical attitude. I didn't think at the time it was helping me.

Charlotte, NC—Dr. Charles Foshee—Ridgeview Baptist Church

Dr. Charles Foshee is one of the best friends I have. He's about fourteen years younger than I am, and we went to Bible school together at Tennessee Temple Bible School. We used to let him ride with us from school in Chattanooga, Tennessee when we would go back home in Graham, North Carolina. He finished his four years in Bible school and left Tennessee Temple a year before I did. I stayed and finished my college degree.

Brother Charles had a church in Cleveland, Tennessee. He had me there in a meeting, with several professions of faith. He was a good pastor, even when he first started out. Then he went to Charlotte, North Carolina and started a church. I was with him six or seven times. Brother Charles ended up just a few miles from the Northside Baptist Church, pastored by Jack Hudson.

In one of the meetings he came to me and said, "Ferguson, we've got to pray seriously for Mr. Tyler - Carl Tyler. This man and his whole family come to the church. His wife is saved. His children are saved. He's a good moral man. He doesn't smoke, drink, or curse, and is more faithful in church than nine-tenths of my members. I can't understand it. We've got to start praying for him now, and if the Lord leads us, let's go and talk to him."

The man came to church every night. I talked to him, but the Lord never directed me to talk to him about being saved. Lots of times men have to be talked to individually, and mostly it's in the home that you'll win a lot of them to the Lord. Brother Charles and I kept praying for Carl Tyler as the meeting was going on. We'd had people saved. One woman who had lived a rough life came every service, and one night after the service I talked to her and she was saved. She was baptized and became faithful in attending church until the day she died.

We decided on a day to go talk to Mr. Tyler. He was working in his garden. I was standing there and he had an extra hoe. I said, "Mr. Tyler, let me see if I can do a little of that." I worked with him a while and dug a little, and he said, "Aw, you don't do that!" And I said, "No, it makes me think of the old days when my Daddy made me hoe corn and I hated that stuff."

So we went over to the house, and I took the Scripture and showed him Romans 5:12: *"Wherefore, as by one man sin entered into the world, and death by sin; and so death passed upon all men, for that all have sinned:"* Then I showed him some other verses and I Peter 2:24: *"Who his own self bare our sins in his own body on the tree, that we, being dead to sins, should live unto righteousness: by whose stripes ye were healed."*

I used several others, which I won't give here, but I used Romans 10:13: *"For whosoever shall call upon the name of the Lord shall be saved."* I explained to him that he was a sinner,

224

although he was a good moral man and went to church. I told him that if he died he would go to Hell, and he said, "I know that." I showed him other verses: 1 John 5:1: *"Whosoever believeth that Jesus is the Christ is born of God..."* and Acts 2:21: *"And it shall come to pass, that whosoever shall call on the name of the Lord shall be saved."* Then I got down on my knees and we prayed.

And then I said, "Are you willing to be saved?" The preacher liked to have had a heart attack, and I did too. We went there believing he would be saved, but then when he said, "Yes," we were surprised. That's like the people in Acts 12 where they were praying for Peter to get out of jail, and then they didn't believe it when he knocked at the door of the house where they were praying for him.

Mr. Tyler accepted the Lord, and I said, "You've been going to church regularly and now you need to go join the church and be baptized," and he did. He's buried now, but that man had a great testimony 'til the day he died. He even tithed his money before he was saved.

This brings up a question as to why he was such a moral man and so close to the church and yet had never been saved. He said, "Most of the people didn't witness to me because I was such a good moral man. When you all came over to the house, that was the first time anybody ever talked to me about being saved. They would talk to me about my need of being saved, but didn't tell me how to be saved."

Later, in a different meeting at the same church, there was a man named James Helms. Mr. Helms had been pretty rough, but he had quit all that stuff and was a pretty moral man. He was really a hard one. I spoke to him every night and talked to him, was friendly with him. Pastor Foshee told me, "I don't think we ought to go see him. I don't think it would do any good." So we didn't go to his house. The church had moved from the longer eight-day meetings to Sunday-through-Wednesday meetings, and you had to do what you were going to do in a hurry.

Going After Helms One More Time.
The last night of the meeting was the only time Mr. Helms didn't come to the meeting. I went home there, and Pastor Foshee

and I talked a while after the meeting was over. I had never been with Foshee when he didn't give me a substantial offering. He believed in that. But as I went to my room I became so burdened about that man that I knew I couldn't have had that much burden. God had put a burden on me for Mr. Helms. I prayed most of the night.

Brother Foshee was supposed to come after me early the next morning. He is a real man of God, but he said, "Brother Paul, I don't think it would do any good for us to go see that man. I don't believe Mr. Helms will ever be saved." I said, "Brother Foshee, I differ on that. You and I always agree, and you're a good man, but I want to go see that man. God has just put that on my heart, and if this man dies and I don't go to see him, his blood will be on my hands. I want to go whether it does any good or not, but I believe it'll do some good." If I hadn't prayed all night I might have believed it wouldn't have done any good, but after praying like that I believed it would do some good.

God had made it plain for me to go, so I went. Mr. Helms invited us into the house. I didn't stay very long. I just said, "Mr. Helms, the Lord willing, I've got to catch a plane but, I know the Lord wants me to talk to you. Will let me talk to you?" He said, "Yes sir." He sat down. I went through the plan of salvation. He knew he was a sinner and that Christ had paid the price for his past, present, and future sins as set forth in II Corinthians 1:10: *"Who delivered us from so great a death, and doth deliver: in whom we trust that he will yet deliver us..."*

I brought God's Word to him and showed him that if he was willing to be saved, he could be saved. I gave him the Scriptures I had given Carl Tyler, but a few more. After I finished, I prayed and asked the Lord to touch him. When I finished praying I noticed that he was stirred. I said, "Are you willing to be saved?" And he said, "Yes sir." He accepted the Lord as his Savior and was baptized.

But before I could read any Bible verses about assurance of salvation, he said, "I've something to do right quick!" He ran to the telephone and called his wife at work, and said, "Honey, I've just accepted the Lord, Praise God! Hallelujah!" He was excited, just praising God. You could hear her over the phone. That man is still in the church today, a faithful member.

That just shows the importance of obeying God and the importance of talking to men one-on-one. He told me later that he believed he would have gone to Hell if I hadn't talked to him that day.

My Grandson Gets Saved!

Isaiah Brown is the pastor now at People's Baptist Church of Dalton, Georgia. I can't remember the name of the former pastor. My youngest boy, Mark, has two sons – Tommy and John. John was five or six years old and wanted to go to a meeting with me. I always bought him a hamburger when we were out together. He and Tommy went with me, and also a friend, Tim Daniel. Tim came from a family of ten or twelve. They were talking about which one would sit in the front seat with me in the car and the others would sit in the back going down there.

I preached a message on salvation and began to give the invitation. The Lord put it on my heart to go to John. Usually you don't go to children when they're young like that, but God put it on my heart to go to him. I walked back and said, "John, are you unsaved?" And he said, "Yes, Granddaddy I am." I said, "Well, would you let me take the Bible and show you how to be saved?"

He went to crying and then he said, "Granddaddy, everybody has been telling me I needed to be saved, but you're the first one that ever offered to show me how." And he went forward and accepted the Lord with a good experience and made a public profession of faith right then. Of course, he didn't join that church, but went where his daddy went to church and was baptized. He's still going on in his walk with the Lord and knows he's saved. You know, a lot of times when children get saved, when they become a teenager they make another profession. Later, they'll realize that they were saved all the time. I was saved young.

Now, let me tell you about the change in the child's life. They were arguing down there about who would sit with me in the front and who would sit in the back. And John said, "Aw, I don't care where I sit. I would be willing to be out in the snow without anything on for two hours just because I'm saved. I don't care

227

whether I sit in the front or the back just so I know I'm saved and going to Heaven through the blood of the Lord Jesus Christ."

That's one of the greatest experiences of a child I've ever seen beside little Sammy that I mentioned earlier. Tommy was already saved. John is about fifteen now, and he's never made another profession of faith and is still living for the Lord. His daddy, Mark, sees to it that he goes to church regularly.

Humor in the Pulpit.

Dr. John Hermann, professor of psychology at Tennessee Temple College, was the first one that talked about how we ought to use humor, especially in the day we are living in now. He said you ought to use humor to get people's attention, and especially young people. Dr. Hermann was a brilliant man and he had a heart for young people. So I would tell good, clean jokes before the services, and I got criticized for it, especially in the south. So I went to the Lord about it, and He put it on my heart as plain as if He had spoken audibly to use humor in my messages, and I've used humor ever since. Now, since I'm older, I don't guess I make many older people mad when I tell jokes, but I used to make a lot of people mad, telling jokes.

Some of them said they would shoot me. They were afraid to jump on me. In some of my best meetings, some of the people would get mad because I told jokes and later, they would come and tell me. I'll tell you, though, that I didn't tell any jokes over at Stevenson, Alabama that night at Centennial Baptist Church when things broke loose over there.

I still tell jokes. I heard about a Temple graduate that went off into the Seventh Day Adventists, who told about a meeting where somebody told a joke and it ruined the whole service and the Spirit left. Now, it wasn't the Spirit of God. I don't think you could tell a shady story and not grieve the Holy Spirit.

I heard a man in Florida talk about how hard he was and how many things he did and said he didn't intend to come to any of the meetings. He had a high-paying job and was a wealthy man. The first night he came was just because his wife wanted him to come, and he came every night then to hear me tell the jokes. He said, "It relaxed me and I could think and hear. I was so busy during the day that I couldn't concentrate when I came to the meetings. I was too tired. But when you told those stories while you were preaching, I'd get tickled and laugh so much I would get something out of the meeting, so I came every night."

Now, stories won't bring the power of God. Stories can get the attention of the people. The power of God comes through prayer and the work of the Holy Spirit. But He'll use those things. Not everybody is alike. I've got a preacher friend, and if he told a joke they'd all freeze to death while he was telling it. He can't tell a joke. He's not made that way. It's just natural for me to tell a joke.

And, some people, if I don't tell a few jokes, will say, "What's the matter with you? You sick or something? You didn't tell anything funny tonight." So I don't think telling jokes is wrong. Some people should and some people shouldn't. I tell people that the reason I can tell a joke and other preachers can't is because, when I tell a joke, the people wanted to laugh anyway, and I'm so ugly it gives them an outlet to laugh.

I told that one time to a woman who criticized me all the time for telling jokes and she got tickled about it. She told me later that, after that, she enjoyed my telling jokes.

Meetings in Other Places.

Brother Paul held meetings in places and with pastors that he could not remember, or he lost the records. He had a lot of preacher-friends and a lot of churches that loved him. In making the audio tapes he was very much concerned that he might leave someone out. Several times he mentioned that. At last, he knew that he was leaving some out. We had met for six days, one day a week for six weeks, ALL DAY – and he labored hard to remember forty years and to put it together in some meaningful way.

If he was with you in a meeting and your name is not in the book, we would like to know. If your name is in the book and you can tell us more, we would like to know about that.

Remembering Names and Places.

I'm trying to remember as many names as I can, but I just can't remember them all. I preached for forty-some years, and I just can't remember it all. I don't want to leave anybody out. I'm concerned about that. I kept records of my meetings, but I lost one of my record books a few years ago, and I regret that very much. I'll try to remember all I can and, also, consult the records I have.

Arizona – Bill Duncan.

That was a real outstanding meeting.

Arizona; and Tennessee, North Chattanooga, – John Brown

Some people saved, but not as many as in some of the other meetings with him.

California, San Diego – John Brown.

That's the home of the San Diego Chargers. I went to the

stadium and watched them play. Good meeting there.

Florida, Gainesville – R. E. Tease

I keep records of my meetings and, in one of the meetings here, we had seventy people make a profession of faith. Brother Tease and I grew to be good friends, and I was with him four or five times. I was never in a meeting with him that we didn't have unusual things to happen. He said, "Every time you've come to the church, we've not had under sixty people make a profession of faith." Brother Tease has gone on to be with the Lord, and his son is pastor there now.

Florida, Miami – Several Meetings.

I was with Marvin Gochenour in Miami, Florida and had several meetings in Miami. I fought my second professional fight in Miami Beach, Florida.

Georgia, Jefferson – Gerald Mitton.

D.C.: *Gerald was a native of Canada and migrated to Tennessee Temple, a good friend of Brother Paul. Do not know about meetings with him. Lives in Jefferson, Georgia.*

Georgia, Monroe – Mina Davis.

Mina lived next door to us in Chattanooga while I was an evangelist, and I was with him in several meetings. I knew his wife, Betty, before they were married. We know their children, Rebecca, Lee, and Ruth. I was with Mina Davis in South Carolina at the Liberty Baptist Church. I met Roger Redman there. Mina has been a close friend to me over several years. He was a pastor also of the First Baptist Church in Creed Coor, Illinois. He was a pastor also of First Baptist Church in Linton, Ohio. I was with him in Louisiana. In nearly every place I was with him, we had people to make a profession of faith. I didn't want to leave him out. *[Mina and Betty live in Monroe, Ga. dc]*

Georgia – Lockhart

Georgia, Valdosta – A Camp.

George Eager had me every year for three or four years, and we always had good meetings there with many professions of faith.

Georgia, Valdosta – Gene Wiseheart.
We had an outstanding meeting there. I lost my book that records that meeting. We had an outstanding number of people saved, well over fifty. Somebody canceled a meeting and I was able to be with him. In the first few years I preached, I had more cancellations than I did in later years.

Illinois – Camps.

Illinois – Chanc Ickes.

Illinois – Loudersport – Davis.

Illinois – Tennessee, Middletown – Dale Montgomery.
I was with him about three different times. Two of his boys live close to me in Chattanooga now. I was with him once in Middletown, Tennessee.

Maryland, Baltimore – Statesboro, Georgia – John Hanna.
I was with John Hanna five times – maybe six times – in Baltimore, Maryland. We had some good meetings there. Then he moved to Statesboro, Georgia, and I was in two meetings with him down there and had good meetings. John Hanna is a real, outstanding man who loves the Lord and wants to do the will of the Lord.

Michigan, Detroit – Tom Turley.
Several meetings.

Michigan, Flat Rock – H. H. Clark – First Baptist Church.
Quite a few people saved in this meeting.

Michigan, Pontiac – W. B. Lawrence – and also Pastor Dickerson.
In one of the meetings at Pontiac, Michigan, the snow was five

to six feet deep. One place in Ohio was deeper.

Michigan, Rochester – Don Evilsizer.
A good meeting, but the weather was real bad. A few more in Michigan.

New York, Johnstown – Maryland – R. R. Richardson.
I was with him two or three times in Johnstown, New York.

North Carolina, Elizabethtown – A Camp.
Al Whitted was an evangelist that operated a camp in Elizabethtown, North Carolina. We had a good number of professions of faith.

Oklahoma, Tulsa – A. W. Lockhart.
A large number of people saved there.

Oklahoma, Tulsa – Charles L. Pack.

Pennsylvania, Novert – Charles Horton.

South Carolina – Arizona – Hamilton.
This meeting was in the early days right after I had finished school. We went about three weeks with many professions of faith. I was with him again in Arizona. Later, Hugh went to Alaska as a missionary.

South Carolina, Charleston – Coast Guard.
I was stationed in Charleston, South Carolina in the Mounted Beach Patrol of the U. S. Coast Guard during the Second World War. My wife and I lived there for a while. I fought several times in Charleston, and won all those fights by a knock-out. Much later I had several meetings in Charleston, with pastors Howard Knowles, Bob Marshall, and Bob Sinset.

South Carolina, Summerville – Jesse Powers.
Tennessee, Chattanooga – A Camp.
I've been to just one service at Camp Joy while David Bragg was the director. Camp Joy is on Highway 58 out from Chattanooga, at Harrison, I believe. Durwood Williams was at the camp while I was still in school at Tennessee Temple, and I went there back then. I've lost one of my record books that records a lot of camps

I went to, but I always had good experiences at the camps. The young people liked me because I used humor.

Tennessee, Chattanooga – Marshall Dykes – Central Avenue Baptist Church.

I must mention Pastor Marshall Dykes, a good man and a teacher at Tennessee Temple. He pastored at Central Avenue Baptist Church and had me for a meeting. He's gone to be with the Lord.

Tennessee, Dickson – George Rye.

I was with George Rye in Dickson, Tennessee. George rented the City Auditorium, and we had several unusual things to happen there. There was a man there who put a loaded gun to his head and snapped the gun five times, and it didn't fire. He decided the gun was no good and turned it away from him and pulled the trigger, and it fired. He got right with the Lord and got up in the meeting and told the story, and he told it again and again to anybody that would listen. He said he knew that God was keeping him for some reason, and he did witness a whole lot.

Tennessee, Tennessee Ridge – Dan Carr.

We had a fairly good meeting there. That's where I met Forest Rye. He was a go-getter and a good man. George Rye was his nephew and was the one who led Forest to the Lord.

West Virginia, Marion – W. H. Anderson

A very good meeting here.

"If you have information on facts, locations, people, spelling, dates or anything else, please send information to: Dan Carr, 1320 County Road 891 - Flat Rock, AL 35966. Email: dan@dancarr.org or "dancarr@farmerstel. com. Phones: (256) 632-3513 (Flat Rock); (910) 692-8311 (Calvary Memorial Church/Calvary Christian School) Mon.-Fri. 8:30-3:30."

May God Bless You—
May God Bless America!

Paul Ferguson the Fighter
Chapter 20

Scriptures used in this book.
(See suggestions for memorizing in Chapter 21.)

Exo 11:6-7 And there shall be a great cry throughout all the land of Egypt, such as there was none like it, nor shall be like it any more. (7) But against any of the children of Israel shall not a dog move his tongue, against man or beast: that ye may know how that the LORD doth put a difference between the Egyptians and Israel.

Num 22:32-33 And the angel of the LORD said unto him, Wherefore hast thou smitten thine ass these three times? behold, I went out to withstand thee, because *thy* way is perverse before me: (33) And the ass saw me, and turned from me these three times: unless she had turned from me, surely now also I had slain thee, and saved her alive.

1Sa 16:7 But the LORD said unto Samuel, Look not on his countenance, or on the height of his stature; because I have refused him: for *the LORD seeth* not as man seeth; for man looketh on the outward appearance, but the LORD looketh on the heart.

2Ch 7:14 If my people, which are called by my name, shall humble themselves, and pray, and seek my face, and turn from their wicked ways; then will I hear from heaven, and will forgive their sin, and will heal their land.

Neh 4:8-9 And conspired all of them together to come *and* to fight against Jerusalem, and to hinder it. Nevertheless we made our prayer unto our God, and set a watch against them day and night, because of them.

Psa 100:4 Enter into his gates with thanksgiving, *and* into his courts with praise: be thankful unto him, *and* bless his name.

Psa 127:2 *It is* vain for you to rise up early, to sit up late, to eat the bread of sorrows: *for* so he giveth his beloved sleep.

Isa 30:21 And thine ears shall hear a word behind thee, saying, This *is* the way, walk ye in it, when ye turn to the right hand, and when ye turn to the left.

Isa 56:7 Even them will I bring to my holy mountain, and make them joyful in my house of prayer: their burnt offerings and their sacrifices *shall be* accepted upon mine altar; for mine house shall be called a house of prayer for all people.

Isa 61:3 To appoint unto them that mourn in Zion, to give unto them beauty for ashes, the oil of joy for mourning, the garment of praise for the spirit of heaviness; that they might be called trees of righteousness, the planting of the LORD, that he might be glorified.

Jer 29:13 And ye shall seek me, and find *me*, when ye shall search for me with all your heart.

Jer 32:27 Behold, I *am* the LORD, the God of all flesh: is there any thing too hard for me?

Jer 33:3 Call unto me, and I will answer thee, and show thee great and mighty things, which thou knowest not.

Eze 9:4 And the LORD said unto him, Go through the midst of the city, through the midst of Jerusalem, and set a mark upon the foreheads of the men that sigh and that cry for all the abominations that be done in the midst thereof.

Eze 22:30 And I sought for a man among them, that should make up the hedge, and stand in the gap before me for the land, that I should not destroy it: but I found none.

Eze 24:15-27 (Ezekiel's wife died and he was not allowed to weep – as a sign to Israel. They would not be able to bury their dead for the judgment that was coming upon them.)

Nah 1:3 The LORD *is* slow to anger, and great in power, and will not at all acquit *the wicked*: the LORD hath his way in the whirlwind and in the storm, and the clouds *are* the dust of his feet.

Mat 9:37-38 Then saith he unto his disciples, The harvest truly *is* plenteous, but the laborers *are* few; (38) Pray ye therefore the Lord of the harvest, that he will send forth laborers into his harvest.

Mat 18:6 But whoso shall offend one of these little ones which believe in me, it were better for him that a millstone were hanged about his neck, and *that* he were drowned in the depth of the sea.

Mat 21:13 And said unto them, It is written, My house shall be called the house of prayer; but ye have made it a den of thieves.

Mat 21:22 And all things, whatsoever ye shall ask in prayer, believing, ye shall receive.

Mat 22:37-38 Jesus said unto him, Thou shalt love the Lord thy God with all thy heart, and with all thy soul, and with all thy mind. (38) This is the first and great commandment.

Mat 27:5 And he cast down the pieces of silver in the temple, and departed, and went and hanged himself.

Mar 1:35 And in the morning, rising up a great while before day, he went out, and departed into a solitary place, and there prayed.

Mar 8:36-37 For what shall it profit a man, if he shall gain the whole world, and lose his own soul? (37) Or what shall a man give in exchange for his soul?

Mar 8:38 Whosoever therefore shall be ashamed of me and of my words in this adulterous and sinful generation; of him also shall the Son of man be ashamed, when he cometh in the glory of his Father with the holy angels.

Mar 9:41 For whosoever shall give you a cup of water to drink in my name, because ye belong to Christ, verily I say unto you, he shall not lose his reward.

Mar 11:17 And he taught, saying unto them, Is it not written, My house shall be called of all nations the house of prayer? but ye have made it a den of thieves.

Mar 16:15 And he said unto them, Go ye into all the world, and preach the gospel to every creature.

Luk 2:19 But Mary kept all these things, and pondered *them* in her heart.

Luk 10:37 And he said, He that showed mercy on him. Then said Jesus unto him, Go, and do thou likewise.

Luk 16:19-31 There was a certain rich man, which was clothed in purple and fine linen, and fared sumptuously every day:..(the rich man who went to hell and talked with Lazarus about bringing him water).

Luk 18:1 And he spake a parable unto them *to this end,* that men ought always to pray, and not to faint;

Luk 19:46 Saying unto them, It is written, My house is the house of prayer: but ye have made it a den of thieves.

Luk 22:44 And being in an agony he prayed more earnestly: and his sweat was as it were great drops of blood falling down to the ground.

Joh 1:11-12 He came unto his own, and his own received him not. (12) But as many as received him, to them gave he power to become the sons of God, *even* to them that believe on his name:
Joh 3:16 For God so loved the world, that he gave his only

begotten Son, that whosoever believeth in him should not perish, but have everlasting life.

Joh 3:36 He that believeth on the Son hath everlasting life: and he that believeth not the Son shall not see life; but the wrath of God abideth on him.

Joh 4:38 I sent you to reap that whereon ye bestowed no labor: other men labored, and ye are entered into their labors.

Joh 5:24 Verily, verily, I say unto you, He that heareth my word, and believeth on him that sent me, hath everlasting life, and shall not come into condemnation; but is passed from death unto life.

Joh 6:37 All that the Father giveth me shall come to me; and him that cometh to me I will in no wise cast out.

Joh 6:44 No man can come to me, except the Father which hath sent me draw him: and I will raise him up at the last day.

Joh 6:47 Verily, verily, I say unto you, He that believeth on me hath everlasting life.

Joh 13:27 And after the sop Satan entered into him. Then said Jesus unto him, That thou doest, do quickly.

Joh 16:8 And when he is come, he will reprove the world of sin, and of righteousness, and of judgment:

Act 2:21 And it shall come to pass, *that* whosoever shall call on the name of the Lord shall be saved.

Act 6:3-4 Wherefore, brethren, look ye out among you seven men of honest report, full of the Holy Ghost and wisdom, whom we may appoint over this business. (4) But we will give ourselves continually to prayer, and to the ministry of the word.

Act 8:1 And Saul was consenting unto his death. And at that time there was a great persecution against the church which was at Jerusalem; and they were all scattered abroad throughout the regions of Judea and Samaria, except the apostles.

Act 8:3-4 As for Saul, he made havoc of the church, entering into every house, and haling men and women committed *them* to prison. (4) Therefore they that were scattered abroad went every where preaching the word.

Act 9:16 For I will show him how great things he must suffer for my name's sake.

Act 14:22 Confirming the souls of the disciples, *and* exhorting them to continue in the faith, and that we must through much tribulation enter into the kingdom of God.

Act 16:29-32 Then he called for a light, and sprang in, and came trembling, and fell down before Paul and Silas, (30) And brought them out, and said, Sirs, what must I do to be saved? (31) And they said, Believe on the Lord Jesus Christ, and thou shalt be saved, and thy house. (32) And they spake unto him the word of the Lord, and to all that were in his house.

Act 20:21 Testifying both to the Jews, and also to the Greeks, repentance toward God, and faith toward our Lord Jesus Christ.

Rom 3:9-12 What then? are we better *than they*? No, in no wise: for we have before proved both Jews and Gentiles, that they are all under sin; (10) As it is written, There is none righteous, no, not one: (11) There is none that understandeth, there is none that seeketh after God. (12) They are all gone out of the way, they are together become unprofitable; there is none that doeth good, no, not one.

Rom 3:22-23 Even the righteousness of God *which is* by faith of Jesus Christ unto all and upon all them that believe: for there is no difference: (23) For all have sinned, and come short of the glory of God;

Rom 5:12 Wherefore, as by one man sin entered into the world, and death by sin; and so death passed upon all men, for that all have sinned:

Rom 5:21 That as sin hath reigned unto death, even so might grace reign through righteousness unto eternal life by Jesus Christ our Lord.

Rom 8:14 For as many as are led by the Spirit of God, they are the sons of God.

Rom 8:17 And if children, then heirs; heirs of God, and joint-heirs with Christ; if so be that we suffer with *him,* that we may be also glorified together.

Rom 8:26-27 Likewise the Spirit also helpeth our infirmities: for we know not what we should pray for as we ought: but the Spirit itself maketh intercession for us with groanings which cannot be uttered. (27) And he that searcheth the hearts knoweth what *is* the mind of the Spirit, because he maketh intercession for the saints according to *the will of* God.

Rom 9:2 That I have great heaviness and continual sorrow in my heart.

Rom 10:9-13 That if thou shalt confess with thy mouth the Lord Jesus, and shalt believe in thine heart that God hath raised him from the dead, thou shalt be saved. (10) For with the heart man believeth unto righteousness; and with the mouth confession is made unto salvation. (11) For the Scripture saith, Whosoever believeth on him shall not be ashamed. (12) For there is no difference between the Jew and the Greek: for the same Lord over all is rich unto all that call upon him. (13) For whosoever shall call upon the name of the Lord shall be saved.

Rom 14:7 For none of us liveth to himself, and no man dieth to himself.

1Co 1:26-29 For ye see your calling, brethren, how that not many wise men after the flesh, not many mighty, not many noble, *are called*: (27) But God hath chosen the foolish things of the world to confound the wise; and God hath chosen the weak things of the world to confound the things which are mighty; (28) And base things of the world, and things which are despised, hath God chosen, *yea,* and things which are not, to bring to naught things that are: (29) That no flesh should glory in his presence.

1Co 3:6-9 I have planted, Apollos watered; but God gave the increase. (7) So then neither is he that planteth any thing, neither he that watereth; but God that giveth the increase. (8) Now he that planteth and he that watereth are one: and every man shall receive his own reward according to his own labor. (9) For we are laborers together with God: ye are God's husbandry, *ye are* God's building.

1Co 5:5 To deliver such a one unto Satan for the destruction of the flesh, that the spirit may be saved in the day of the Lord Jesus.

1Co 12:7-8 But the manifestation of the Spirit is given to every man to profit withal. (8) For to one is given by the Spirit the word of wisdom; to another the word of knowledge by the same Spirit;

2Co 1:9-10 But we had the sentence of death in ourselves, that we should not trust in ourselves, but in God which raiseth the dead: (10) Who delivered us from so great a death, and doth deliver: in whom we trust that he will yet deliver *us;*

2Co 5:21 For he hath made him *to be* sin for us, who knew no sin; that we might be made the righteousness of God in him.

Gal 1:4 Who gave himself for our sins, that he might deliver us from this present evil world, according to the will of God and our Father:

Gal 2:20 I am crucified with Christ: nevertheless I live; yet not I, but Christ liveth in me: and the life which I now live in the flesh I live by the faith of the Son of God, who loved me, and gave himself for me.

Gal 4:6 And because ye are sons, God hath sent forth the Spirit of his Son into your hearts, crying, Abba, Father.

Gal 6:9 And let us not be weary in well doing: for in due season we shall reap, if we faint not.

Eph 6:18 Praying always with all prayer and supplication in the Spirit, and watching thereunto with all perseverance and supplication for all saints;

Phi 1:6 Being confident of this very thing, that he which hath begun a good work in you will perform *it* until the day of Jesus Christ:

Phi 1:29 For unto you it is given in the behalf of Christ, not only to believe on him, but also to suffer for his sake;

1Th 5:17 Pray without ceasing.

2Ti 1:12 For the which cause I also suffer these things: nevertheless I am not ashamed: for I know whom I have believed, and am persuaded that he is able to keep that which I have committed unto him against that day.

Heb 2:8 Thou hast put all things in subjection under his feet. For in that he put all in subjection under him, he left nothing *that is* not put under him. But now we see not yet all things put under him.

Heb 4:16 Let us therefore come boldly unto the throne of grace, that we may obtain mercy, and find grace to help in time of need.

Jam 4:8-11 Draw nigh to God, and he will draw nigh to you. Cleanse *your* hands, *ye* sinners; and purify *your* hearts, *ye* double minded. (9) Be afflicted, and mourn, and weep: let your laughter be turned to mourning, and *your* joy to heaviness. (10) Humble yourselves in the sight of the Lord, and he shall lift you up. (11) Speak not evil one of another, brethren. He that speaketh evil of *his* brother, and judgeth his brother, speaketh evil of the law, and judgeth the law: but if thou judge the law, thou art not a doer of the law, but a judge.

Jam 4:15 For that ye *ought* to say, If the Lord will, we shall live, and do this, or that.

1Pe 1.5 Who are kept by the power of God through faith unto salvation ready to be revealed in the last time.

1Pe 2:24 Who his own self bare our sins in his own body on the tree, that we, being dead to sins, should live unto righteousness: by whose stripes ye were healed.

1Pe 3:7 Likewise, ye husbands, dwell with *them* according to knowledge, giving honor unto the wife, as unto the weaker vessel, and as being heirs together of the grace of life; that your prayers be not hindered.

2Pe 3:9 The Lord is not slack concerning his promise, as some men count slackness; but is longsuffering to us-ward, not willing that any should perish, but that all should come to repentance.

1Jo 1:7 But if we walk in the light, as he is in the light, we have fellowship one with another, and the blood of Jesus Christ his Son cleanseth us from all sin.

1Jo 3:23-24 And this is his commandment, That we should believe on the name of his Son Jesus Christ, and love one another, as he gave us commandment. (24) And he that keepeth his commandments dwelleth in him, and he in him. And hereby we know that he abideth in us, by the Spirit which he hath given us.

1Jo 5:1 Whosoever believeth that Jesus is the Christ is born of

God: and every one that loveth him that begat loveth him also that is begotten of him.

Jud 1:20 But ye, beloved, building up yourselves on your most holy faith, praying in the Holy Ghost,

Jud 1:24 Now unto him that is able to keep you from falling, and to present *you* faultless before the presence of his glory with exceeding joy,

Rev 2:10 Fear none of those things which thou shalt suffer: behold, the devil shall cast *some* of you into prison, that ye may be tried; and ye shall have tribulation ten days; be thou faithful unto death, and I will give thee a crown of life.

Rev 3:20 Behold, I stand at the door, and knock: if any man hear my voice, and open the door, I will come in to him, and will sup with him, and he with me.

Rev 22:17 And the Spirit and the bride say, Come. And let him that heareth say, Come. And let him that is athirst come. And whosoever will, let him take the water of life freely.

Suggestions for Memorizing Scripture are in Chapter 21. More suggestions can be found in www.dancarr.org.

Hiding God's Word...
(As Part of Your Lifestyle)
Chapter 21

Paul Ferguson Memorized Over Eight Thousand Verses of Scripture and used them in his sermons, his personal witnessing, and in living the Christian life. He told me he read in one of John R. Rice's books that preachers tend to be lazy and therefore neglect to memorize the Word of God. That statement had a great influence on Paul's life. He would not be lazy. In Chapter 20 we listed all the verses gleaned from *Paul Ferguson the Fighter*.

If you are interested in memorizing Bible verses, you will find simple and effective suggestions below to help you memorize. More information can be found at www.dancarr.org. Click on *Bible Memorization*. That section will continue to grow as continue writing and gathering good material. There is no right way and wrong way to memorize. However, some methods are more productive than others.

Dr. Lee Roberson Believes in Memorizing Scripture. On December 3, 2005, at the Southwide Baptist Fellowship in Chattanooga, Tennessee, Dr. Lee Roberson (age 96) preached on: "*Thy Word have I hid in mine heart that I might not sin against thee" (Psalm 119:11)*. He still believes we should memorize and obey the Word of God.

This short chapter is all you really need to successfully memorize the Word of God. At www.dancarr.org there will be an ongoing posting of good suggestions on memorizing.

The Most Important Thing in Memorizing Bible Verses is your own personal desire and commitment. The Bible tells us to hear, read, study, memorize, and meditate on the Word of God. So then, memorizing—hiding the Word in our hearts—is commanded by and commended by the Lord. (Deut. 6:6,7; Psalm 119:9,11; Hosea 4:6; Jer.15:16; Psalm 19:14; Mal. 2:7; Mat.4:4; Col.3:16; 2 Tim.3:15; 2 Tim. 2:15; Heb.4:12; 1 Peter 2:2; 2 Peter 3:18; Isaiah 55:11.)

If You Know Your Name, Phone Number, and Where You

Live, it's because you have memorized that information. It also suggests that you probably can memorize Bible verses. I've been gleaning ideas for memorizing for many years, and it comes down to a few practical things. It begins with a firm decision to do it. It is reasonable to think about eventually memorizing at least 300 verses that are well-memorized and maintained for easy recall and use. Most people can memorize 1,000 verses. That is NOT unreasonable. But, to be of any value, the verses must become a part of you. Love the Word of God. Obey the Word of God.

Soak Several Verses Ahead of Time by Reading the Verses Aloud Every Day. Read 10-20 verses aloud every day for two weeks without trying to memorize them. Pay close attention to key words. Focus on the key words but don't try to memorize the verses. Just read them aloud. Pick out one of those verses and finish memorizing it.

Will it be One Verse Per Week? That's 52 verses per year, and it can make a big difference in your life. After you have successfully memorized 20 verses at one verse per week, you may want to consider two verses per week, but don't hold yourself to it. Hold yourself to one verse per week. If a verse begins to roll out without effort, you can move it to weekly review and replace it with another verse. Do quality work. Avoid haphazard, shoddy work.

It Usually Takes 60 days to Thoroughly Memorize a Verse of Scripture. This is especially true if the verse has not been "soaked" for a couple of weeks. A passage may contain 2 or 3 verses that will fit on one card. You count the card as one passage and memorize the whole card in one week. You continue to RE-memorize the verse every morning for 60 days. A verse is not memorized until it will flow out of your mouth and through your mind without effort or hesitation. Begin with five verses in five weeks. Concentrate on just five verses for five weeks.

All Verses are Not Equally Easy or Equally Difficult to Memorize. Some verses are very easy to memorize. Some verses are harder to memorize and some verses are downright HARD to memorize. *Similar* verses are harder to memorize than verses unlike each other. Similar references tend to run together and are harder to recall.

Each Sunday Evening, break in your new verse for the coming week. Hold to that schedule. If you want to succeed in memorizing you must build habits that will produce for you. This simple practice on Sunday afternoon will serve you well.

Say the Reference Before and After the Verse. Repeat the newest verses at least five times per day for a month, then once a week for a month, once a month for a year, and once a year for life. *Anytime a verse does not spill out without effort, return it to your new-verse group until it flows without effort*.
 Practice until the reference quickly triggers the first words of the verse. Then, practice until the words of the verse will recall the reference. Eventually, you will want to remember where a few verses are found on key subjects or themes. Memorize a list of verses on Creation, the Cross, Sin, the Word, Prayer, etc.

Write the Newer Verses Several Times on a Sheet of Paper. Write the verse with references before and after. Turn the paper upside down and write it again. Turn the paper upside down and write again. Do this until the paper is full all the way to the middle from both ends. Turning the paper helps to prevent your eyes from copying the verse above, since the verse above is upside down.

After you can Say the Verse Well, get someone to listen to you recite with the paper or cards in hand. Don't do this on a new verse. It will be too frustrating. Ask the person listening to you to require you to be 100% accurate. When you miss, recite that phrase, then go back and recite the whole verse.

Cards Are Best For Memorization, but cards are not absolutely essential. If you are writing verses by hand, 3x5 cards are the most practical. You can find packs of 3x5 cards in many stores.

Use a black ball-point pen. Yellow and pink cards are easier to read and easier to find if you misplace them. Put a medium rubber band around the cards. On one outside card, write your name, address, and phone number and: "THESE CARDS BELONG TO _____. IF YOU FIND THEM, PLEASE CALL ME AND I WILL PICK THEM UP. THANK YOU!"

Use of the Computer Has Some Advantages if you can do it, but it is too complicated to present here. Computer programs are not standardized and they are constantly changing. Subdividing a page into 2 ¾ x 4¼ size cards is easy on WordPerfect, very difficult on Microsoft unless you use Avery label sizes. Programs don't talk to each other much, and you must have WordPerfect installed on your computer to open WP documents. The various versions of Microsoft will not open on some computers if you don't have that exact program installed. I encounter this often when sending documents. Please see www.dancarr.org and look for "Bible Memorization."

You May Also Print a Sheet of Verses and Fold Them in Half in Your Bible and you are ready to begin memorizing. This works better than cards if a class or congregation is rehearsing verses. Keep them in your Bible and they will be handy for group participation. (You can't carry cards in your Bible, but you can carry two folded sheets in your Bible very easily without damaging your Bible.) You can copy the verses in Chapter 20 from the book or download the verses from the above web site and print them if you are computer savvy.

Memorize Chapters as a Family, Sunday School Class, or Congregation.
Chapters are easier than individual verses because you don't have so many numbers. One chapter with no more than 12-15 verses or so every two months would be a good goal. Begin with Psalm 23. The late Evangelist Lester Roloff had his workers to drill the young people at his homes at the City of Refuge in memorizing and reciting Bible chapters. Chapters and uplifting songs were an important part of their spiritual diet. He sent me his list of "60 Chapters in 60 Months." These are found in

chapter 22 and will be posted on the above web site.

When I was growing up in country churches, some of the preachers could quote the Bible by the yard as they exhorted and told Bible stories in great detail. They memorized without cards or paper. They simply went at it with great determination, sometimes pacing the floor with a Bible in hand, or walked in the woods with an open Bible. Perhaps they copied President Abraham Lincoln who wrote Bible verses on pieces of paper and memorized them that way.

They proved to me as a boy that there is no excuse for the Lord's people to be lazy about reading and memorizing the Word of God. Some of these men never finished the 8th grade which, in those days, required a lot for 8th grade graduation. This was not true in every school, but it was not uncommon. The Blue Back Speller and the McGuffey Readers were a tough act to follow.

Where to Find Verses to Memorize. You can find the best verses while reading the Bible, listening to sermons and Bible lessons, from Bible memorization courses, reading books, tracts, booklets, devotional booklets and books, and reading and singing hymns. Carry a small notebook for writing down verses or references. Keep a 3x5 card in your Bible, shirt, or purse for writing verses or references.

Bible Reading is Important. Carry a pocket Testament with Proverbs and Psalms. You'll always have Bible verses to read to shutins, and those who need a witness. By making a habit of carrying the Testament, you will find it easier to read more of the Word of God. Carry a pen with you to underline verses. Speed reading the Bible with no study is a good way to read. Reading slowly, marking, looking up word meanings and commentary is also important. Read alone. Read in family devotions. Don't leave your Bible in the back window of your car. That's a bad testimony of disrespect for the Word of God.

We use the King James Bible because we believe it is the most reliable and the most beautiful in its rhythm and majesty. It is the greatest used in history and is readable for today. It is the most trusted and is the most accepted without having to defend it. It was the most-used book in stabilizing the English language and it was the greatest influence in writing the foundational documents of American government.

For study Bibles, we prefer: King James Study Bible, New Defenders Study Bible (Henry Morris), the old Scofield, the MacArthur Study Bible (notes only). We use the e-sword for computer: www.e-sword.net. It is free, "feature-rich and user-friendly". It includes a host of study books and commentaries to be downloaded free. We recommend that you use it and help support it financially.

Memorize the Great Hymns.

May we suggest that you memorize the great, old, time-tested meaty hymns and songs of the Christian faith. One hymn a month or every two months would be a great blessing to you and those around you. You can copy the old hymns whose copyright dates are no longer valid. If the original copyright date on a hymn is 1911 or older, it probably is now in the public domain (95 years from the original copyright). A good place to find old hymns is in old hymnals. Some of the more recent hymnals have good collections of old hymns and a short section containing all its authors with the birth and death dates. Some books give the name and death date of the author/composer on the same page as the song. Almost all of the great Christmas songs are public domain. The arrangements of the songs may be copyrighted.

For example, Robert Lowry died in 1899. Fanny Crosby died in 1915. Isaac Watts died in 1748. Charles Wesley died in 1788. John Newton died in 1807. Obviously, they will have no copyrighted works after they died and they wrote some of the greatest hymns. These are only a few names. There are scores of names whose music is no longer copyrighted. You can do a Google search with the word: "Copyright," and find about everything you want to know about copyright.

You may want to make up your own personal notebook of old hymns. Get a 3-ring snap notebook and a pack of paper.
Print the songs you select. Buy a pack of plastic notebook folders that fit your notebook. Slip your songs into the folders and you are in business. All of that can be done for about $10.00.

Some of the most beautiful harmony comes from the men singing the melody and the ladies singing a harmony part above. Two-part harmony. Some hymns lend themselves better for this than others. <u>Lower the key about two steps</u>. The ladies may have to dip under the melody for a short while and then back to the upper level. If you reach a place that is awkward, both sing in unison until you pass that spot and go back to harmony. One or two altos may want to sing melody with the men. It doesn't have to be perfect. Sing it slow and deliberate. It will carry itself. You don't even have to have a piano or guitar, but it's ok if you do.

62 GREAT HYMNS TO LIFT YOU UP

Amazing Grace
Am I A Soldier of the Cross?
Are You Washed In The Blood?
At The Cross
Blessed Assurance
Brethren We Have Met To Worship
Close To Thee
Come Thou Almighty King
Come Thou Fount
Fill My Cup, Lord
Great Is Thy Faithfulness
Have Thine Own Way
Higher Ground
His Name Is Wonderful
How Firm a Foundation
How Great Thou Art
I Am Thine O Lord
I Know Whom I Have Believed
I Must Tell Jesus
I Need Thee Every Hour
I Surrender All
Jesus Paid It All
Just As I Am
Just Keep On Praying
Just When I Need Him Most

Lord, I'm Coming Home
Love Lifted Me
My Faith Looks Up To Thee
My Hope Is Built
Near The Cross
No, Not One
No One Ever Cared for Me like Jesus
No One Understands Like Jesus
Nothing Between
Nothing but the Blood
O For a Thousand Tongues
O God, Our Help in Ages Past
On Jordan's Stormy Banks
Only Believe
Pass Me Not, O Gentle Savior
Precious Lord, Take My Hand
Rock of Ages
Savior, Like a Shepherd Lead Us
Set My Soul Afire
Softly and Tenderly
Spirit of the Living God
Take It to the Lord In Prayer
Tell It to Jesus
The Blood that Stained the Old Rugged Cross
The Old Account Was Settled
There Is a Balm in Gilead
There Is a Fountain
There's Just Something About That Name
'Tis So Sweet To Trust In Jesus
Under His Wings
What a Friend We Have In Jesus
When I Can Read My Title Clear
When I See The Blood
Where Could I Go
Where He Leads Me
Whisper a Prayer
Wonderful Words of Life

Sixty Chapters in Sixty Months
Evangelist Lester Roloff

Forty years ago I became a stand-in pianist to accompany Evangelist Lester Roloff in Bible conferences and other meetings where I happened to be in attendance. The difficulty was that Brother Roloff never bothered with written music for himself or for anyone who played for him. He might sing a familiar song or one not so familiar. He sang most everything in the Key of F. He also had his own timing and paused where he pleased. It wasn't that he couldn't sing. He could sing very well and on key. (Some people didn't think he could sing a lick, but he had them fooled.) To him, music was a tool for enhancing speech. He was a preacher, the thunder of a prophet, and music was his servant—not his master.

There was just one Lester Roloff. He reminds me of Paul Ferguson in that they were both mavericks and both practiced an unusual standard of reading and memorizing Scripture. They both had strong faith in God.

Once when Brother Roloff's plane ran out of gas outside of Chattanooga, he landed on the highway and rolled to the side of the road. People stopped their cars and assembled around his plane out of curiosity. He crawled out of the plane with his Bible in hand and began to preach to them. When the highway patrol came on the scene, Brother Roloff raised his hand and said, "Just a minute Officer, please. I'm just getting ready to give the invitation."

In meetings, he would say, "Brother Dan, I want to sing that old song…" and would give the title. Half of them I had never heard of so I would give him a C7 chord and run it up the keyboard. He would begin and I would play a split-second behind him, figuring out some chords, and guessing the rest. My main job was to follow his speed and rhythm and not to force a chord on him that would clash with his tune.

The remedy to that was to mix in a bit of a second harmony (they call it "poly-tonality") so that a wrong chord wouldn't be a full clash. Then, I could quickly go into the right chord when I knew what it should be. A bit like landing a Cessna in a sweet potato patch. He must have thought it worked OK, because if he spotted me in the audience, I was the usual candidate to play for him. He sang and I invented the accompaniment as we went along.

Often he brought young people with him from the Roloff Home in Texas or Mississippi, who would sing and quote a chapter of Scripture in unison. They were good at it. They sang three-part harmony with no accompaniment. I was impressed by the way Bible chapters rolled out with real gusto. I discovered that Brother Roloff had a plan of Sixty Chapters in Sixty Months. They were memorizing a Bible chapter every month. I asked him in Jacksonville, Florida if I might have a copy of the chapters in his plan and he sent them to me. He gave me permission to reprint them and they are listed below.

I suggest that you look them over and pick out the chapters that best suit your needs. You may want to write the chapter references in the inside of your Bible. Begin reading one of the chapters aloud every day. That will enable you to remember bits and pieces of the text. Then, begin memorizing it word-for-word. At the same time, begin reading a second chapter aloud for a month.

The Roloff Homes had a high success rate in helping troubled youth to stay out of prisons. I believe the memorizing of Scripture chapters and the positive, encouraging songs they sang was a vital part of their success. The environment was highly structured, but so were other institutions that had less success than the Roloff Homes. He believed that filling their mouths with the Word of God and faith-building songs was a strong part of the core of what he was doing.

They also had strong, daily Bible preaching and teaching, but those things can be tuned out. It is much harder to tune out memorizing and reciting Scripture and faith-building music that commands the speech center of the brain. I heard a doctor on radio from the Minnereth Myer Clinic in Texas, say that the most effective thing they had found to reprogram people who were addicted to pornography was a robust program of memorizing selected Bible verses over a period of time. "It has the power to reprogram the mind," he said.

I list for you below a total of 63 chapters.

Deut. 28.

Psalm: 1, 2, 3, 8, 14, 15, 19, 23, 24, 27, 34, 37, 40, 41, 42, 46, 51, 63, 67, 73, 85, 90, 91, 92, 93, 100, 103, 116, 117, 121, 122, 124, 126, 127, 131, 133, 134, 150.

Proverbs: 3, 16, 22.

Matthew: 5, 6, 7, 28.

John: 3, 10, 14, 15, 17, 21.

Romans: 5, 8, 10.

1 Cor. 13.

Eph. 2, 3, 6.

Phil. 3, 4.

Col. 3.

Heb. 11.

James 1.

1 Peter 1.

1 John 1, 5.

Paul Ferguson the Fighter
Appendix

Dr. Bob Jones, Sr. said, *"I am not everybody, therefore I cannot do everything. But I am one and I can do something. What I can do, I ought to do, and by the grace of God I will do it."*

What Did Paul Ferguson Do by the Grace of God?

Mainly he obeyed what God showed him. We can do that. You can do that. We can all pray and listen to the Holy Spirit and witness as God expects us to. We can all obey God as completely as Brother Paul. Studying his life and ministry may help us do that.

Paul's Birth Traits.

His birth traits undergirded his strict training and discipline in sports. He was born with lightning reflexes, a capacity for physical coordination, and a thirst for competition. All these things worked for him at forty when he turned to memorizing the Word of God, a life of prayer, preaching, and personal witnessing. He memorized over eight thousand verses, and most of his well-ordered sermons consisted of memorized Scripture organized into an outline and spiced with stories and humor.

Paul loved good stories and jokes and shared them with the people he preached to in over forty states. That was his nature from earliest days. He told jokes to relax the audience and to draw their minds and emotions into the meeting. Occasionally someone thought he was unspiritual because he told jokes in the pulpit. There was no end to his picking on people if he could get a story on them. But when he began to "plow their corn" with the Word of God, they soon forgot about his jokes and "lack of spirituality."

The Holy Spirit.

As Paul labored to study the eternal security of the believer in Christ and went through the life-changing experience of understanding John 5:24, he became acquainted with the Holy Spirit in a practical way. The Holy Spirit was a close teacher, and this was new to him. As he witnessed to individuals, he relied heavily on the Holy Spirit to guide him, but he also studied the face and speech of the person he was witnessing to, the same as in boxing. Some people were spiritually tough and hard. Sometimes he sat patiently for an hour or more, engaging in small-talk, slowly gaining the confidence of the man, and praying within himself what to do and when to do it. He learned to rely upon the prompting of the Holy Spirit in his witnessing.

Paul believed that his *most important job* was prayer. Without earnest prayer there would be no power in his preaching, even though he used much Scripture. Without prayer, there would be no conviction of sin and righteousness and judgment by the Holy Spirit. Without prayer, people would not be saved. Without prayer, he could not have much of a meeting.

A Little Background.

Paul Ferguson stayed in our home for a week in 1992 while preaching in nearby revival services. We began sharing some unusual things each of us had experienced with the Lord that we seldom talked about publicly. Our hearts burned and we wept many times.

By the end of the week, I knew we had to highlight Paul's experiences with the Lord and to open the curtain on his prayer life. He was reluctant because he didn't want to appear to be bragging. We talked by phone several times and finally he agreed. We both understood that the purpose was to get across a much larger truth: *If we draw near to God, He will draw near to us.*

Most of the *Paul Ferguson the Fighter* book is the transcript of nine 90-minute audio tapes, recorded during six days of interviews with him - thirteen hours of recordings from forty eight hours of conversation. Another twenty hours of conversation preceded the recordings. I've attempted to round out the tapes with additional information about the boxer-preacher. For example, *why did Paul Ferguson pray so long? Why did he tell jokes in the pulpit? Why did he sit with hardened lost men and talk with them about baseball instead of getting right into the Gospel?*

I have woven into the story several conversations with Brother Paul that did not get into the audio tapes and things from my personal knowledge of him over a period of several years.

Talking It Over.

Talking with Paul Ferguson for sixty-eight hours about his life and ministry was a major lifetime experience for me. Here was a man of prayer who's praying and results were akin to E. M. Bounds, Charles Finney, Praying Hyde, Cam Thompson, and many others like them. As we talked, the Holy Spirit swept over us several times so that we wept and sometimes trembled with more than human emotion. The Spirit of God needs no introduction.

In the still-popular 19th century hymn, *Wonderful Peace*, the chorus says: *"Peace! Peace! Wonderful peace, Coming down from the Father above; Sweep over my spirit forever, I pray, In fathomless billows of love."* The writer, W. D. Cornell, must have known the presence of the Lord.

Fanny Crosby (1820-1915), the blind song writer, wrote in another popular hymn, *I Am Thine O Lord: "O the pure delight of a single hour that before Thy throne I spend; When I kneel in prayer, and with Thee, my God, I commune as friend with friend!"* The idea of this popular song is conscious communion with God—conscious communion.

A much-loved chorus is sung in hushed tones: *"Spirit of the Living God, Fall fresh on me; Spirit of the Living God, Fall fresh on me. Melt me, Mold me; Fill me, Use me. Spirit of the Living God, fall fresh on me."* In one church, the Holy Spirit did, indeed, fall upon them as they sang this chorus, and it spread. If you have sung the above songs or songs like them, you must believe that the Spirit of God is known to sweep over His children, and we know it consciously when that occurs.

Brother Paul and I were going to talk and record for a single week, but at the end of the first day we were both physically exhausted from the unexpected emotional and spiritual exercise. We changed our plan to one day a week for as long as necessary. It took six days—six weeks.

Some people believe a visitation of the Holy Spirit *always* lifts one up, and the theme song will be *"...the garment of praise for the spirit of heaviness;" (Isa.61:3).* I know a few such visitations of the Holy Spirit that I cannot describe. D. L. Moody and others speak of such visitations of the Holy Spirit.

Gethsemane.

But the visitation of the Holy Spirit does not always bring joy and a *"garment of praise."* There's another side of the Spirit's work that brings us into Christ's sufferings at Gethsemane. He may bring us into the garden of intercessory prayer. By its very nature, intercessory prayer most often focuses on dire need, on the undone.

It is fitting that Jesus should bring His disciples into the Garden of Gethsemane on the Mount of Olives. Gethsemane is a word from the Aramaic language meaning *oil press.* This garden of the oil press was located in the midst of the grove of huge olive trees, convenient for pressing out the oil from the olive harvest.

Here, Jesus was pressed out in soul and spirit as He prayed until His sweat was as great drops of blood falling to the ground (Luke 22:44). Did Jesus lack the Spirit of God in that hour because he was in great heaviness and not wearing *"the garment of praise?"* I think not.

The Holy Spirit may, at times, bring heaviness and render us exhausted instead of refreshed. If we engage in intercessory prayer, or if we rehearse times of intercessory prayer and spiritual wrestling, we may not always experience *the garment of praise* and *great joy.* Rather, we may find ourselves in the *Garden of Gethsemane.* He may deal with us about the hidden things of the heart that we have pushed aside or buried rather than face it.

Witnessing.

Wives of lost husbands were sometimes upset with Paul. He felt there was no need to *rush into combat* with a man in his own home until he sensed a signal from the Lord or from the man himself that he was ready to discuss his eternal soul. This really upset some women who invited Brother Paul to visit their unsaved husbands. They would tell a friend, "I was just so disappointed in Preacher Ferguson. I thought he would come in and witness to my lost husband and get him saved. But, instead, he just sat there and talked about baseball for almost an hour

261

until I was so frustrated and aggravated and disappointed—and mad—!"

Sometimes a wife would rush in from the kitchen to try to push Paul into getting the job done. She would usually blow it, of course, and waste his time and effort toward getting her husband saved. Early in his ministry, Brother Paul learned to get a promise from the wife that, if possible, she would leave the house while he talked to her husband. You'll read more about that. If Paul sensed that a man was not open for a witness, he would leave on good terms, pray hard for him, and go back again during the meeting.

Paul Prayed At Home.

One day I went by Brother Paul's house in Chattanooga to share some fresh produce and to visit a few minutes. Mrs. Ferguson was working at the Temple dormitory behind their house. I knocked on the door, knocked again, knocked again. He finally came to the door barefoot, hair disheveled, and eyes blinking at the light. He had some sheets of curled-up paper in his hand, worn and soiled from use. It took him a few seconds to recognize me and invite me in.

As I went in, I realized that the papers were handwritten lists of the names of people. Our names were somewhere on one of those sheets – several hundreds of names that he prayed over every day. When I knocked, he was on his knees in the den in the back of the house, calling out names to the Lord. Prayer takes time. Prayer is hard work. If it were not so, more people would do it.

I felt bad about interrupting Paul's prayer time, but I also felt good about being there. He said he was not an early-morning "pray-er." He had too much trouble falling asleep if he prayed early in the morning or after eating a meal. Ten o'clock in the morning was a much better time for him. He said he had memorized most of the names on his papers and the order they were written in.

He held the papers in his hand in case he should forget where he was on the list. He moved down the list in his mind and would call each name in prayer. If the Holy Spirit stopped him at a name, he would pray for that person until he was free in his spirit to go to the next name. Sometimes he might need to look at the list to find the next name.

When Paul was in a meeting, it was obviously God's will for Paul to pray long, to pray into the night while others slept enough to work the next day. He prayed while people worked at their jobs. One of Paul's favorite prayer positions was to stretch out face-down on the floor or ground, sometimes for hours at a time. We can't all pray that long or pray that way, but everyone can draw near to God in prayer so that God will draw near.

Why Did Paul Pray So Long?

Paul told me several times that he had to pray a long time— not to persuade God, but to get himself out of the way so God could work through him. It's sobering to think that it may be that way for all of us. We want to believe we are nice people, that a little nod toward Heaven will put us in touch with God. There seems to be a level of minimal fellowship with God that we are comfortable with and that God accepts to a certain degree. But if we want to get down to business with God, it will take more than a smile and a nod to get there.

We may need to take some time to search out the hidden secrets in our hearts and to dispose of some of the wood, hay, and stubble. My old nature, my pride, my self-will, they all keep getting in the way of praying in the Spirit.

● Every Christian can *"Pray without ceasing"* (ad-ee-al-lipe'-toce - *uninterruptedly, i.e. without omission (on an appropriate occasion) - Strongs*) (I Thessalonians 5:17).

● Every Christian can *"pray in the Holy Ghost"* (Jude 1:20).

● Every Christian can allow the Holy Spirit to: "**cry**: (kradzo - *to scream as a raven, to call aloud, shriek, intreat, cry*) **Abba, Father**" (pat-ayr': *father, daddy, parent*) "**God hath sent forth the Spirit of his Son into your hearts, crying, Abba, Father**" (Galatians 4:6).

This is the Spirit crying "Father-Daddy" through us, and not an urging of our own making. As we sincerely seek the Lord in prayer, we should expect the Holy Spirit to gently lead us in our praying.

Once, during a very difficult time in my life, I could not pray. I would attempt to pray, but could only utter, "Father." As I slowly, earnestly repeated "Father" as my one and only prayer, there came from the top of my head an energy flowing through me, a movement to cry out, "Father. Father!" And the Spirit of God covered me like a blanket. For a month or so, this went on every day. I knew it was the Holy Spirit, but somehow the text of the above verse did not occur to me.

One day, I remembered the verse and it all fit together. I had known the verse for years, but for a month I did not think to connect the verse with what was going on. How did I know it was the Spirit of God? Like I recognize the noon-day sun. The Holy Spirit is His own signature.

Paul Ferguson knew the real score. It took time to get himself out of the way, but I believe it was more than that. Beyond getting himself out of the way, I believe God had chosen Paul to be an instrument of intercessory prayer more than the average Christian. However, everyone can pray so that God will draw near. Every Christian should engage in intercessory prayer for others.

Paul's Greatest Teacher on Prayer.

Paul's favorite authors on prayer were E. M. Bounds and Charles Finney. But his greatest teacher on prayer was Jesus. He read the gospels and searched out every reference on Jesus' teachings on prayer and His practice of prayer. "Jesus spent a whole night in prayer," he said. "Why would it be strange if I need to spend a night in prayer?"

Obviously, Jesus did not need to spend a night in prayer to get Himself out of the way so the Father's will could be done. Jesus needed communion with His Father, and He drew much-needed strength from that all-night of prayer.

In Gethsemane He displayed an awesome scene of prayer while His disciples slept. He prayed on the cross in a few words, prayed as no one has ever prayed. But He prayed.... and it shook the crowd. Earlier, "...he spake a parable unto them to this end, that men ought always to pray, and not to faint;" (Luke 18:1).
Paul Believed In Prayer.

Paul Ferguson believed that his most important job was prayer. His second job was to preach the Word of God toward getting others to pray in his meetings. His third job was to preach the Gospel and to witness to individuals.

He said that it was usually not possible to get people under a prayer burden in short meetings. A two-week meeting was almost always necessary to get anything done. He believed that the power for his meetings was more through prayer than through his preaching, even though he had memorized over eight thousand verses of Scripture and his sermons were mostly Scripture. This reminds me of what I once heard Dr. John R. Rice say to a thousand preachers in Chicago: "*If you preachers don't learn how to pray, you needn't bother to learn how to preach.*"

Why Does God Want Us To Pray For Laborers To Be Sent Into His Harvest? (Mark 9:38)

We spent some time discussing this issue. God appeals with great passion to His redeemed ones to share His burden and labor in redeeming the lost world. Why should we work in HIS harvest? Because it is our privilege to share in the heart of the Father. Though it was not our lot to go to the Cross, yet we are appointed and privileged to enter into the sufferings of Christ.

"...unto you it is given...to suffer for his sake," (Philippians 1:29).
"...I will show him [Paul] how great things he must suffer for my name's sake" (Acts 9:16).
"...be thou faithful unto death, and I will give thee a crown of life" (Revelation 2:10).
"...we must through much tribulation enter into the kingdom of God" (Acts 14:22).
"...if...we suffer with him, ...we... also... glorified together" (Romans 8:17).

Giving a gospel tract surely draws the attention of Heaven. Giving a cup of water in His name is noticed and marked for reward (Mark 9:41). Intercessory prayer is the casting of our spirits into the bosom of the Father, that He may cause us to share in His compassion and suffering for a lost world. Without intercessory prayer for others, we will have little of God's compassion and suffering for a lost world. Religious exercise in the energy of the flesh is not the same thing as intercessory prayer, not the same thing as exercise in the Spirit.

Intercessory prayer is a very special thing with God. Reading and speaking are wonderful, but God has appointed praise and thanksgiving as the means of entering into His courts (Psalm 100:4). By prayer we come to His throne of grace to obtain mercy and grace to help in time of need (Hebrews 4:16).

Good preaching has always been the joy of my heart, but "House of Prayer" is the most scriptural name for the House of God. (Isaiah 56:7, Matthew 21:13, Mark 11:17, Luke 19:46.) I can't find any place in the Bible where God or His servants ever called God's house the "House of Preaching." We all believe in preaching - love preaching - but the "House of Prayer" is God's name for His house.

We Are Writing About More than Paul Ferguson.

Our purpose in writing this story goes beyond the life of Paul Ferguson. It is about the power of God, available today to ordinary Christians who are willing to give themselves to the Word of God and earnest, fervent, persistent, believing, expectant prayer. It is to encourage me—and you— to give ourselves to prayer and the Word of God - to obey the Spirit of God. Brother Paul and I agreed that this should be the theme and purpose of the writing: *"Draw nigh to God and He will draw nigh to you."* If that is not true and practical, then you can't depend on anything else in the Bible.

He was not interested in a monument to his name. He strongly emphasized to me that what was done in his ministry was through the power of the Holy Spirit, and he knew he could take no credit for it.

America Hangs in the Balance.

He understood that our nation is in severe moral crisis involving millions of young people trained in evolution and humanism, and that the only way out—if there is a way out— is to enlist God's people in persistent, prevailing prayer. Although our nation is being swallowed up by satanic power, God still answers prayer.

As much as he believed in preaching, he believed that it was not possible to preach America out of its self-destruction without strong prayer. Preaching will have power only if Christians can be stirred to pray as though our next breath depends on it. With that in mind, he agreed for us to review some highlights of his life and ministry to the end that some may be encouraged to engage in serious prayer.

All things are possible with God and He can revive America - save America - if He chooses. However, if God's dealing with nations in the Bible, if the records of secular history have any meaning for America, it is that America will behave like all other nations that God has destroyed. America is rotting from within. We are our own worst enemy. Money is flowing. Who needs God?

We are now greatly outnumbered by unbelievers. True Christians are a shrinking minority in America, and the one-world government is quickly coming together. But the Great Commission has not changed. God has not changed. God's program for His church has not changed.

Revival and Non-standard Things.

Many things in Paul Ferguson's ministry were ordinary. He didn't have revival every place he went. He didn't win everyone to the Lord he witnessed to. But some very *non-standard* things took place in his ministry. They may seem radical, hard to believe, and even offensive to some people, especially those who want God to do only *standard* things. No attempt is being made here to establish new doctrine or to suggest an unrealistic standard for serving God. We're simply reporting the facts and pointing to the Scripture for their meaning.

Nevertheless, if God should break forth upon us, doing *non-standard* things, would we be offended or embarrassed by it? We humans prefer to keep things nice and orderly so we can look respectable and feel secure. We may feel more secure with familiar, fruitless church services than to have revival and its strangeness. We humans love to be in charge. Sometimes we don't want God to break us into new territory.

Meeting Paul Ferguson in the Gospel Tent—1954.

Fifty-two years ago, I met Paul Ferguson in the back of a Gospel tent somewhere in the Chattanooga valley. It was expected in tent meetings that people would be saved. Everything was geared to that end. Lost people were invited to attend and much prayer was offered on their behalf.

A fellow-student and I entered the tent and sat on the right side near the aisle, about three benches from the back. On the outside end of the back bench sat a man in a grey suit, holding a big Bible. My friend nudged me and whispered, "That's Paul Ferguson. He attends meetings and prays, and then does personal work during the invitation."

I thought something like, "That's good. Somebody needs to do that. I guess he doesn't get an opportunity to preach, so he does what he can in that way. He's starting out at the bottom as a humble servant. Bless his heart." He was about twenty years older than me and I figured he hadn't been saved long. But he had been saved more than twenty years. My friend introduced me to Paul Ferguson before we left the tent and I shook hands with him. I didn't yet know about his past boxing career or his long journey to understanding the eternal security of the believer.

Paul and Preaching and Pulpits.

Soon after meeting Paul, I was at another place and he was there praying for the meeting and doing personal work at the altar. He talked to individuals wherever he could and inquired about their spiritual condition.

What Is Preaching? At the time, I was sorting things out about preaching and God's work in general. I didn't quite know what to do with Paul. He was clearly dedicated to serving the Lord. *Would he end up preaching? If you're going to preach, it's done behind a pulpit. Anybody knows that.* I learned it from preachers. *Sacred Desk*, they called it. Preaching is done behind the *Sacred Desk*.

There is, indeed, that special call of God upon certain men to publicly preach His word and to lead a congregation of believers. There are other gifts and callings, but we are talking about preaching. I honestly did not know that preaching was anything other than talking with a raised voice while standing

268

behind a pulpit—to an audience.

Then, in the Bible, I found Jesus sitting at a well in Samaria, talking to—preaching to— a mixed-up, discouraged woman. No pulpit, no building. There's no mention in the Bible of any of the prophets or the apostles using a pulpit. Apparently, they all preached from memorized Scripture. Furthermore, I found that *pulpit* occurs only one time in the Bible (Neh.8:4), when Ezra the scribe stood on a pulpit. Of course, if reading was done from a large scroll, it most certainly would have required a table on which to lay the scroll. From that, we seem to have inherited the pulpit tradition we enjoy today.

A Turning Point in My Life.

Brother Paul made a strong impression on me in those two or three services in tent meetings by his earnest witnessing and praying for individual lost souls. I was slowly realizing that some of the greatest, most important, most effective preaching is— to individuals. To me, this was a revolutionary truth, a turning point.

I came to realize that witnessing to people, wherever you can find them, is a form of *preaching.* I wonder how many Christians know this. The call of God, the commandment of God is upon every Christian to *preach as you go throughout the world,* is virtually unknown.

Every Christian should *preach,* even through a gospel tract. Christians should work hard at praying and preaching—all Christians. There's a special call of God on some people to preach in public meetings, to pastor, to be an evangelist, to teach, to be a missionary. In addition to that, every Christian is called of God, commanded of God to bear witness of the Gospel—to preach.

Hardly any of the lost world today is going to come and sit in front of a modern pulpit to hear the gospel preached. That's a great place to preach if you can get people into the room to listen. Comfortable pews are a great place to listen to preaching, but the vast majority of Americans never darken a church door. We must *preach*—out there! Every Christian.

If preaching has to be done behind a pulpit, only a handful of Christians on planet earth will ever preach anything. We have

269

unintentionally so under-defined the word *preach* - have so removed it from its Biblical setting - that most Christians don't know they are commanded to preach. Please bear with me a little longer at this point. I may not be as pitiful as you think.

Please look at this:

"**And Saul was consenting unto his death. And at that time there was a great persecution against the church which was at Jerusalem; and they were all scattered abroad throughout the regions of Judea and Samaria, except the Apostles**" (Acts 8:1).

Who was scattered? Not the Apostles. The Apostles stayed in Jerusalem to face the music, even death. But there was a wholesale exodus of *all Christians* out of Jerusalem to escape death and imprisonment. Verse 3 explains the reason why the Christians left Jerusalem.

"**As for Saul, he made havoc of the church, entering into every house, and haling men and women committed them to prison.**" The next verse says, "**Therefore they that were scattered abroad went every where preaching the word**" (Acts 8:3,4).

As they fled for their safety, they preached. These were not the special-called preachers, not the Apostles. The point is: There are two kinds of preaching. Every Christian is called and commanded to preach the gospel. Among us, there are people whom God has called and equipped to preach in public meetings and to lead the rest.

"**Preaching....**" (Acts 8:4). Greek: *Euaggerlizo (yoo-ang-ghel-id'-zo). "to announce good news (evangelize) especially the gospel:–declare, bring, preach (the gospel).*

Where did all these people get the idea they were suppose to preach as they fled for their lives? Jesus had commanded: "**Go ye into all the world, and preach the gospel to every creature**" (Mark16:15). "**Go**" is from Greek: poreuomai. "*travel, depart, go (away, forth, one's way, up)."* It can be translated: "As you Go."

They had been taught to preach, teach, wherever they were,

wherever they traveled. Let's get with God's plan. Let's preach the gospel every way we can, to every creature.

If You Would Like to Help.

Brother Paul didn't brag about anything except that he could beat your socks off at hand ball. But he knew that God's hand had done some unusual things in his ministry that might be of some value if he told it. We didn't discuss how we might get it done.

I've fulfilled the promise I made to Brother Paul to write the story and to write a limited amount of my own comment. I commit it to the Lord to do with it as He will. After you've read the story in book form or at www.dancarr.org, if you want to help with the distribution of the book version, we welcome your help as unto the Lord.

I do need your help. It will help if you will buy several copies for family and friends. We will keep the cost of the book as low as we can. The money will be recycled for more books to be printed. Short printing runs cost more per book. Obviously, we cannot distribute further than available funds will allow. *Dan Carr will receive no money from the book.*

The Theme of This Book.

We are not charismatic. We must have God's power to do God's work. Mary, the mother of Jesus, pondered some things in her heart rather than talk about them (Luke 2:19). There is something about witnessing God's hand that restrains utterance. It doesn't always produce a song.

I am not a charismatic. I don't believe healing is in the atonement, but I've experienced instant healing and have seen several instant healings. Neither do I believe that *tongues* are Biblical proof of being filled with the Holy Spirit. But I know about the presence of the Holy Spirit in unusual ways - enough to establish a landmark of His presence. D. L. Moody wrote about this happening to him on Wall Street in New York as he was raising money to rebuild his church after the Chicago fire. When we draw nigh to God, we have His unfailing promise that He will draw nigh to us.

We can't win increasingly hardened hearts with merely

271

learned techniques. We cannot bypass the convicting power of the Holy Spirit and get anything but false professions. We must get serious about our prayer life.

I believe that most Christians are on a spiritual starvation diet by neglect or by choice. American Christianity, as a whole, is in such spiritual rags, in such a beggarly state that we live as though we have no Heavenly Father. We are like orphans in the street, simply because we ignore the Word of God and do not pray. We should pray until God's presence is a reality. *Just Keep On Praying. Wallow in the Word of God.*

"If My people, which are called by My name, will humble themselves, and pray, and seek my face, and turn from their wicked ways; then will I hear from Heaven, and will forgive their sin, and will heal their land" (II Chronicles 7:14).

Christians are under increasing attack by the satanic vultures of the American culture. We are at war!

Martin Luther of five hundred years ago is credited with saying: *"The man that defends every truth but the truth that's under attack at the present hour, that man is found a traitor before God."*

Biblical Separation in Evangelism
Dan Carr

Paul Ferguson mentioned Billy Graham several times in six days of interview, and some of those references appear in various chapters. I never asked Paul anything about Billy Graham, but it was on his mind. Many pastors now in their prime know nothing about it. A quick glance is in order. Billy Graham is just the tip of the iceberg. I heard him for the first time on the radio in my dad's new 1950 Ford pickup and tuned in as often as I could to the "Hour of Decision." It could have been called the "Hour of Fireball." I learned quickly to love Billy Graham and will love him 'til I die. Years later, he made a change in the direction of his meetings that many pastors and church people could not follow.

Two verses are uppermost in our living the Christian life and our Christian service: *"...We ought to obey God rather than men (Acts 5:29),* and *"Whether therefore ye eat, or drink, or whatsoever ye do, do all to the glory of God"* (1 Co 10:31).

Paul's Ferguson's ministry paralleled the prime days of Billy Graham. Paul wanted nothing to do with yoking up with churches or pastors who did not believe the Bible, the sinful nature and lost condition of man; the virgin birth of Christ, His sinless life and vicarious atonement, His bodily resurrection from the dead and His imminent return to earth to catch away His own. These have been the cardinal doctrines agreed on for the past 100 years as a basis for cooperation of groups of believers in cooperative evangelism, missions, and Christian school associations.

In addition to the above cardinal doctrines for cooperative efforts, there are other doctrinal issues important to many churches, evangelists and missionaries today: The security of the believer; the seven-year tribulation as introduced by the Prophet Daniel and expanded in the book of Revelation; Christ's literal thousand-year reign on the earth; and the new heaven and new earth that follows the thousand-year reign of Christ on the earth.

Almost all the people Paul Ferguson personally knew who believed in the fundamental doctrines of the Bible were conservative Southern Baptists and Independent Baptists.

Because of that, he did not like to go outside of that camp to hold meetings. Of course, there are other churches that believe those things, but he didn't know about them.

The Background.

The background begins in the 1800's when German Rationalism was corrupting American seminaries, publishing houses, and some of the pulpits of the mainline denominations, including: Methodist, Presbyterian, Northern Baptist, Lutheran, and at last—Southern Baptist. The attack was on the integrity and reliability of the Bible; the sinful nature of man and his lost condition; Christ's virgin birth; the deity of Jesus Christ, his sinless life, vicarious atonement for sin, and his literal bodily resurrection from the dead and his return for the redeemed church. Church leaders realized they were losing their denominations to infidels, but they were slow to counter the corruption. About 1860, Charles Darwin's *Origin of Species* entered the war. Christianity in America was under tremendous assault.

Concerned church leaders realized that they had to pull together if they were to counter the tide of unbelief. They agreed on the major doctrines that could not be compromised if they pooled their efforts. The fundamental doctrines agreed upon were published in little booklets and distributed widely in the 1890's. Christians who embraced these cardinal doctrines were then called "Fundamentalists." They believed the fundamentals of the faith. Lesser issues would not separate them. They united—they stood—they fought… as one man.

It was still going on when Billy Graham arrived on the scene in 1949. He had spent a short time at Bob Jones University and longer at Florida Bible College. He had earned a degree in Anthropology at Wheaton College. Dr. John R. Rice was living in Wheaton, and had his Sword of the Lord headquarters in Wheaton. As Billy Graham became more prominent as an evangelist, he was recruited by Dr. W. B Riley to become the young president of the conservative Northwest Seminary in Minneapolis. That didn't last long, but long enough for the Billy Graham headquarters to be established there. John R. Rice and Bob Jones, Sr. were two of Billy Graham's closest mentors. Dr.

Rice went to Scotland, at Billy Graham's invitation, about 1954 and sat on the platform of the Billy Graham meeting there and reported on the Scotland Meeting in the Sword of the Lord. You will recognize Rice and Jones as signers of the joint resolution at the end of this Appendix II.

In just four years after the meeting in Scotland, Billy Graham made a sudden turn in how his meetings would be organized. Instead of working under the sponsorship of men and churches that held to the Cardinal Doctrines of the faith, he would also include sponsors who did not hold to the Cardinal Doctrines. He would include those who found fault with the Bible, those who denied the virgin birth of Christ, those who might fall short in other areas of unbelief. These were called Liberals, or Modernists. The deliberate courting of unbelieving church leadership into his meetings was an idea generated by Harold Ockenga of New York. This approach came to be called "Neo-Evangelicalism," or "New-Evangelicalism." The plan was to include Modernists in his meetings to get a chance to preach to them.

The swap-off was "to preach less message to more people." Trim the message. Don't offend the masses. Preach the simple Gospel message, which he has done. But there is more to the Bible than the Gospel, and we call that "the whole counsel of God." That disappeared from his preaching.

Including Modernists in his meetings obligated him to send new converts back into those corrupt churches and to welcome unbelieving church men as "Christian brothers" and to have them lead in prayer on the platform. Some of these corrupt leaders had written books and made public statements so that there was no guessing what they believed. Not only so, but once he had included unbelieving church leaders in his meetings, he could not very well criticize them or preach against their sins of denying the Bible and the fundamentals of the faith.

This is the "Billy Graham issue," and it has accelerated the confusion in churches today. In principle, it is the "scrambled egg" of American Christianity. Dr. Graham has never raised his voice against the American abortion holocaust that has slaughtered over 43 million living babies; has had nothing to say about the atheism of public education or the sins of Sodom and

Gomorrah. The old-time evangelists preached hard against the sins of their day. They fulfilled the role of the prophet as well as the role of the evangelist. He has shied away from that. Billy Graham has embraced the Catholic Church as equal to his own Christian heritage. That gesture brought many Catholics to his meetings. The old-time evangelists NEVER did any of this.

Underneath all of this was the ongoing struggle between fundamentalists and modernists within the major denominations for control. Many Southern Baptist churches came out of the Southern Baptist Convention to avoid paying seminary professors to destroy the faith of young preachers who went there to be trained. The same struggle was going on in the Southern Baptist colleges on the state level. I elected (in 1952) to attend neither Carson Newman College in Tennessee nor Howard College in Alabama for that reason.

In the wake of this warfare are many Independent Baptists who came out of the Southern Baptist Convention to maintain "purity" in their sanctuaries, which see no problem in sending their children to public schools to be trained in atheism. Many of them make no effort to counter the religious humanism being spoon fed daily to their children.

In 1958, shortly after Billy Graham announced his change in policy, an emergency meeting was called during the Christmas holidays by several leading fundamentalist pastors and other Christian leaders, including Dr. John R. Rice and Dr. Bob Jones, Sr. The resolution they all signed can be found in Dr. Rice's book: *Come Out or Stay In*. I have included excerpts from that book, below (pp 80-95). Even though Billy Graham's name is not mentioned, there is no question about where the resolution was focused.

The signers include Dan Graham of Bristol, Tennessee. I was saved at the age of nine under Dan Graham's preaching in a bean market in Mountain City, Tennessee in October, 1943. He was a rough preacher.

COME OUT
OR STAY IN

By Dr. John R. Rice © 1974

Published by Thomas Nelson, Inc., Nashville, TN

Chap V. SEPARATION FROM UNBELIEF AGE-LONG PRACTICE OF BEST CHRISTIANS

Chapter V. Headings:

I. HOW MANY MARTYRS DIED BECAUSE THEY WOULD NOT COMPROMISE CONVICTIONS, WOULD NOT GO ALONG WITH CROWD!

II. LUTHER RISKED LIFE TO COME OUT OF ROME

III. WESLEY UNWILLINGLY BROKE WITH UNGODLY CHURCH LEADERS

IV. SPURGEON CAME OUT OF BAPTIST UNION BECAUSE OF THEIR UNBELIEF

V. D. L. MOODY TOOK HISTORIC STAND IN SEPARATION FROM UNBELIEVERS

VI. BILLY SUNDAY, OUTSPOKEN FOE OF MODERNISM

VII. JAMES M. GRAY OF MOODY BIBLE INSTITUTE TOOK CLEAR STAND, HAVING NO TIE, NO YOKE, WITH LIBERALS

VIII. H. A. IRONSIDE TOOK EARNEST STAND AGAINST YOKING UP WITH UNBELIEVERS

Dr. H. A. Ironside would not join the ministerial association in Chicago, which included liberals. He continually took an open, plain stand against yoking up with unbelievers. For the religion Analysis Service he wrote the article, "Exposing Error: Is It Worthwhile?"

Exposing Error: Is It Worthwhile?

Dr. H. A. Ironside

Objection is often raised—even by some sound in the faith—regarding the exposure of error as being entirely negative and of no real edification. Of late, the hue and cry has been against any and all negative teaching. But the brethren who assume this attitude forget that a large part of the New Testament, both of the teaching of our blessed Lord Himself and the writings of the apostles, is made up of this very character of ministry —namely, showing the satanic origin, and therefore the unsettling results, of the propagation of erroneous systems which Peter, in his second epistles, so definitely refers to as "damnable heresies"

Our Lord prophesied, "Many false prophets shall rise, and shall deceive many." Within our own day, how many false prophets have risen; and oh, how many are the deceived! Paul predicted, "I know this, that after my departing shall grievous wolves enter in among you, not sparing the flock. Also of your own selves shall men arise, speaking perverse things to draw away disciples after them. Therefore watch." My own observation is that these "grievous wolves," alone and in packs, are not sparing even the most favored flocks. Undershepherds in these "perilous times" will do well to note the apostle's warning, "Take heed therefore unto yourselves and to all the flock over which the Holy Ghost hath made you overseers." It is important in these days as in Paul's—in fact, it is increasingly important–to expose the many types of false teaching that, on every hand, abound more and more.

We are called upon to "contend earnestly for the faith once for all delivered to the saints, "while we hold the truth in love. The faith means the whole body of revealed truth, and to contend for *all* of God's truth necessitates some negative teaching. The choice is not left with us. Jude said he preferred a different, a pleasanter theme–"Beloved, my whole concern was to write to you on a subject of our common salvation, but I *am forced* to write you an appeal to defend the faith which has once for all been committed to the saints; for certain persons have slipped in by stealth (their doom has been predicted long ago), impious

278

creatures who pervert the grace of God" (Jude 3, 4, Moffatt). Paul likewise admonishes us to "take no part in the unfruitful works of darkness, but instead expose them" (Eph 5:11, R.S.V.). (Even the faulty R.S.V. is clear here. J.R.R.)

This does not imply harsh treatment of those entrapped by error—quite the opposite. If it be objected that exposure of error necessitates unkind reflection upon others who do not see as we do, our answer is, it has always been the duty of every loyal servant of Christ to warn against any teaching that would make Him less precious, or cast reflection upon His finished redemptive work and the all-sufficiency of His present service as our great High Priest and Advocate.

Every system of teaching can be judged by what it sets forth as to these fundamental truths of the faith. "What think ye of Christ?" is still the true test of every creed. The Christ of the Bible is certainly not the Christ of any false ism. Each of the cults has its hideous caricature of our lovely Lord.

Let us who have been redeemed at the cost of His precious blood, be "good soldiers of Jesus Christ." As the battle against the forces of evil waxes ever more hot, we have need for God-given valor. There is constant temptation to compromise. "Let us go forth therefore unto him without the camp, bearing his reproach." It is always right to stand firmly for what God has revealed concerning His blessed Son's person and work. The "father of lies" deals in half-truths, and specializes in most subtle fallacies concerning the Lord Jesus, our sole and sufficient Saviour.

Error is like leaven, of which we read, "A *little* leaven leaveneth the whole lump." Truth mixed with error is equivalent to the entire error, except that it is more innocent looking, and therefore more dangerous. God hates such a mixture! Any error, or any truth-and-error mixture, calls for definite exposure and repudiation. To condone such is to be unfaithful to God and His Word, and treacherous to imperiled souls for whom Christ died.

Exposing error is most unpopular work. But from every true standpoint, it is worthwhile work. To our Savior, it means that He receives from us, His blood-bought ones, the loyalty that is His due. To ourselves, if we consider "the reproach of Christ greater riches than the treasures of Egypt," it insures future reward, a thousandfold. And to souls "caught in the snare of the fowler"—how many of them God only knows—it may mean light and life, abundant and everlasting.

IX. BOB JONES, SR., MADE EARNEST FIGHT IN DEFENSE OF THIS BIBLE POSITION

The position of Dr. Bob Jones, Sr., who went to be with the Lord on January 16, 1968, made a strong fight against yoking up with unbelievers. At a called meeting of evangelists at the Hamilton Hotel in Chicago, December 26, 1958, a resolution was formed, prepared by Dr. Jones [Sr], with my help [Dr. Rice] and signed by all the evangelists present. It said:

Resolution

We, evangelists, pastor-evangelists, and educators of soul-winners assembled in Chicago, Dec 26-27, facing our responsibilities to God and Christian people for scriptural leadership in evangelism, hereby adopt and establish the following resolution.

I. Whereas; America needs an old-time Bible revival with hard-hitting, Holy Spirit empowered, true-to-the-Bible preaching, living, and witnessing, to meet the wide-spread breakdown of morality and Christianity which is evidenced by overwhelming sins of divorce, drunkenness, crime, juvenile delinquency, adultery among the people; with shocking unbelief, worldliness, and cold formalism in the churches.

II. Whereas; We solemnly believe any evangelism which does not deal honestly and scripturally with the sin and the unbelief and disloyalty to the Bible prevalent in religious circles cannot bring about the true scriptural revival America and the world needs.

III. Whereas; We agree in believing, proclaiming, and contending for certain basic Bible doctrines as essential to the Christian faith. As do all major creeds of Christianity, and as orthodox Christians have unitedly agreed since the apostles, we affirm that without these fundamental truths, any religion is not the historic Christian religion, the religion of our Lord Jesus Christ. These absolute essentials are, we believe:

1. The verbal inspiration, the absolute authority, and infallible

accuracy of the Bible as God's Word in original manuscripts.

2. The deity, the virgin birth, the vicarious atoning death, the bodily resurrection of Jesus Christ, and His return.

3. In the fallen nature of man, the absolute need for regeneration, in salvation by grace through faith in Christ, and in the Great Commission to preach the Gospel to every creature.

IV. Whereas; We believe that with brotherly love, Christians, as individuals, may properly cooperate with all who (1) claim and evidence in life saving faith in Christ, as Savior, (2) firmly believe and profess the above essentials of the faith, and (3) though they may differ on lesser matters of faith, do not make "doubtful disputations."

V. Whereas; We believe it unscriptural and wrong to yoke up with unbelievers and thus put unsaved men or enemies of the historic Christian faith in partial control of, or influential in any kind of Christian work, whether in evangelism or Christian schools or denominational work or ministerial associations or local churches. We rejoice in the Gospel, whoever preaches it, and in souls saved, however won. But we believe that any evangelist who calls unbelievers Christians, who has enemies of the Bible lead in prayer, or who sends new converts or inquirers to churches which do not believe and preach the Bible as the perfectly revealed Word of God, and where their faith is likely to be destroyed, does wrong, whether his motives are good or bad. By so doing, we believe one violates the plain command of God in 2 Cor 6:14-18, Eph 5:11, 2 Jn 7-11, and Gal 1:8,9.

Thus to receive to our pulpits or platforms and to give Christian recognition to men who "do not abide in the doctrine of Christ" is to "bid them Godspeed" and to "be a partaker of their evil deed," as 2 Jn, vv 7 to 11, plainly forbids. To help erase the line between those who believe the Bible is the Word of God, and those who believe the Bible may or may not CONTAIN the Word of God along with uninspired material is forbidden in the Bible. Even though the Gospel is preached, any occasion when modernists and unbelievers are made more popular and influential and Bible-believing preachers are left in reproach, it is wrong.

The Bible says, "Blessed is the man that walketh not in the counsel of the ungodly, nor standeth in the way of sinners,

281

nor sitteth in the seat of the scornful" (Ps 1:1). The Bible is as clear on the question of bad company, of wrong associations, of spiritual compromise, as on the gospel message itself, or on the fundamental doctrines accepted by all Bible-believing, orthodox Christians. It is never right to do wrong in order to get a chance to do right.

We believe it right to preach to all sinners. We believe it is never right to put lost men, enemies of the Bible, in places to partially control or sponsor a revival campaign, a local church, a ministerial association, or a denomination or religious institution.

THEREFORE, BE IT RESOLVED:

1. That we affirm our whole-hearted loyalty to these truths–the verbal inspiration and authority of the Bible, the deity, virgin birth, vicarious blood atonement, bodily resurrection, and second coming of our Lord Jesus Christ.

2. That we, with humble confession of our failures and weaknesses, earnestly dedicate ourselves anew and with holy zeal to soul winning and evangelism at home and abroad, in obedience to Christ's Great Commission, and as the main thing Jesus died for.

3. That we humbly ask God to make us worthy of the reproach of Christ, and to make us willing to suffer for the holy faith, as have prophets, apostles and martyrs and saints who were true to Christ in all ages. Since this is the age for crosses, not crowns; since we are commanded to go outside the gate with Christ instead of staying in with the majorities of this world, we humbly ask God to give us grace to stand fast, suffering, if need be, for Christ.

4. We solemnly resolve that we will not knowingly support, with gifts, or influence or labor, any religious program or institution or man which denies or contradicts or perverts any of the essentials of the faith mentioned above. By God's help we undertake to match our holy convictions with our living and giving.

5. We solemnly resolve that we will not knowingly give Christian recognition to those who are unconverted or who deny any of the basic essentials of the Christian faith; that we will not knowingly work under the sponsorship of these unbelievers, nor join them in sponsorship of any religious program, whether evangelistic campaign, ministerial association, denominational

or local church programs. We resolve not to disobey the plain commands of the Bible in order to get a chance to preach the gospel.

6. We solemnly resolve that we will endeavor to go anywhere God leads, for revival and soul winning, as He opens the doors and makes His will clear by the Holy Spirit, whether opportunities appear great or small, and as the opportunities conform to the requirements for cooperation or sponsorship.

7. We declare our intention to promote and pray for cooperation in evangelism with true Christians on a scriptural basis, while we also earnestly promote local church and individual evangelism. End.

THE RESOLUTIONS COMMITTEE WAS COMPOSED OF THE FOLLOWING:

Dr. John R. Rice (Chairman) evangelist, and editor and publisher of *The SWORD of the LORD*, Wheaton, Illinois.

Dr. Bob Jones, Sr., president of Bob Jones Univ.

Rev. Joe Boyd, moderator, Southern Baptist Fellowship, pastor, The Open Door Baptist Church, Dallas, Texas.

Dr. Horace Dean, pres., Christ for America, Philadelphia, Pennsylvania.

Dr. W. O. H. Garman, pres., Associated gospel Churches, Wilkinsburg, Pennsylvania.

Dr Harry McCormick Lintz, director, Victory Crusade Evangelistic Association, Redlands, California.

Rev. Henry P. Lovik, general director, Conservative Baptist Association of Illinois, Oak Lawn, Illinois.

Dr. Ernest Pickering, national executive secretary, Independent Fundamental Churches of America, Chicago, Illinois.

Rev. Harold Sightler, past moderator, Southern Baptist Fellowship, and pastor, Tabernacle Baptist Church, Greenville, S. Carolina.

Rev. Charles A. Thigpen, moderator and chairman of the general board, National Association of Free Will Baptists, Nashville, Tennessee.

Dr. James A. Franklin, business manager, Westminster College and Bible Institute, Tehuacana, Texas.

Rev. Dan H. Graham, president, Graham Bible Institute and Bible College, and pastor, Walnut Hill Presbyterian Church,

Bristol, Tennessee.

Dr. Henry Grube, president, Greystone Christian School, and pastor, The Tabernacle, Mobile, Alabama.

Dr. Linton C. Johnson, president, Free Will Baptist Bible College, Nashville, Tennessee.

Dr. Allen MacRae, president, Faith Theological Seminary, Philadelphia, Pennsylvania.

Dr. Tom Malone, chairman of the board and president, Midwestern Baptist Seminary, and pastor, Emmanuel Baptist Church, Pontiac, Michigan.

Dr. John Murray, president, Shelton College, Ringwood, New Jersey, and pastor, Church of the Open Door, Philadelphia, Pennsylvania.

Dr. Monroe Parker, president, Pillsbury Conservative Baptist Bible College, Owatonna, Minnesota.

Dr. Lee Roberson, president, Tennessee Temple Schools, and pastor, Highland Park Baptist Church, Chattanooga, Tennessee.

Rev. G. Beauchamp Vick, president Baptist Bible College, Springfield, Missouri, and pastor, Temple Baptist Church, Detroit, Michigan.

Dr. G. Archer Weniger, chairman of the board, Conservative Baptist Theological Sem'ry, San Francisco, CA, and pastor, Foothills Boulevard Baptist Church, Oakland, CA.

Rev. W. B. Bedford. Pastor, Christian and Missionary Alliance Church, Greensboro, N. C

Dr. James E. Bennett, counselor-at-law, New York, New York.

Rev. Kenton Beshore, pastor, First Baptist Church, Oceanside, California.

Dr. Fred Garland, evangelist, Roanoke, Virginia.

Rev. Robert C. Gray, Jr., editor, THE BAPTIST BEACON, treasurer, The Southern Baptist Fellowship, and pastor, Trinity Baptist Church, Jacksonville, Florida.

Evangelist Oliver B. Greene, director, "The Gospel Hour," Greenville, South Carolina.

Rev. Jack Hyles, pastor, Miller Road Baptist Church, Garland, Texas.

Dr. John F. MacArthur, pastor, MacArthur Memorial Bible Church, Glendale, CA.

Rev. Ford Porter, president, Berean Gospel Distributors, Inc., and pastor, Berean Gospel Temple, Indianapolis, Indiana.

Dr. Bill Rice, president, Cumberwood Christian Retreat, Murfreesboro, Tennessee.

Dr. William H. Lee Spratt, pastor, Grace Baptist Church, Decatur, Alabama.

Dr. William McCarrell, pastor-emeritus of Cicero Bible Church, Cicero, Illinois.

Paul Ferguson
April, 1958

Paul Ferguson and John Paul Ferguson
McConnell Road Baptist Church

Bro. Tom Ellis, Pastor of McConnell Road Baptist Church
Pastor when Paul was called to preach.